General Editors

MALCOLM BRADBURY
AND DAVID PALMER

Also available in this series

Under the General Editorship of Malcolm Bradbury and David Palmer

CONTEMPORARY ENGLISH DRAMA

ASSOCIATE EDITOR
C.W.E. BIGSBY

Holmes & Meier Publishers, Inc.
New York

© EDWARD ARNOLD (PUBLISHERS) LTD 1981

First published in the
United States of America 1981 by
HOLMES & MEIER PUBLISHERS, INC.
30 Irving Place, New York
N.Y. 10003

In memory of Larry Holland

Library of Congress Cataloging Publication Data
Contemporary English drama. — (Stratford-
upon-Avon studies; 19).
1. English drama — 20th century — History
and criticism
I. Bigsby, Christopher William Edgar
II. Series
81–81341

ISBN 0-8419-0716-1
ISBN 0-8419-0717-X Pbk

Printed in Great Britain

Contents

Preface

In 1962, John Russell Brown and Bernard Harris, the then editors of the Stratford-Upon-Avon Studies series, devoted their fourth volume to the subject of *Contemporary Theatre*, giving the series a contemporary dimension it has maintained ever since. This was a timely volume for, though the span was international, it was able to stress and display all the new excitement that had come into postwar theatre, but above all into British theatre after the key date of 1956—the year when, with the Royal Court Theatre's production of John Osborne's *Look Back in Anger*, a whole new phase of British theatre seemed to begin. The essays in that volume are an early record of the resulting new curiosity. They reflected the sense that new playwrights and new theatrical forms and ideas were emerging. But it is a signal of the extent to which that excitement and sense of possibility has continued and developed, with new playwrights, new theatres, new opportunities in television creating a continuously energetic scene, that that volume is now out-of-date—well worth consulting for its record of the times, and its analysis of the then new developments, but requiring today another volume that extends the story, looks at the further development of careers by then already started, identifies the importance of many subsequent ones, and concentrates itself totally on British drama. So the aim of this volume is to advance the record and look at British theatre up to 1980, gazing across a period of remarkable growth.

The previous volume in this series, number 18, was devoted to *The Contemporary English Novel*, and there it was noted that many of the developments in recent British fiction have not had wide recognition in the international scene. One can hardly say the same about British theatre, which has generated a good deal of interest abroad as well as at home. Contemporary British poetry may be found modest, contemporary British fiction less vigorous overall than current American, Latin American, African or French fiction. But British theatre is clearly visible internationally, whether it be in the theatres of Broadway or Germany—a visibility often selective, however, and concentrated on certain particular reputations. If it is possible that in the postwar years it has been theatre that has attracted some of the best literary talents, who have then had the support of a remarkable generation of directors, actors, companies, theatrical organizations, drama magazines, the fact remains that, as with all contemporary careers, there remain considerable problems of assessment. It is not in fact easy to see the direction that new British theatre has taken, or, now that many of the reputations of the 1950s have been altered, who are the leading and most significant figures. The excitements of the 1950s have been replaced by new ones, and the nature of theatre has changed. As Christopher Bigsby points out in the opening essay in this book, in the 1950s the main significance attached to the new theatre of Osborne, Wesker, Delaney and others was that it was political, a theatre of anger and revolt. In fact much of the protest was reformist rather than revolutionary in spirit, and much the same might be said of the form of the plays, though they did contain a powerful reaction against the way theatre had become fixed as an anodyne and middle-class institution. But it was in many ways a very traditional drama, realist or naturalist in spirit, that emerged, taking much of its energy from the social range it attended to and the new social experiences it explored.

But this mood was soon complicated—by the growing influence of continental theatre, of foreign playwrights and companies, of Brecht, Artaud, Grotowski, by the growth of fringe theatrical institutions, above all, perhaps, by the impact of the Theatre of the Absurd, and the shock of the London production of Samuel Beckett's *Waiting for Godot* in 1953, though such are the elements of insularity in British theatre that these influences were rather less powerful than they might have been. Indeed, as is suggested in the opening chapter, perhaps the most striking thing is that beneath the general questioning of theatrical ideas and the stirring of innovation was an underlying continuity. The very strength of the British dramatic tradition made it more resistant than the American—which has always been eclectic, desperately anxious to appropriate and adapt European experimentalism. Even so, English theatre in the 1960s was more open to outside influence than it had been for much of its history. British directors travelled to and worked in Europe and America more frequently; the World Theatre season at the Aldwych brought major foreign companies to London; the impact of American fringe companies became strongly felt. The 1966 production of *US* brought together Peter Brook, Jerzy Grotowski and Joseph Chaiken. Chaiken's Open Theatre Company visited Britain in the following year, staging *America Hurrah!* at the Royal Court, and bringing home some of the new developments in performance theatre that had been reshaping American drama from the end of the 1950s onward, and which expressed many of the ferments that passed through western Europe and peaked in 1968. The birth of the 'fringe,' originally inspired by American theatre and peopled by expatriate Americans like Charles Marowitz, Ed Berman and Jim Haynes, established an alternative outlet to the major subsidized companies. This tendency was very rapidly Anglicized and to an important degree politicized, and it grew greatly in influence during the early 1970s.

And, though it has been reasonably argued that British theatre has been a theatre of language rather than performance, these influences have undoubtedly qualified the British line. As in British fiction, British theatre has displayed markedly realistic and social preoccupations, and questions of representation rather than form have played a heavy if not overweighty part. But there have been many signs of pluralism and experimentalism (though Peter Brook, the most radical of British directors, has now effectively moved his centre of operations to Paris, finding there the international actors who are amenable to the subjects and approaches that have come to concern him). As several of the following articles suggest, there has as a result been evidence of some outward, and in the case of some writers an inward, tension between the claims of realism and politics on the one hand and theatrical formal experiment on the other. The results, however, have often been very creative. British theatre can claim the powerful talents of politically committed writers like John McGrath, Caryl Churchill or Trevor Griffiths, discussed here by Christian Thomsen; it can also claim the outstanding talents of Harold Pinter, Tom Stoppard and Samuel Beckett (admittedly an Irishman who writes in French) who are central figures in any notion of a late twentieth-century 'post-modernist' drama. (Pinter and Stoppard are discussed here by Guido Almansi and Ruby Cohn.) Yet in fact both parties seem always to feel the compelling pressure of the other, and this has done a great deal to sustain the complicated and enquiring texture of the work of the best young British dramatists.

And it is this tension which is displayed through most of the essays in this book. Thus, as Martin Esslin shows, Joe Orton responded to the pressure by an anarchic personal and literary style, deliberately subversive and linguistically perverse. For Edward Bond, Jenny Spencer suggests, the pressure encouraged him to confront questions of public value and private responsibility; and, though theatre for him was charged with a social function, tension ensues between a clear-sighted social rationalism and the irrationalism of dramatic effects, between the prophet and the poet, a tension that is the essence of his art. John Arden, as Julian Hilton points out, is more emphatic in his social assumptions, more determined to locate an audience that will respond directly to the political substance of his work; so is John McGrath. The risk of ethics being deflected into aesthetics is recognized by both, but is largely evaded by addressing subjects and audiences for whom the pressure of the real is a matter of daily substance. But this is not to suggest that contemporary British theatre is predominantly political in the narrow ideological sense. Theatre always does respond, perhaps more directly and immediately than other genres, to the present moment—the present is the natural tense of drama. But for the most part the response is oblique. For, if the theatre displays cultural energy, it has displayed it in socially uneasy times, when the key images in theatre have been those of decline and decay. One response is the sharp ideological thrust, though for a number of writers here this has been blunted over the decade into a privatized view of experience; however other writers, like Stoppard, seem to have moved along virtually the reverse path. Social, political and metaphysical spaces have opened up, and another response has been an attempt to bridge the spaces with words, a fascination with epistemological questions and the humour of absurdity and unease. The British dramatic tradition of comedy of manners has been transformed into an agent of metaphysical enquiry, a deeply ironic dismantling of assumptions about private and public order, or about language itself.

At the moment, this seems to be the dominant spirit in British theatre, a theatre where a profound sense of unease has surfaced in disturbing images of violence and of a brutalized landscape peopled by self-deceiving individuals. The lie—once, as David Hare suggests in his television play *Licking Hitler*, simply a necessary tool of the state—has been internalized, until questions about the nature of reality become simultaneously social, metaphysical and psychological. The schizophrenia of Keith Waterhouse's and Willis Hall's *Billy Liar* (1960) has become, it seems, almost a necessary cultural strategy. Yet, as David Edgar and David Hare have suggested, theatre is ideally placed to expose the lie, for it can dramatize both the reality and the illusion, it can put opposing fictions in conflict. This can generate a political theatre, observing this conflict as a dialectical process; it can also create a reflexive drama, as with Tom Stoppard's *Travesties* (1975) and *Every Good Boy Deserves Favour* (1977), or Caryl Churchill's *Traps* (1978). What, though, is clear is that English theatre has generated a wide range of original writers acutely attuned to the resonances, the tensions, the colliding myths, values and symbols of the society in which they live, and whose preoccupations are perhaps unavoidably their own. Almost unanimously disturbed by a present in which values are surrendered to the press of the material, and the imagination is threatened by a bland technology, a brutalized vision of individual and social potential, an empty positivism, they have, over the last decade, created a drama charged with social and cultural alarm. It is the spirit of this drama and its lively variety which we have sought to explore in this book.

MALCOLM BRADBURY
CHRISTOPHER BIGSBY

Note

For general studies of the period see: Peter Ansorge, *Disrupting the Spectacle: Five Years of Experimental and Fringe Theatre* (London, 1975); John Russell Brown, ed., *Modern British Dramatists* (Englewood Cliffs, 1968); John Russell Brown and B. Harris eds., *Contemporary English Theatre* (1962); Terry Browne, *Playwrights' Theatre* (1975); John Chiari, *Landmarks of Contemporary Drama* (1965); John Elsom, *Theatre Outside London* (1971); Martin Esslin, *The Theatre of the Absurd,* revised ed. (1968); Martin Esslin, *Reflections: Essays on Modern Theatre* (New York, 1969); Lawrence Kitchen, *Mid-Century Drama* (1960); Charles Marowitz *et al.*, eds., *The Encore Reader* (1965); Charles Marowitz and Simon Trussler, eds. *Theatre at Work* (1967); Charles Marowitz, *Confessions of a Counterfeit Critic* (1973); John Russell Taylor, *Anger and After,* 2nd edition (1969); John Russell Taylor, *The Second Wave* (1971); Katherine Worth, *Revolutions in Modern English Drama* (1973).

For the work of individual writers see: Michael Anderson, *Anger and Detachment* (1976); Ronald Hayman, *Playback* (1973); Andrew Kennedy, *Six Dramatists in Search of a Language* (1975). See also the British Council/Longman *Writers and Their Work* series.

For more theoretical studies see: Antonin Artaud, *The Theatre and its Double* (New York, 1958); Peter Brook, *The Empty Space* (1972); Jerzi Growtowski, *Towards a Poor Theatre* (New York, 1968); Raymond Williams, *Drama in Performance* (1972).

Basic reference books: Phyllis Hartnoll, ed., *The Oxford Companion to the Theatre* (1967); James Vinson, ed., *Contemporary Dramatists* (1973); *Who's Who in the Theatre* (1972).

Britain's principal theatre magazine, *Theatre Quarterly,* regularly contains extensive interviews with contemporary writers as well as accounts of individual productions and theatre documents. Its associated publication, *Theatre Facts,* offers full bibliographical information on individual authors, while the new ITI (International Theatre Institute) publication *British Theatrelog* gives details of new productions and revivals. Another valuable source is *Plays and Players* which regularly reviewed productions and print play texts, until it ceased publication in 1980.

The Language of Crisis in British Theatre: The Drama of Cultural Pathology

C.W.E. BIGSBY

Words, words, they're all we've got to go on.

Tom Stoppard, *Rosencrantz and Guildenstern Are Dead*

Words are important. They may be dispensed with but it seems to me they're the last link with God. When millions of people seem unable to communicate with one another it is vitally important that words are made to work. It may be old-fashioned, but they're the only thing.

John Osborne

Words can *only* be tested by being spoken. Ideas can *only* be worked out in real situations . . . the theatre is the best court society has.

David Hare

. . . the only thing that binds us together today is a profound unease, and laughter is the language of that unease.

Howard Brenton

I

In his book *Political Theatre*, Erwin Piscator lamented that the working class had been excluded from theatre, both by price and by a tradition that saw theatre as a social event requiring certain niceties of dress and behaviour. He likewise objected to the exclusion of that class as subject-matter, and the assumption that the theatre exists as an entertainment for the middle class or a shrine of pure art. Such comments might have been directed at English theatre as it was up to the middle 1950s. Actually Piscator's book appeared in 1929, and it described the situation of German theatre in the nineteenth century.[1] And this perhaps explains why the change that came over English theatre in the later 1950s was seen initially as social in character, and potentially political in consequence, for, up to then, the working class had been virtually absent as a force in English drama. When they did appear, as in Shaw's *Pygmalion*, it was in sentimentalized and patronized form. They were seen as admirable either because, like Eliza Doolittle's father, they played the role of earthy vulgarity and attractive stupidity, touched with a certain primitive wit and wisdom, or because, like Eliza herself, they could be transformed into good bourgeoises: a transformation effected and confirmed by a shift of linguistic register. But in the 1950s the working class

[1] Erwin Piscator, *The Political Theatre: A History 1914-1929*, trans. Hugh Rorrison (New York, 1978).

appeared in more dignified, significant form: they had at last apparently penetrated English theatre as subject and artist. The change seemed significant, a trigger for a new phase in drama. It appeared that the long-looked-for consequences of the 1944 Education Act had arrived. Subject, attitudes, and above all writers themselves were no longer being drawn almost exclusively from that narrow social stratum which has, in England, traditionally dictated the nature of social action and public forms. Now new writers, whose experience was profoundly different and whose subjects and methods were therefore likely to be equally new, had emerged. In the middle of a decade whose self-image was of growing affluence presided over by a benign but decadent conservatism, there was to be a welcome irritant.

It is not hard to see where this idea came from. English culture has indeed been remarkably homogeneous, produced essentially by people from the same background as those who dominated all the major institutions of British life. In *The Long Revolution* Raymond Williams offers an analysis of the educational (and largely, as a result, the social) background of English writers over several centuries. Examining those writers listed in the Oxford *Introduction to English Literature* and the *Dictionary of National Biography*, he points out that of the fifty-three writers listed in the period 1880-1930, for example, thirty-two had been to Oxford and Cambridge universities, and six to other universities.[2] In another such study, based on the *Cambridge Bibliography of English Literature*, a sample of seventy-two 'imaginative' writers listed for the period since 1900 results in thirty-six Oxbridge graduates, eight graduates of other universities and a total of forty-four who had been to public (fee-paying) schools.[3] The theatre, in the first half of the century, was effectively dominated by figures like Galsworthy (Oxford), J.M. Barrie (Edinburgh), J.B. Priestley (Cambridge), Somerset Maugham (Heidelberg, though he was supposed to go to Oxford), Auden and Isherwood (Oxford and Cambridge respectively), T.S. Eliot (Harvard, Sorbonne, Oxford), Graham Greene (Oxford), and Terence Rattigan (Oxford)—a tradition in stark contrast to that offered by Irish playwrights like Shaw, Synge, Yeats and O'Casey. It is no wonder, then, that the emergence of young, working-class writers should present the appearance of a social and artistic revolution. Indeed there was a clear messianic tone in Bernard Kops's enumeration, in 1962, of Arden, Wesker, Owen, Bolt, Willis Hall and himself as writers who had ensured that the theatre would never again be the 'precious inner-sanctum for the precious few', and his belief that by tackling issues of an immediate social concern they could change the face of things, 'we hope for all time'.

The coincidence of the emergence of this new theatre precisely at a time when British military ascendency was finally exposed as a sham at Suez, and when political divisions ran deep, lent conviction to this sense of a profound change. The abortive Suez venture—which provides the background to Osborne's second play, *The Entertainer* (1957)—not only split the country

[2] Raymond Williams, *The Long Revolution* (1961), pp. 230-93.
[3] Malcolm Bradbury, *The Social Context of Modern English Literature* (1971), pp. 137-43.

politically but revealed a widening gulf between the generations, between those who had fought in the war, and could regard themselves as the inheritors of an imperial past, and those born during or just after the war, who found many of the values of their society quaint, outmoded or enervating. This was the feeling which John Osborne appeared to catch so effectively in *Look Back in Anger* in 1956. But in fact, as John Russell Taylor himself pointed out in his 1962 book *Anger and After*, it is deceptive.[4] Below the surface is a profound nostalgia for those values acknowledged to be slipping away—a nostalgia as apparent in Wesker's living recreation of the battles of the 1930s, of a communality which he fears to be crumbling under the assault of the modern, as it is in Osborne's respectful portrait of an older generation. Indeed, for the most part, the so-called 'new' theatre of the late 1950s was 'new' only in its subject matter, not really in its style (though Pinter was a notable exception). It was new only in an English context. Surely only in England could it be thought revolutionary to write about working-class characters in a naturalistic way. Ionesco put things in a different perspective when he dismissed the 'new wave' simply as 'one-dimensional bourgeois triviality'. And it is worth remembering that while the English were busy congratulating themselves on their belated discovery of naturalism, the rest of Europe was witnessing the emergence of writers like Beckett and Ionesco whose first dramatic works were actually written in the 1940s.

In fact, when we look at Bernard Kops's original list of authors from the perspective of the 1980s, we can see that, if these writers ever constituted a social or political movement, it was one without a coherent philosophy, and one which rapidly fell apart. The real politicizing of the English theatre was still well over a decade away. Indeed, it has also become apparent that the idea that there had been a radical change in the social background of English writers, at least as judged by their education, is also false (in fact C.H. Halsey's research, published in 1980, suggests that the 1944 Education Act had itself surprisingly little effect on the class structure of English society). There were a number of working-class writers who appeared in the final years of the 1950s. But if we were to assemble a list of English dramatists of the last twenty-five years who shared a university background, or were one of the five per cent of the population who attend public schools, it would make a significant catalogue of the leading figures of contemporary theatre. The Oxbridge axis, in particular, has clearly not been broken: thus John Antrobus (Sandhurst), John Arden (Oxford), Alan Ayckbourn (public school); John Bowen (Oxford), Howard Barker (Sussex), Alan Bennett (Oxford), Howard Brenton (Cambridge), Bridget Brophy (Cambridge), Caryl Churchill (Oxford), Brian Clark (Nottingham), David Cregan (Cambridge), Keith Dewhurst (Cambridge), David Edgar (Manchester), Stanley Eveling (Durham), Michael Frayn (Cambridge), Pam Gems (Manchester), Simon Gray (Cambridge), David Hare (Cambridge), William Douglas

4 W.J. Baumol and W.G. Bowen, 'A Survey of American and British Audiences for the Performing Arts (1966)', in *The Economics of the Arts*, ed. Mark Blaug (1970), pp. 148-74.

Home (Oxford), Christopher Hampton (Oxford), Trevor Griffiths (Manchester), Anne Jellicoe (public school), Henry Livings (Liverpool), Wolf Mankowitz (Cambridge), John McGrath (Oxford), David Mercer (Durham), Adrian Mitchell (Oxford), John Mortimer (Oxford), John Osborne (public school), Stephen Poliakov (Cambridge), Anthony Shaffer (Cambridge), Peter Shaffer (Cambridge), James Saunders (Southampton), John Spurling (Oxford), Tom Stoppard (public school), N.F. Simpson (public school), David Selbourne (Oxford), Snoo Wilson (East Anglia), A.E. Whitehead (Cambridge). It seems clear that there is still a homogeneity to English cultural life in general, and perhaps the theatre in particular —though obviously my thumb is securely on the scales, since the above list would exclude, among others, Edward Bond, Steve Berkoff, Barrie Keefe, Steve Gooch, David Halliwell, Peter Nichols, Harold Pinter, David Storey and Arnold Wesker.

But theatre is a collaborative art, and it is perhaps worth stressing that plays written by Oxbridge graduates stood a very good chance of being directed and even reviewed by Oxbridge graduates. Indeed the homogeneity is even more remarkable if one lists the leading English directors over the last two decades: Peter Brook (Oxford), John Barton (Cambridge), Lindsay Anderson (Oxford), Robert Chetwyn (Oxford), Michael Blackmore (Sydney), George Devine (Oxford), Peter Dews (Oxford), Michael Croft (Oxford), William Gaskill (Oxford), Peter Gill (St Illyd College, Cardiff), Peter Hall (Cambridge), David Jones (Cambridge), Terry Hands (Birmingham), Robert Kidd (secondary school), Trevor Nunn (Cambridge), Jonathan Miller (Cambridge), Anthony Page (Oxford), Val May (Cambridge), Tony Richardson (Oxford), Max Stafford Clark (Trinity), Peter Wood (Cambridge).

There are at the present moment 44 universities in Britain, educating something less than eight per cent of the population. On the whole they have not provided that stimulus for eroding the class system which many had hoped. The percentage of working-class students attending those universities, indeed, was the same in 1976 as it had been, on average, during the period 1928-47. Those attending Oxford and Cambridge constitute some eight per cent of all those attending university in Britain. In other words, approximately half of one per cent of British people attend those two universities, with half of that number coming from fee-paying schools. And it is from this group, by and large, that the English theatre draws its strength.

It is more difficult to know what to do with this information. A number of Oxbridge playwrights like to stress that their presence does not necessarily imply anything about their class or economic background. For John McGrath, indeed, it was his experience of the army and of Oxford which alerted him to the nature and power of the British class system. And certainly if Oxbridge had produced a high percentage of Tory members of parliament*

---

*Of the Conservative MPs elected in 1970, in Feb and October 1974, 76 per cent had been to public school and 52.6 per cent to Oxbridge. The figures for Labour MPs were 17.1 per cent and 20.7 per cent respectively. See S.A. Walkland and Michael Ryle, *The Commons in the 70s* (1977).

and a substantial part of the civil service, the media, the military and the Church, it has also bred a fair number of KGB colonels. But I think it does make plain that assumptions about a fundamental change having occurred in the background of English dramatists and in the ethos of the English theatre were based on inadequate data. The fact is that, as an institution, the social composition of theatre resembles to a remarkable degree the other institutions of British life—the majority of people involved being drawn from a remarkably narrow social and educational range.

There is, however, clearly no reason why we should expect writers or directors to be in any way representative of the population at large. Indeed there is probably every reason for assuming otherwise. But the coincidence, in Britain, of educational and class backgrounds distinguishes it from most other systems in the world. If the above details do anything at all, it is probably to indicate an underlying continuity rather than a sudden disjunction in the kind of person drawn to write for the theatre. It may also explain why the British theatre has remained so resolutely literate and articulate; so dedicated to the word, so distrustful, on the whole, of physicality, of a vision of the theatre as non-rational, as dedicated to the dismantling of boundaries, the celebration of shared values and experiences. It is also, perhaps, worth reminding ourselves that a mid-1960s analysis of British theatre audiences discovered the perhaps unsurprising fact that, at a time when 68.9 per cent of the male population were engaged in such jobs, only 4.6 per cent of male theatregoers did blue-collar jobs,[5] and that 40 per cent of the non-graduates in the audience at the Royal Court Theatre were students. Indeed 86 per cent of men and 90.3 per cent of women in a survey of audiences for the performing arts in Britain had left school after the minimum school-leaving age, while nearly a half were graduates or held professional qualifications (as judged by the fact that their full-time education ended at the age of twenty or over). Theatre, at least in the mid 1960s, was not only produced by graduates, it was also, it seems, watched by them—when they could displace some of the foreign visitors, 38 per cent of whom visited the theatre despite the obvious foreign-language difficulties, at some time during their stay (at a time when 12 million visitors came to Britain). It was this fact which, in the 1960s, provided some of the impetus for the fringe theatre which sprang up in London, and, in the 70s, for the establishment of socialist theatres intent on creating new audiences. For the failure of Wesker's attempt to create a working-class theatre, Centre 42, through the trade unions, an attempt finally abandoned in 1970, was followed by the creation of a number of socialist touring theatres.

But, for all this, some things did change in 1956, even if that change was not quite what it appeared to be at the time. For this was not only the year of *Look Back in Anger*; it was also the year in which Joan Littlewood's company at Stratford East produced, and to a certain extent rewrote, Brendan Behan's *The Quare Fellow*; the year in which the Royal Court Theatre opened in its

[5]A.H. Halsey, A.F. Heath, J.M. Ridge, *Origins and Destinations: Family, Class, and Education in Modern Britain* (1980).

present form; the year in which the Berliner Ensemble visited Britain, and the sudden and extensive programme of provincial theatre building was symbolized by the beginnings of the Belgrade Theatre, Coventry. Only the year before, Independent (usually, in Britain, a synonym for commercial) Television had begun, and expanded at one go both the demand for drama and its social range. In London, the Royal Court was joined in 1960 by the Royal Shakespeare's new base at the Aldwych, and subsequently, in 1963, by the National Theatre. The Royal Shakespeare Company alone, dedicated in its London theatre to producing new playwrights as well as classic drama, averaged one new production a month, and by the late 1970s boasted an annual audience of one and a half million. Government gave increasing amounts of financial aid, not only to the principal companies, but to some 80 per cent of provincial repertory companies, and to an increasing number of 'fringe' theatres as they appeared in the late 1960s. In other words, a new and expanded market for plays appeared, a market sustained in some large degree by subsidies to companies, productions and individuals. The theatre increasingly seemed the natural place for the new young writer to turn. And for those interested in propagating social theories, or intent on securing a hearing for those previously driven to the edge of British cultural life, or even parodied by it, the very social fact of theatre proved a powerful attraction.

The changes which came about in the English theatre in the late 1950s do not, however, seem to have extended to the emergence of women writers. To be sure, Ann Jellicoe and Shelagh Delaney attracted some attention but neither have really sustained their early promise, and the latter owed a great deal to the admittedly female-dominated Theatre Workshop at Stratford East. It is difficult to know why women have on the whole been so little evident as playwrights (though they did play a significant role in the late seventeenth-century theatre, and approximately 20 per cent of plays produced in Britain in the period 1900-1930 were by women). Conventional wisdom suggests that women avoid drama as a social art requiring the strength and personal acerbity necessary for sustaining one's views in a public arena. The playwright has to battle with producer, director, and actors, and this may be contrasted with the quieter life of the poet or novelist. Yet this is not a view which can easily be sustained. In the first place, not all playwrights choose to shepherd their works through the production process; in the second, women have played a vital and uncompromising role in a number of major theatrical organizations. In America it was a woman, Hallie Flanagan, who ran the entire Federal Theatre, a diplomatic task of considerable complexity and toughness. It was a woman, Ellen Stuart, who played a central role in the emergence of the Off-Off-Broadway theatre of the 1960s. It was a woman, Nancy Fischandler, who founded Arena Stage. In Britain, Lillian Bayliss was the founder of the Old Vic, and Joan Littlewood created and ran Stratford East. But the fact remains thay they have not been notable either as playwrights or directors.

Moreover, it is possible, in the twentieth century, to identify women writers of considerable subtley. In America, Susan Glaspell's early plays were, arguably, better than the first plays of Eugene O'Neill—both writers sharing the stage of the Provincetown Theatre, birthplace of the modern American theatre. But in truth Lillian Hellman's neat moral parables, like those of Lorraine Hansberry, made her natural kin to William Inge and Robert Anderson rather than Miller, Williams or Albee. In England it is difficult to adduce any woman dramatist of equal significance.

Perhaps there is some small truth in Germaine Greer's observation of women painters that they had subordinated their career to private life, their own talents to those of husband, son or friend. Certainly Susan Glaspell conceded too much to her dramatically less talented husband, George Cram Cook, founder of the Provincetown Playhouse. Conversely, however, Lillian Hellman's best work occurred under the tutelage of Dashiell Hammett; if he did not create her career, he did at least propose it to her. Nor did domesticity in any way inhibit women from playing a critical role in the post-war English novel, though Pam Gems has spoken of the problems which she has in this regard. Peter Conrad, in a review of Germaine Greer's book, argues with what he takes to be her conviction that women have been prevented from making great art because their egos have been bruised and their wills pulverized. 'Certainly', he admits, 'they haven't made great painters and musicians but the reason in these cases is simple and practical: these arts depend on technical skill, and women until recently have been denied access to vocational training. In literature, which requires no such apprenticeship, they haven't suffered any disadvantage from what Miss Greer calls their compulsory enculturation.' This scarcely meets the case of drama, which equally requires no specialist training. When Arthur Miller wrote his first play, he had only been to the theatre on one occasion, and had to ask a friend the conventional length of an act.

Peter Conrad then reminds us of Madame de Staël's argument 'that women are the presiding spirits of modern literature and the inventors of its most characteristic form, the novel' because 'classical literature is masculine, extolling a heroism which is either martial or statesmanlike; but modern literature devotes itself to the internal emotional crises which are the feminine correlative of masculine adventure.'[6] Apart from the fact that this must rest on a cliché, notions of a sexually-based aesthetic are suspect. Modern literature does, indeed, engage an internal world, but the male sensibility (in the form of Poe, Melville, Conrad, Lawrence, Joyce) has shown little hesitation about engaging that world, while, despite the apparent sociality of the theatre, it too has concerned itself with internal emotional crises. Indeed, the irony, given Peter Conrad's view, is that it was the increasing consciousness of women's social role which eventually led to the establishment of various feminist groups, performing plays by women. It was in the 1970s that women writers of the calibre of Caryl Churchill, Pam Gems, Micheline Wandor and Mary O'Malley finally emerged.

There is no simple answer. Historically, of course, the theatre has been a male-dominated form, to the extent even of entirely excluding women for a

[6] Peter Conrad, *The Observer*, 28 October 1979, p. 39.

considerable period. But the historical association of theatre with lewdness hardly offers a convincing reason for the lack of interest by women writers in the twentieth century. Perhaps there is a minor explanation in the significance of Oxbridge as a source of writers; not simply in the male dominance at those institutions, though this is important, but in a tradition which takes seriously products of the Oxbridge system in this area as in the area of satirical revue. The strength of Oxbridge's hold on British institutions is as likely to prove beneficial to the young student playwright as to the budding civil servant. (John McGrath's first play, for example, a student production at Oxford, was reviewed by Kenneth Tynan, himself an Oxford man, in the *Observer*. The result was that George Devine—Oxford—asked him to work on a play with Anthony Page—Oxford—at the Royal Court. Students at Leicester should be so lucky.) It is perhaps less a matter of bias than of expectation. The lack of women playwrights creates a situation in which women simply don't think of themselves as potential playwrights, or see their way into a system which seems manifestly uninterested in them. Thus, only when specifically feminist theatre groups are founded is there a manifest market, a means of access. It is not a convincing explanation, but I have no other.

Of all the new women playwrights, Caryl Churchill seems to me the most powerful and original, and is dealt with at greater length elsewhere in this book. Neither she nor Pam Gems is primarily a militant feminist writer (in the sense that Joan Ware, Catherine Webster, Michelene Wandor and Dinah Brooke might be so described). Nonetheless Pam Gems in particular is interested in examining the nature of what—perhaps in common with Peter Conrad—she would indeed call the feminine sensibility, in a world in which public and private roles are in a state of flux and the reassuring if constricting boundaries which shape experience are in a state of collapse.

Pam Gems's characters in *Dusa, Fish, Stas and Vi* (1976) seem to cover the range of possibilities which she sees available to women: mother, mistress, whore, intellectual, neurotic. All are deeply vulnerable. It is a female world: men are the objects of pursuit or scorn. No one is happily married. They all pay some kind of price for their sexual identity. One, Violet, an anorexic, is actually destroying herself through irrational attachment to models of feminine attractiveness; a second, Fish, kills herself in despair at a life which is falling apart. And her suicide note stands as some kind of epitaph for all four of them, who happen to be living through a time when changes in sexual role are destroying a sense of order which, however frail or misguided, previously offered an identity which was secure and socially sanctioned. 'My loves, what are we to do? We won't do as they want any more, and they hate it. What are we to do?'[7] And behind that collapse is another. As Stas remarks, 'there is a tendency, in the physical world, for things to collapse.' It is a truth which rings through the work of virtually all the writers considered here but one perhaps felt more acutely by women who traditionally have been charged with sustaining the principle of continuity,

[7] Pam Gems, *Dusa, Fish, Stas and Vi* (1977), p. 43.

with providing a social and even a metaphysical anchor.

In *Piaf* (1978), Gems writes of a woman who was the adjunct to nothing but her own incredible talent and appetite for life, but who at the same time saw sexuality as the central fact of her existence. Though her own sensibility meant that she lived at a neurotic pitch which made lasting relationships virtually impossible to sustain, as dramatized by Pam Gems she was never apologetic about her pursuit of relationships which were unequal only because her fame and her talent inevitably distorted the context of those relationships. Gems is unafraid to underscore Piaf's crudity because that was always the source of her power. By the same token her articulateness exists mostly in the songs through which she communicates so much of her genuine feelings. Much of the dialogue is deliberately fragmented, brief, prosaic, and direct. Piaf exists not primarily through spoken language, but through her emotions and her songs. It is the special achievement of *Piaf* that this becomes both a dramatic strategy and a subject.

Mary O'Malley's *Once a Catholic* (1977) is a humorous and, one suspects, barely satirical portrait of life in a convent in the early 1950s. But her humour becomes more functional in *Look Out . . . Here Comes Trouble* (1978), which dramatizes the dislocations of life in a mental hospital which scarcely differs from life outside. Librium is passed out liberally but scarcely more so than in the society beyond the walls. Mary O'Malley lacks the symbolic imagination of David Storey. She is far more concerned with locating and dramatizing a barely controlled sense of desperation and pain than with pressing through the fact to the image. Her technique, which seems to derive from television, is particularly apt as brief spasms of experience are pulled together by the writer, creating a collage of emotional events. Plot is minimal. The focus of the play and its methodology centre on emotional states, on rhythms of desperation disrupted by occasional bursts of pointless activity. But the play does operate on a symbolic level, and the symbol which it elaborates is one which has clearly proved a compelling one for those who share a conviction that the self is under extreme pressure.

For a period in which boundaries are indeed dissolving, in which roles are no longer as clearly definable and acceptable, in which the dominant images seem to be those of decay and degeneration, and in which society is perceived as a conspiracy against the self or against a class, it is perhaps not surprising that the mental hospital should have become a favourite image and setting for the playwright of the 60s and 70s. It is evident, for example, in Dürrenmatt's *The Scientists*, Peter Weiss's *Marat/Sade*, Ken Kesey's *One Flew Over the Cuckoo's Nest*, Edward Albee's *Listening*, David Storey's *Home*, Joe Orton's *What the Butler Saw*, Peter Shaffer's *Equus*, David Edgar's *Mary Barnes*, Tom Stoppard's *Every Good Boy Deserves Favour* and Mary O'Malley's *Look Out . . . Here Comes Trouble*. It is a telling image and, indeed, its potency underlines a thematic continuity which can be seen as connecting the early plays of Osborne, Wesker and Stoppard with the work of writers like David Hare, David Edgar, Howard Brenton and Barrie Keefe two decades later. Beyond everything they express a powerful sense of cultural and personal collapse.

II

In one sense the 'new' playwrights of the late 1950s were more conservative than the press and critics were prepared to acknowledge. Readily making the classic mistake of assuming that plays featuring the working class are necessarily revolutionary, journalists and critics collaborated in creating the fiction of an iconoclastic drama. But the sound which they heard was not that of falling idols; it was more often a wistful regret at lost opportunity, a bitter despair at the inability of their own age to generate myths with the same compelling quality as those of the past. Whether it was Wesker, looking back to the unambiguous battles of the 1930s or recalling with nostalgia the blueprints and commitments of a time when revolutionary change was something more than a rhetorical flourish, or Osborne, observing the slow deracination of social forms, these writers challenged the indifference which they saw around them and the particular texture of the social organism, rather than the nature of authority itself. Wesker's quarrel with society is a lover's tiff over who shall plan, build and operate the golden cities of the future which in his heart he is convinced will never be constructed. And that combination of hope and despair is an essential characteristic of his work which in fact finds its central source of value less in a socialist objective than in the nature of the struggle.

As he himself once admitted, and as is apparent in his developing career, his plays are less concerned with a radical reconstruction of the public world than with finding ways for the individual to survive, to imprint his or her own identity, to deal with a life in which the moral being is assaulted from within and without. What primarily disturbs him is the sleep of the spirit which allows the individual to surrender either to social dictat, a debilitating homogeneity, on the one hand, or a brutalizing fanaticism on the other.

As he said of his play, *The Old Ones*, in 1971:

> This play is about survival, like all my plays. There are many kinds of survival. We need to survive our disappointments with ourselves, with our lovers, with our ideas, or perhaps it is with the way we've attempted to carry out these ideas. We need to survive the knowledge of our weaknesses, mistakes and our death. But it seems to me that looming over all these things is the need to survive those who on the one hand are in power and abuse that power and those, on the other hand, who, with fanaticism, try to defend us. It's not easy to steer between the two—but I would like to think my plays helped to protect man from the twin passions of corruption and fanaticism, of inequality and violence. Extremists exorcise only the devil within themselves not the devil within our society.[8]

Coming one year after his final acceptance of the failure of Centre 42, this marked not so much a new stage in his career as a new perception of a theme which had always been central to his work.

The clearest change in Wesker's work since the mid 1960s, apart from the obvious shift in the class of the people he writes about (a shift paralleled in

[8] Letter to the author, 1971.

Pinter's work), is that his plays have become more self-consciously poetic, that the energy of his work is refracted now through a more precise sensibility. Much of his original power was socially derived; it emanated from the friction between classes, or between the individual and his political ideals. That has mostly gone. His work is now more concerned with an internal world, with the low-voltage world of memory, of physical and emotional entropy. He still insists on the need for his protagonists to speak with their own voice—in that respect *The Old Ones* (1971) scarcely differs from *Roots* (1959)—but structure now dominates material as material once dominated his structures. His work is now more finely calculated. For David Edgar, the passion has gone out of Wesker's drama. He has, moreover, become less a social than a metaphysical writer. For the early Wesker, the struggle towards articulateness, the release of personal energy, seemed always in some way directly linked to the emergence of a class. Now he is more concerned with language as a strategy, an evasion, as public evidence of a private sense of vulnerability. The issues which always existed beneath the carapace of class have broken through to the surface.

The revival of social realism, when it came in the late 1950s, was, indeed, a response to a more fundamental sense of unease than is inspired by a feeling of social inequity. It expressed not merely the conviction that power and control were slipping away but the belief that no one was exerting control and no one could. Beckett's clowns, Osborne's music hall entertainer, and Pinter's caretaker (as, later, David Mercer's Flint or Joe Orton's retired worker, Mr Buchanan) are not simply images of a society which has lost all purpose and direction, of people dislodged from history. They are images of a world in which the idea of identity and individuality are themselves ironic.

The fascination of *Look Back in Anger* lay precisely in the fact that it reflected a sense of cultural dislocation. The anger of the play was only ostensibly a class anger. Its chief characteristic was that it was unfocused. The discontent, misdirected into physical violence, was in fact a profound dissatisfaction which sought a target, reached for a language, which could give it shape. It was not the injustice of his society which angered Jimmy Porter, but the vacuousness of his own life. Education had given him articulateness but nothing to be articulate about. The old England was dead but no convincing new one had taken its place. The country seemed like an endless succession of Sunday afternoons (an image close to that used by Alan Sillitoe in his novel *Saturday Night and Sunday Morning* (1958)). It was its triviality, its pointlessness, which appalled Jimmy Porter, who was in effect an absurd hero rather than a social rebel. His anger was his attempt to simulate life; his violent language an effort to insist on his existence. The natural analogue in 1970s drama is Stephen Poliakov's *Hitting Town* (1975), Barrie Keefe's *Gimme Shelter* (1977), Howard Brenton's *Magnificence* (1973), and, in the 1980s, Poliakov's *Bloody Kids* (1980).

What Osborne responded to was a system in a state of collapse (an image which he successfully elaborates in *The Entertainer*). But his was not just a sudden awareness that time had exposed a fundamental provinciality formerly concealed behind the caul of imperial pretensions. He detected a profound sense of cultural disruption of a kind which Beckett had proposed. The conventional form of Osborne's play concealed its potential profundity, as the more recent collapse of his work into triviality has discouraged serious critical attention. For a few brief years (in *Look Back in Anger, The Entertainer* and *Inadmissible Evidence*, 1964) he wrote a series of plays which captured a sense of disintegration felt equally on a social and a metaphysical level. Those who saw his work only in a social context were simply registering the aftershocks of a disturbance taking place much deeper in the cultural substrata, and captured perhaps most obviously in Beckett's work. Beckett expresses a sense of cultural paradox, a paradox implicit in the disjunction between language and action ('Let's go.' *They do not move.*) A metaphysical tension, it also addresses a fundamental ambivalence about the utility and indeed the propriety of action. The lesson of history, apparently, does not propose the consonance or the progress implied by political theories or the structure of language, but simply a nullifying stasis. Its painful contradictions are those of a culture. For Beckett, at least, there were simply no sanctions for theories of social advance, moral autonomy or even the freedom necessary for change.

The evidence of this paradox is equally visible in England which simply becomes a province of the modern. It is visible in the deconstruction of character in Orton, in the dissolving certainties of Pinter, the logical contradictions of Caryl Churchill, the supposedly inevitable collapse of aspiration in Keefe, the apparently irredeemable corrosion of language identified by Hare and Poliakov, and, perhaps more poignantly, the subversion of radical polemics by a suspect literateness. It is not simply that there are a series of minor ironies: Oxbridge graduates assaulting the system which gave them direct access to their craft; radical drama being subsidized by the state it wishes to destroy or, in the case of Wesker's Centre 42, by a friendly millionaire; Bond's assertion of a rational art in a drama whose poetic images operate on an emotional level. It is that the tensions go to the heart of a fundamental cultural uncertainty, an eclecticism, a heterogeneity, suggesting a system in a state of flux, uncertain as to the shape and meaning of the past (exploded by Bond in *The Pope's Wedding*, Pinter's *Old Times* and Caryl Churchill's *Cloud Nine*), the nature of a present in process of mythicizing itself (Poliakov's *City Sugar*), a world, in short, dissolving into planes of language (N.F. Simpson's *Resounding Tinkle*), simple role (Orton's *What the Butler Saw*), or self-referential action (Stoppard's *After Magritte*). The future is seldom imagined. The key to it is restlessly sought elsewhere. There is, indeed, even a profound doubt about the function and morality of art itself (Hampton's *Savages*, Stoppard's *Every Good Boy Deserves Favour*). The writer fears that he may be an accomplice to a process of manipulation which is perceived in the external world, but which invades an art which no longer has the autonomy proposed by modernist aesthetics. Even Bond's plays allow for greater ambiguity than do his prefaces, an admission of the failure of art to convey a political analysis without subverting its own certainties with a problematic model of character and action. The prefaces attempt to close the spaces opened up by art. And those spaces are feared.

Ideological drama, whatever else it may be, is the expression of the need to close aesthetic and social spaces. Appearance and essence must be made to coincide; the kinetic energy which is generated by different economic and class levels must discharge itself completely as it will, one day, in revolution. So that it is entirely logical that social realism should be the favoured style for socialist art and ambiguity be seen as the source of threat since that admits to the survival of the irrational; it concedes an experience not wholly subordinated to analysis and hence potentially disruptive of a system claiming to offer total explanations. And disruption, disintegration and decay were the dominant images of the 1960s and 1970s alike.

Yet, for all this, English drama tends to grant an authority and a power to the environment and to the constraining arabesques of the social system that is not felt by most European and American dramatists. On the whole (and Orton, Pinter, and early Stoppard are the most conspicuous exceptions), issues are perceived at a social or psychological rather than metaphysical level. Reality (for all but a few writers) is simply not seen as being problematic. Experience is susceptible of rational analysis. Manipulation is a product of economic or class injustice. Personal dislocations can be explained in terms of social or spiritual deprivation (Bond's *Saved*), or extreme psychological pressure (Shaffer's *Equus*). Either way an historical consciousness, a clear-eyed rationalism, can identify if not resolve the problem. Herein lies some of the banality of *Equus*, surely the most overrated play of the 1970s. For Beckett, for Ionesco, Genet, Handke, for late Albee, for Robert Wilson, the problem lies elsewhere. The realities of the British class system, evidenced in the educational background of those who create English theatre, are, it seems, simply too apparent, too immediate, too real to permit the writer to see beyond them to more fundamental issues, or at least too manifest to allow an approach to the metaphysical which does not engage a social reality first.

The constraining power of the environment is acknowledged in American writing—in fiction no less than in drama. Indeed it is an essential image in plays like *The Glass Menagerie*, *A Streetcar Named Desire*, *The Iceman Cometh* and *Death of a Salesman*. But it tends to become a symbol of the given, of a metaphysical rather than a social determinism, which must be resisted by a self which responds with desperate fictions (*Salesman*, *Streetcar*, *Who's Afraid of Virginia Woolf?*), or with a defiant and subversive eccentricity, a neurotic energy and a linguistic inventiveness which creates a space denied by the environment. The challenge is to strike through the pasteboard mask. The imagination creates values. It becomes evidence of rebellion. Conspiracies exist, but they tend to be metaphysical rather than social —except where black writers are concerned. And that is perhaps the clue. For there the enemy is less cosmic, more immediate and identifiable. And that I take to be the reason for the more directly social thrust of English drama. Social and economic injustice is real if not massive. The system lacks the fluidity which can discharge that energy in action or, indeed, in movement. England never had the physical space which in America was once fact and is now metaphor—myth. Space in England fails to operate on either a literal or symbolic level. Thus awareness of metaphysical constraint tends to be seen as a secondary stage, a luxury for those who suffer no other kind.

III

The theatre begins with space. For the French theatre theoretician Antonin Artaud, the very existence of that space creates a potential, a necessity for the theatrical event to expand to fill it. Though it occurs in time, its own time is conventionally regarded as relating only analogically to that which its audience experiences. But to Artaud, 'theatre is not the imitation of life, but life is the imitation of transcendental principle which art puts us into communication with once again'. Theatre and life thus become part of the same process. This was a conviction eagerly embraced by the American theatre of the 1960s, and in particular by Off-Broadway groups in reaction, theatrically, against the solemn profundities of O'Neill, Hellman, Miller and Albee, and, socially, against a supposedly defunct rationalism. They responded in particular to the emphasis on physicality, on spectacle and on performance which they found in Artaud. They responded, too, to his reaction against the dominance of language, and to his insistence on the theatre's unique command of the present tense, which potentially turns art into epiphany. Artaud specifically wished to galvanize the theatre, to mobilize the present moment. His imagery was drawn from dance and from the circus. The word was not to be removed but it was to be cut down to size. The language of theatre lay primarily elsewhere. As he observed in *The Theatre and its Double* (published in America in 1958, and thus available as a handbook for the new developments which began in American theatre in the following year),

> The theatre, an independent and autonomous art, must, in order to revive or simply to live, realize what differentiates it from text, pure speech, literature, and all other fixed and written means. We can perfectly well continue to conceive of a theatre based upon the authority of the text, and on a text more and more wordy, diffuse, and boring, to which the aesthetics of the stage would be subject. But this conception of theatre, which consists of having people sit in a certain number of straight-backed or over-stuffed chairs placed in a row and tell each other stories, however marvellous, is, if not the absolute negation of theatre— which does not absolutely require movement in order to be what it should —certainly its perversion.[9]

But, in this respect, as in so many others, the British theatre remained remarkably resistant to outside forces. The resistance stemmed primarily from the strength of the English tradition of highly verbal theatre and from an insistence on the factitious nature of the theatrical moment, its power to create structure, to contrast language with event. As Iris Murdoch's narrator in *The Sea, The Sea* observes:

[9] Antonin Artaud, *The Theatre and its Double*, trans., Mary Caroline Richards (New York, 1958), p. 106.

even a middling novelist can tell a lot of truth. His humble medium is on the side of truth. Whereas the theatre, even at its most 'realistic,' is connected with the level at which, and the methods by which, we tell our everyday lies. . . . Drama must create a factitious spell-binding present moment and imprison the spectator in it. The theatre apes the profound truth that we are extended beings who yet can only exist in the present. It is a factitious present because it lacks the free aura of personal reflection and contains its own secret limits and conclusions. Thus life is comic, but though it may be terrible it is not tragic.[10]

Peter Brook may have looked forward to the time when normal life might be seen as theatre and have pursued that conviction into a concern with anthropology, pressing drama back towards its roots in myth and ritual—but noticeably he chose to do so outside England, basing himself in Paris and touring through Iran and Africa. For the most part the British have remained committed to a more conservative view of theatre, one in which language continues to have a primary role, in which the present moment is charged with ambiguities.

And, paradoxically, though primarily a visual medium, television has tended to reinforce this emphasis on language. Jack Gold, the television and film director, has suggested that there are budgetary and logistical reasons for this. Filmed sequences cost fifty per cent more than electronic ones and, since television lacks the sensual impact of the cinema, it substitutes intensity for scale. Its own scale makes it less effective as a means of creating action sequences; it lacks epic potential, having to rely on sheer accumulation for its effects, a collage of incidents, intimate moments, fragments of experience, to build its sense of process. Space has to be recreated in time. The simultaneous becomes the sequential. And one of the mechanisms for that elongation is language. British television drama is heavily linguistic. Words are set against images, close-ups permitting an ironic contrast of expression and word difficult to approximate in the theatre and which in the cinema tends to defer to ironies of action.

Indeed, in many respects contemporary English drama is *about* language. It is not merely that the English dramatic tradition has always been self-consciously literate, that articulateness is seen as a primary virtue. Words have in many ways become the focus. For Osborne and Wesker they remain a link, a bond at a time when social cohesiveness is in a state of collapse. The appalling *A Sense of Detachment* is, in fact, Osborne's misguided attempt to rescue words from their denaturing by pornography and casual abuse. Language, indeed, and its connection with both social and physical manipulation, has been a central concern of a number of writers in the 1960s and 1970s. For Orton and Stoppard the viscosity of language, its ambiguities, its availability as an instrument of social control and moral evasion, is a clue to a more fundamental betrayal of morale and morality. Orton's response is to lurch into a world of fictions, a vortex of language in which infinite linguistic resonances imply infinite lexical regress, and thereby deny any concept of

[10] Iris Murdoch, *The Sea The Sea* (1978), pp. 33, 36.

order, form, definitional boundaries. His response to authoritarian systems which effect their power through language is to explode that primary mechanism of control. And so he detaches words from their context, allows them to collapse as their meaning fragments. His characters inhabit separate linguistic universes (a trick he learned, with much else, from Pinter). And because it is impossible to tie down the real, it is equally impossible to force the individual into a coercive straight jacket of role, identity or type. Orton was a genuine anarchist and recognized that the first and primary sacrifice required by his revolution had to be the word.

Stoppard's alarm is of a different kind. Beginning his career with similar doubts, he has become increasingly disturbed by the implications of his own logic. An antinomian world, a relativistic linguistic world, such as that proposed in *Rosencrantz and Guildenstern are Dead*, consisting only of opposing fictions, leaves little space for moral value. The hangman and the victim become indistinguishable except as types of linguistic statement. Art, as in *After Magritte* and *The Real Inspector Hound*, becomes hermetic. Everything, finally, becomes a question of aesthetics. As a consequence, Stoppard has found himself in his more recent work (certainly in *Professional Foul, Every Good Boy Deserves Favour* and *Night and Day*), trying to re-establish both the absolute need for moral responsibility and the necessity to acknowledge language as in some way both rationally and morally linked to a world whose reality must be assumed even if it cannot ultimately be proved.

Edward Bond attacks Stoppard on the one hand as a facile wordsmith and on the other as a dangerous reactionary—thus, unsurprisingly, mirroring those East European critics who once denounced him for his lack of social awareness and moral commitment only to find that, once discovered, that moral vision focused on their own evasions. Stoppard acknowledges the link between language and power. It is not for nothing that he makes the KGB Colonel in *Every Good Boy Deserves Favour* into a semanticist. Indeed, he confesses, as Bond does not, to the coercive power even of his own work. His social criticism may in recent years have located a precise target (in the suppression of human rights in eastern Europe and the loss of personal freedoms at home) but he knows and acknowledges, as few English writers do, the contradiction and even the moral evasion (the 'professional foul') implied by challenging other people's fictions, other people's coercive language, with one's own; the totalitarian gesture with an art whose imaginative power is not unconnected with the totalitarian spirit, in its dictation of values, manipulation of character and dramatization of history. Art is perhaps no less peremptory than the political dictat—simply less immediately powerful. Its only defence lies in its willingness to confess as much by foregrounding technique, drawing attention to its theatricality, as Stoppard does in *Travesties* and *Every Good Boy*. Its avowed theatricality, its admitted travesty of the real, becomes a confession of that urge to manipulate, to shape the imaginative world in which people are invited to live out their real lives, which makes the writer unavoidably to some degree an accomplice of the forces he would denounce. This is a truth seldom confronted by those so confident of their own vision that they become blind to the nature of theatrical power. To corrupt an audience in the direction of truth—a phrase unblushingly used by the American dramatist Edward Albee—is legitimate to the degree that the writer defines that truth in such a way as to include an inspection of his own motives or methods.

A concern over the function of art also characterizes Christopher Hampton who, when he was not writing uneasy comedies, was engaged in a continuing debate over the function of art, the morality, indeed, of his own enterprise. Fully aware of opposing temptations, not only in his own creative imagination but equally in the nature of writing itself, he has, in *Total Eclipse*, to some degree in *The Philanthropist*, and most clearly in *Savages*, questioned the morality of art. For indeed to give social experience linguistic form is already partially to appropriate the ethical to the aesthetic. The British diplomat, in *Savages*, who turns the real experiences, the myths, the values, the lives of the Brazilian Indians into carefully sculpted poems is committing an act of aggression not only against reality, forcing it to accommodate itself to the aesthetic and moral purposes of the writer, but against the living truth of people whose existence is in some way denied by decontextualizing them, by making entertainment out of pain. As Iris Murdoch has suggested, 'Form itself can be a temptation, making the work of art into a small myth which is a self-contained and indeed self-satisfied world.' This is in essence the fear acknowledged in *Savages*—whose truth derives less from its portrait of Indians rendered inarticulate by the enormities of progress, than from the deforming power of language, the coercive fact of appropriation implicit in the act of writing. Reality is reduced to allegory. Pain is aestheticized.

But if art can displace experience from the world of fact into that of sensibility, it can also act as an agent of truth. Again as Iris Murdoch has said,

> Through literature we can rediscover a sense of the destiny of our lives. Literature can arm us against consolation and fantasy and can help us to recover from the ailments of Romanticism. If it can be said to have a task, that surely is its task. But if it is to perform it, prose must recover its former glory, eloquence and discourse return.[11]

Where Eliot had seen prose as merely a slight by-product of verse drama, and had insisted that prose was adequate only to the ephemeral and the superficial, the revolution which took place in English drama in the 1960s and 1970s, whatever else it did, re-established the power and the seriousness of prose. Of course, recognition of the coercive power of language can lead to another conclusion and this, in some ways, is the subject of *Total Eclipse*. For perhaps the only response with any integrity lies in the silence for which Rimbaud, one of the protagonists, opts. It is certainly an option canvassed by Theodor Adorno for whom the horrors of recent history have anyway constituted a fundamental denial of cultural prerogatives.

And Edward Bond is not unaware of that paradox. Indeed in *Bingo* he examines directly the nature of the writer's responsibility to the real,

---

[11] Iris Murdoch, 'Against Dryness', *in The Novel Today* by Malcolm Bradbury (1977), p. 30.

contesting not so much the playwright's right to use experience as his responsibility to recognize a moral continuum between art and life. Shakespeare is arraigned in that play, less for writing work which evades the real issues of his contemporary society than for the hypocrisy which made him elaborate a morality in his art which he failed to enact in his life. For Bond—as for many of the younger committed playwrights of recent years—it is not possible to conceive of a morally responsive and responsible art which is insulated from social experience and from the inner life of the writer. Values cannot exist in art as a virus survives in a culture dish. If art is to be a living organism, it must be coterminous with the life which it purports to describe, and which it is dedicated to transforming. And transformation, logically and morally, must begin with the writer, who can scarcely commend values to which he or she does not subscribe. The writer is only justified in abstracting himself from the immediate problems of transforming the social and economic world if art is seen as being integral to that world. Then the withdrawal, the isolation, which is the usual, though by no means invariable, prelude to creation (see the various cooperative drama groups and collaborative texts of the 1970s), is no longer seen as an ambiguous defection. There is a recognition that language is not a simple tool, not a neutral instrument, but that it has to be reforged, invested with other values, infused with other myths and qualities than those with which it is presently charged if it is to play a useful role as a mechanism of change. You cannot build a new world with old bricks.

This had been a perception at the heart of much black American drama of the 1960s; but it is, perhaps, a legitimate criticism of the committed British playwrights of the 1960s and 1970s that this kind of radical reconstruction has not for the most part been attempted (though there is some evidence of such an interest in the work done by CAST, Jeff Nuttall's The People Show, Steve Berkoff, Snoo Wilson and some of the fringe companies). The German playwright Peter Handke, in Kaspar (1968), wrote a subtle and original play suggesting the intimate connection between language and social control. Ten years before, Kenneth H. Brown, the American playwright, had, in The Brig (1964), created a powerful metaphor of that control and had attempted to resolve the paradox by deploying a wide range of theatrical resources while minimizing the incidence of language. But there are few examples in English drama of language being placed under such extreme pressure. Yet the issue is clearly of central significance—and is perceived as such by, among others, both Joe Orton and Caryl Churchill.

For Joe Orton, however, there were other strategies available. Instead of diminishing his spatial, temporal and linguistic world—instead of allowing silence increasingly to invade his work as the source of some final irony—he drives his characters at a frantic pace, hollows out their language, has the ground literally collapse under their feet, implodes character, expels silence, creates, in other words, an act of pure surface whose anarchistic undertow subverts all meaning. Even the tenuous structure implicit in the act of writing becomes ironic—his central image being that which concludes his only published novel, Head to Toe, that of a man writing on a blackboard in black chalk. Ionesco, of course, in a different mode, did something similar, and the element of farce in absurdist drama is itself significant, with its implications of character deprived of its third dimension and a humour turned against its characters. But, Kenneth Tynan's proscriptions notwithstanding, there was always something of the satirist in Ionesco, of the man who saw absurdity as in part rooted in the social system. For Orton, despite his own vendetta against authority, there was no immunity to the absurd, except in a kind of homeopathic absurdity. Anarchy was the only truth which he would acknowledge, a breaching of all boundaries, so that the world could only adequately be described by images of total flux and contingency. In his world, the mask was the only reality. Since society chose to regard his sexual identity as deviant, and his personal mode of existence as eccentric, he set out to assert the centrality of deviance and eccentricity. In his last play, *What the Butler Saw* (1969), he even coerced his audience into responding enthusiastically to rape and incest, mocking, as ever, that return to consonance which had formerly made farce such a reassuringly conservative form. In Orton's world there is no tranquil norm to which the characters may return at the end of the play. Orton's anarchic farce is not the description of a momentary disruption of order—it is a total world from which there is no escape. Madness is a basic condition. Though it is tempting to see him as very much a product of a period in which boundaries of all kinds were under assault—sexual, class, generational—and though his anarchic rebellion was of a piece with that more cynically deployed by Andy Warhol in another medium in America, and not unrelated to the aesthetics of 'happenings', his was (his borrowing from Pinter once left behind), in its essentials, a unique voice. And his assault was more profound than that of those playwrights who attacked authority in its capitalist guise, but left the authority of the theatre, of character and of language largely untouched. For Orton, history was no less fictional than his own work, and character simply a series of carelessly deployed roles. Language, meanwhile, was hopelessly plastic, the source of a never-ending series of double entrendres, misunderstandings and deceptions.

Caryl Churchil is more insistent on the social component of linguistic control, but she too is fascinated by language as evidence of a desire for rationality. Interested, as she is, in the historical 'enclosure' system, whereby land was commandeered from the people, she has been equally drawn to dramatize the linguistic enclosure whereby experience is appropriated through language. In *Light Shining in Buckinghamshire* (1976), set in seventeenth-century England, she makes her characters sensitive to the language of power—the Norman language is shown being consciously employed to reinforce class division by linguistic means. Men are denied the vote—but women, significantly, are denied a voice. Indeed the voicelessness of women (a radical minister will accept questions from men but not from women) is a political and linguistic fact which her plot is designed to deny. But of course her own articulateness only demonstrates her participation in the system, not her power to dislodge it. By locating the dilemma in the past she demonstrates the roots of what, to some degree, is presented as a contemporary issue, but inevitably that distance also cauterizes the wound. The device is in some senses self-defusing. Indeed Caryl Churchill is not primarily a radical playwright (though she feels that that element has recently intensified in her work) and her interest in language goes beyond its social utility or its availability as an agent of power. In *Traps* (1977), she creates a Mobius strip of language which can have no reality outside of the theatre. As she indicates in a note:

> It is like an impossible object or a painting by Escher, where the object can exist like that on paper, but it would be impossible in life . . . the time, the place, the characters' motives and relationships cannot all be reconciled . . . the characters can be thought of as living many of their possibilities at once.[12]

Traps is a trap not only for her characters, but for the audience. Just as the eye tries to reassemble a Mobius strip, to make it obey rational expectations, so does the member of the audience attempt to sustain control by reducing possibilities to possibility, character to type, event to plot, language to manifest meaning. Caryl Churchill is one of the few English playwrights to show any interest in investigating the process of perception (Pinter is obviously another). The conventional sight-lines are removed. There are no stylistic clues which assert themselves against the sheer flow of experience—continuously created acts with no necessary connections. The impulse to freeze that experience, to negate flux, to deny the incoherence and plasticity which underlies the process of social organization and art alike, is re-experienced by the audience and reader, who equally cannot tolerate an experience which does not render up its meaning. As in Kafka's *The Trial* or Albee's *Quotations From Chairman Mao*, we are forced to enact that struggle to impose order on chaos which is the essence of the absurd.

If writers like Beckett, Pinter and Orton suggest that language is exhausted, that words have been drained of meaning, detached from any world of verifiable reality, the socialist playwright clearly has to respond otherwise. That much was plain in *Light Shining in Buckinghamshire*. As Sartre has said:

> If words are sick, it is up to us to cure them. Instead of that, many writers live off this sickness. In many cases modern literature is a cancer of words. . . . If one starts deploring the adequacy of language to reality . . . one makes himself an accomplice of the enemy, that is, of propaganda. Our first duty as a writer is thus to re-establish language in its dignity . . . I distrust the incommunicable; it is the source of all violence. When it seems impossible to get others to share the certainties which we enjoy, the only thing left is to fight, or burn, or to hang.[13]

This is, of course, a profoundly materialist view. The assumption that all meaning must be voided through language denies both the force of religion and mystery. Indeed, it is arguably non-revolutionary to wish to insert the

---

[12] Caryl Churchill, *Traps* (1978), n.p.
[13] Jean-Paul Sartre, *What is Literature?* (New York, 1965), pp. 260-1.

word between the self and its realization, between the action and the reaction. But Sartre's response to the latter charge is to see the word as act, to transform the treason of the clerks into the revolution of the clerks. Thus he wishes to see a literature of praxis, that is one in which 'perception itself is action', in which 'to show the world is to disclose it in the perspectives of a possible change' through revealing to the reader, or the audience, 'his power in each concrete case, of doing and undoing, in short of acting'. In an age of 'an unfindable public'—and this was a central problem for the committed playwright in Britain—a literature of praxis becomes, for Sartre, a moral necessity. And he looked forward to a 'theatre of situation' rather than a theatre of character:

> No more characters; the heroes are freedoms caught in a trap like all of us. . . . Each character will be nothing but the choice of an issue and will equal no more than the chosen issue. It is to be hoped that all literature will become moral and problematic like the new theatre. Moral—not moralizing; let it simply show that man is *also* a value and that the questions he raises are always moral. Above all, let it show the inventor in him.[14]

This, indeed, is the sense in which so many English playwrights have set about re-inventing .the past, creating a drama of imminence in which an image of a proximate future is implied, urged, prophesied and enacted, albeit a future usually displaced into a past in which its contours have already been traced out in actions and characters which contained the essence of the new world, and which had only been defeated because they embodied ideas whose time had not yet come.

It is true to say that the single most significant development in British theatre in the decade 1968 to 1978 was the rise of socialist theatre. Despite appearances, the period from 1956 to 1968 had not produced such a theatre —Wesker's well-meaning attempt, in the form of Centre 42, being moribund long before its official death in 1970. But 1968 was a psychological, if not social, economic and political, watershed. Thereafter an increasing number of 'fringe' companies were formed (at first as an off-shoot of American experimentalism, the early companies being founded or sustained by expatriate Americans). Some of these subscribed to socialist principles, while several of the more interesting and accomplished new writers chose to describe themselves as socialists (Arden, Bond, Hare, Brenton, Edgar, McGrath, Griffiths, Churchill). John Arden's career changed direction at this time, while David Edgar, Trevor Griffiths and Howard Brenton have attested to the significance of a year which saw social and political revolt spilling onto the streets of eastern and western Europe as well as of the United States.

It was a movement already on the wane by the middle of the 1970s. In 1975 Howard Brenton announced the death of the 'fringe' and while re-dedicating himself to a social analysis requiring 'communist tools', himself

---

[14]*Ibid.*, pp. 278, 285, 287.

described these tools as 'bloody and stained. . . . Not pleasant'.[15] In 1978, David Edgar was lamenting the failure of socialist theatre. Two years later David Hare declared a fundamental change in his approach. This was clearly not unconnected with the shift to the right of political opinion in Britain and the manifest failure of socialist theatre to provoke a change in working-class consciousness. David Edgar has pointed out that, while in 1967 there was only one independent socialist theatre group in the United Kingdom, the Cartoon Archetypal Slogan Theatre group, whose very title expressed a 1960s version of revolt, he could by 1978 identify at least eighteen full-time subsidized socialist groups, receiving £500,000 in public money, and a long list of socialist playwrights who had succeeded in infiltrating the dramatic Establishment. Yet at the same time he felt obliged to confess that 'while the scale of socialist theatre work is impressive, it is obvious that its intervention in the working-class struggle itself has been at best patchy and peripheral' and that 'socialist theatre has remained at a remove from revolutionary organizations'.[16] This was a view challenged by John McGrath, who regarded Edgar, along with Howard Brenton and David Hare, as evading the central task of the committed playwright: that of creating a new working-class audience for plays, raising the consciousness of those who were potentially the fuel of revolution.

For a number of British playwrights, then, 1968 was a crucial year. Events in Vietnam, in Ireland, in France, Germany and even Czechoslovakia injected a political component into public life and rhetoric which had simply been absent before. It was, to be sure, a somewhat confused and unfocused politics, less ideologically based than reactive. The real revival of the Left was the product of the early 1970s rather than the 1960s, which elaborated instead a counter-cultural, utopian philosophy and language. The revolts of 1968 were, indeed, in some respects akin to Baudelaire's (admittedly somewhat aberrant) conception of the 1848 revolution. It had been a romantic rebellion with a strong literary component, 'amusing only because people made utopias, like castles in Spain'.[17] As Richard Klein has suggested, Marx was not far from sharing this belief, stressing the non-ideological component of that revolution and the degree to which it borrowed language and ideas from an earlier era. It would not be hard to find elements of this in the 1968 rebellions—with their slogans derived from the surrealists, their curious gurus, and their serious political objectives. Of course there was more than this to it in France (and a number of the new playwrights spent time in France in 1968); but in England it was provincial in the extreme. It was vague as to its objectives. It was, indeed, a revolt to some degree against precisely that world which Baudelaire had predicted, a world in which technology 'will have so Americanized us, progress will have

[15] Howard Brenton, 'Petrol Bombs Through the Proscenium Arch', *Theatre Quarterly*, V, xvii (March-May 1975), 10.

[16] David Edgar, 'Ten Years of Political Theatre', *Theatre Quarterly*, VIII, xxxii, (Winter 1979) 25.

[17] Quoted in Richard Klein, 'Baudelaire and Revolution', in *Literature and Revolution* by Jacques Ehrmann, ed. (Boston, 1967), p. 93.

so atrophied our spirit, that nothing in the sanguinary, sacriligious, or anti-natural dreams of the utopians will be comparable to these positive results.'[18]

And that, indeed, was the problem for a Left more concerned with the ownership of technology than its desirability. But it was precisely this sense of the atrophy of the spirit which seized the imagination of writers as various in other respects as Stoppard, Hampton, Brenton, Hare, Poliakov, Keefe and Berkoff, and which connected them in some degree to the work of Wesker and Osborne. The compelling power of avowedly socialist writers like Brenton and Hare lay finally less in their elaborations of Marxist paradigms than in their creation of images of moral and spiritual collapse. Marxism was, after all, materialist philosophy, and at a deeper level they were as profoundly suspicious of that materialism as they were of the vapid consumerism of western society. What was lost was any concept of transcending values. The deconstruction of the public, private and linguistic world was not, finally, a simple product of capitalism but a dimension of the modern. The alarm which they feel begins at a social level but—in particular with Brenton, Hare and Poliakov—it ends with an apprehension that the collapse is more radical in nature and more profound in origins. We may be witnessing the decay of a system, but more disturbingly, they suggest, we can observe the collapse of character, of words and of the whole notion of a morally sensitized existence.

IV

Drawing on distinctions which Raymond Williams makes in his book *Marxism and Literature*, John McGrath identifies three main elements of literary production: 'the *residual*, which draws its sources from a previous period but is still effectively alive in the present; the *dominant*, which exercises hegemony over the period culturally; and the *emergent* element, by which, and I quote, "new meanings and values, new practices, new relationships and kinds of relationships are being created" '. In terms of the English theatre this corresponds structurally with the West End (residual), the major subsidized companies (dominant) and the fringe (emergent). As far as political theatre is concerned, McGrath identifies three main areas of activity:

> Loosely speaking, they are: first, the struggle within the institutions of theatre against the hegemony of the 'bourgeois' ideology within those institutions; secondly, the making of a theatre which is *interventionist* on a political level, usually outside those institutions; and thirdly and most importantly, the creation of a counter-culture based on the working class, which will grow in richness and confidence until it eventually displaces the dominant bourgeois culture of late capitalism.

In terms of socialist writers, this would correspond with writers like John Arden, David Edgar, Trevor Griffiths, Edward Bond, Howard Brenton and David Hare, whom he sees as representing the challenge to bourgeois ideology within the theatre, and those (sometimes, it must be admitted, the

[18] *Ibid.*, p. 95.

same people) who write for groups like 7:84, Red Ladder, Belt and Braces, Monstrous Regiment, Common Stock and other politically committed companies, whose purpose he sees as being directly interventionist,

> polemical, openly political, and whose avowed aim is to gain support for a particular party or position inside the working class, and among its potential allies . . . its ultimate purpose [is] agitational. It uses theatrical devices to explain, elucidate, remind, and eventually persuade its audience to think or act differently.

From this will grow the true counter-culture—which clearly is no longer the vague romantic reactivism of the 1960s. He admits that no political fringe group of which he is aware is linked with a party, but confesses that this is substantially a consequence of what he calls 'Labourism' and Stalinism, which has brought about 'the evacuation of Marxism from working-class politics in this country'.[19] And this is a crucial observation. For the left-wing theatre in Britain has to deal not only with indifference to Marxism but positive hostility. It also has to deal with the fundamentally reformist nature of the welfare state which intervenes between social discontent and the ideological apprehension and expression of that discontent in revolutionary terms.

The welfare state does indeed constitute a problem for the left-wing writer. Its authority is such that it is difficult for either left or right wing to challenge its fundamentals. It operates in a kind of ideological vacuum. Iris Murdoch has argued that its existence has created 'a lassitude about fundamentals', a 'reward of "empiricism in politics" ', and the consequence has been the erosion of the 'theoretical wing of our political scene'.[20] Much the same point is made by the political playwrights of the 1960s and 1970s. What Osborne and Wesker had noted is now acknowledged by a new group of writers, themselves more clearly the result of that system: namely that the welfare state has destroyed ideology, drained the left of its revolutionary rhetoric, and undermined the confident individualism of liberal and conservative alike. And this is why political rhetoric in recent years has seemed so hopelessly dated, so unresponsive to a situation in which the real source of malaise was not ideological conflict, but the absence of any real conceptualization of the function, purpose and destiny of the individual or the group. Right and left joined in expressing their ideals in terms of money and the satisfaction of needs, real or invented. It needed no theory to express such aims: utilitarianism becomes the meeting ground of political forces which only seem to be antithetical. And this is the special problem of a writer like McGrath. It is no longer adequate to assault capitalism for working-class audiences who only wish to be cut in more fully on the profits; it is no longer possible to attack a welfare state which is only the worker's just reward for his labour, and which the left wing has anyway validated by referring to it as the 'social wage'. As a consequence these plays tend to be

[19] John McGrath, 'The Theory and Practice of Political Theatre: the bourgeois versus the popular tradition in committed theatre work'. *Theatre Quarterly*, IX, XXXV (Autumn 1979), 43-54.
[20] Iris Murdoch, 'Against Dryness', p. 26.

baffled accounts, unable to find a way out of the paradox except by stepping backwards in time, beyond the era of Marcuse's 'repressive toleration,' a phrase not empty of meaning but difficult to explain to an audience alive to the more immediate and real repressions of Eastern Europe.

For Iris Murdoch one consequence of the welfare state, and the utilitarianism which lay behind it, was 'a general loss of concepts, the loss of a moral and political vocabulary'.[21] Despite its achievements, the weakness of the left in the theatre is, indeed, that it settles too easily for creating pure myths, crystalline social shapes, self-contained, separated from the present by time and a leap of imagination which the audience is asked to make. Those myths may be situated in the past, a past seen in clear outline, complete, rendering up its meaning without residual mystery: or the necessity for actualizing socialist myths may be demonstrated by creating apocalyptic images of a closed future in which such transformations will become increasingly impossible (Howard Brenton's *The Churchill Play*). The past is unambiguous: it is a platonic paradigm, pure, ideologically neat. The revolutionary future is almost never visited: it defines itself through opposition, through exclusion. It is what is left when greed, a corrupt language, a distorting egotism, a false relationship to self and society, a misguided bourgeois individualism have dropped away. Hence, in *Trees in the Wind* (1971), by John McGrath, a torrent of language (derived from advertising) is vomited up so that words can assume their proper function, can become the precise tools of social analysis once again. But it is the clarity of these myths, their hermetic brilliance, which is potentially their flaw. The mechanism for breaking into these myths, for moving out of the confusions and frustrations of a degrading and spiritually unrewarding present, is by no means clear. Since language has lost its edge, since ideological rhetoric no longer corresponds to a world which has grown if not more complex then at least more confusing, just how can a path be beaten to a world which can only be defined in terms of its discontinuity with that present?

And, as suggested above, there is an aesthetic problem. For political and social reasons these playwrights require a transparent language, a clear glass through which to observe social realities. That this is a naive view of language matters less than the fact that it produces a denial of imaginative depth to experience. Since the political conviction implies that experience and value are definable in terms of material conditions, that the surface is both a determining and an oppressive reality, it follows that the aesthetic presumption is likely to be similar. Ambiguity is not a virtue, mystery has no place, an unconfident deconstructing art becomes a denial rather than an expression of human reality. Communication cannot be seen as problematic, since it is the *sine qua non* of committed art. For this reason the mode more usually favoured by the left-wing theatre is realism—perhaps even a modified version of socialist realism. And one is not obliged to accept Trotsky's jaundiced view of this as a simple version of Stalinism: 'Realism consists in imitating the provincial clichés of the third quarter of the last

---

[21] *Ibid.*

century; the "socialist" aspect is visibly expressed, in that events which never took place are reproduced with the help of touched-up photographs.'[22] More useful is Brecht's definition:

> Realism means, revealing the mask of causes in society/unmasking the dominant viewpoints as viewpoints of those who dominate/writing from the point of view of the class which, for the most urgent difficulties, holds the broadest solutions/emphasizing the moment of the development/ concrete character and possibility of abstraction.[23]

But for Sartre, this is based on a false premise:

> The error of realism has been to believe that the real reveals itself to contemplation, and that consequently one could draw an impartial picture of it. How could that be possible, since the very perception is partial since by itself the meaning is already a modification of the object?[24]

There is, indeed, a real risk in clarity, in a history determined to reveal its own mechanisms, in characters who feel impelled to expose their motives too completely—indeed in a socialist realism whose objective is self-revelation, a direct entry into the mind, by-passing the imagination, and fearing opacity. As Barthes has said, 'It is because socialist realism, in its very aims, does without mediation (at least in the west) that it is asphyxiating itself and dying; it is dying because it refused the thing that hides reality in order to make it more real, which is literature.'[25] The unease expressed here lies not simply in a ruthless drive towards exposure but in the notion that truths apprehended so directly are not likely to be profound truths. As Jean-Pierre Morel has suggested, the real problem is that for the 'real' one can in effect read 'ideology',[26] while the supposed analogy between scientific methodology and socialist realism is untrustworthy, precisely because science lacks an ideological component (Soviet attempts to inject one into the study of biology proving disastrous).

For Piscator, the writer's function was primarily political. He must 'learn to put his own ideas and original touches to the back of his mind and concentrate on bringing out the ideas which are alive in the psyche of the masses'.[27] The play is an instrument for conveying information. For him 'man portrayed on the stage is significant as a social function'. In a reversal of Eugene O'Neill's famous comment, he asserts that 'it is not his relationship to himself, nor his relationship to God, but his relationship to society which is central.'[28] Man is not made into a political animal by political theatre, however, but by a social world which ineluctably charges him with political

[22] Jacques Ehrmann, *Literature and Revolution*, p. 160.

[23] *Ibid.*, p. 170.

[24] Jean-Paul Sartre, *What is Literature?*, p. 55.

[25] Ehrmann, p. 177.

[26] Jean-Pierre Morel, 'A "Revolutionary" Poetics', in Jacques Ehrmann, *Literature and Revolution*, pp. 160-79.

[27] Erwin Piscator, p. 47.

[28] *Ibid.*, p. 187.

significance. Indeed his own statement of his political views could stand as an accurate summary of the stance of contemporary left-wing drama in Britain:

> We, as revolutionary Marxists, cannot consider our task complete if we produce an uncritical copy of reality, conceiving the theatre as a mirror of the time. We can no more consider this our task than we can overcome the state of affairs by theatrical means alone, nor can we conceal the disharmony with a discrete veil, nor can we present man as a creature of sublime greatness in times which in fact socially distort—in a word, it is not our business to produce an idealistic effect. The business of revolutionary theatre is to take reality as its point of departure and to magnify the social discrepancy, making it an element of our indictment, our revolt, our new order.[29]

But Piscator's theatre was subject to precisely the same problems which afflicted Centre 42 forty years later, and which create the ironies which surround the efforts of people like John McGrath:

> The contradiction in the structure of the theatre is nothing more or less than a contradiction in the times as a whole: it proves to be impossible to build up a proletarian theatre within the framework of our current social structure. A proletarian theatre in fact presupposes that the proletariat has the financial means to support such a theatre, and this presupposes that the proletariat has managed to make itself into a dominant social and economic power.[30]

The existence of local and state government subsidy in Britain scarcely diminishes the irony, but that irony cannot be accepted as wholly incapacitating, for the left poses a problem which is entirely cogent and which, once again, Piscator had himself posed. Can the theatre, he asked,

> take the liberty of ignoring the lives of those people down there while it indulges in a display of intellectual abstractions, formal arabesques, changelings from its own imagination? It must be real, real to the last detail, unreservedly true, if it wants to capture even a reflection of these people's lives. And if it is to become a motive force in their lives, how much more real and true it must be.[31]

If it was a good question to pose in 1920s Germany, it was an even better question for Britain in the second half of the twentieth century. But the word 'truth' is used with a casualness which is more likely to be regarded with suspicion in the late twentieth century, at a time when rationalism and even the authority of the assured ideologue and the artistic voice are held to be deeply suspect.

Piscator was not primarily calling for realism as a style, but for the infiltration of an experience which begins as fact and ends as truth:

[29] *Ibid.*, p. 188.
[30] *Ibid.*, p. 173.
[31] *Ibid.*, p. 329.

Political drama must, if it is to fulfill its pedagogic aim, make document-ary evidence its point of departure, and not the individual. On the con-trary, it must maintain the most impersonal, 'objective' attitude to the characters in the subject, not in a neutral sense, but in the sense of a mate-rialistic conception of history.[32]

It is in this sense that John McGrath quotes approvingly Lasalle's dictum, 'to tell the truth is revolutionary.' He might well have added Sartre's observation that demythologizing is also a revolutionary act, for the recon-struction of an alternative history was accepted by the left-wing theatre in Britain as a primary responsibility, and is embodied in works like John Arden's *The Non-Stop Connolly Show*, Caryl Churchill's *Light Shining in Buckinghamshire*, David Hare's *Fanshen*, Steve Gooch's *The Women Pirates Ann Burney and Mary Read*, Trevor Griffiths's *Taking Our Time*, and John McGrath's *The Cheviot, The Stag and the Black Black Oil*.

The obsession with history as subject and explanation is entirely explu-cable. As Jacques Ehrmann has pointed out, 'the true subject of revolution is history.'[33] The revolutionary writer invokes history against language. It is offered as truth, as a sacrament in the revolutionary ritual, as an insight into the hidden logic in which we are trapped and for which we stand as evi-dence. And, because the 1970s Marxist playwright has no available working model to which he can point, either the plays have to operate on an abstract level—the linguistic structure standing in for the political structure—or they have to locate a world less liable to ambiguity and collapse of ideological purity. And this provides another stimulus to turn to the past, to invoke a social context in which class antagonisms were closer to the surface, eco-nomic injustices more apparent, and in which, it is presumed, the working class had not yet internalized the values of the dominant group. Thus John McGrath turns to the days of the 'Red Clyde' because those were 'days when the naked greed and ruthlessness of the capitalist system were plain to see'.[34]

Yet there are problems in the assumption of socialist theatre that it is based on a 'rational' analysis of the processes of history. For Edward Bond, the very word 'rational' becomes a kind of mantra, as if the very evocation of it could ensure agreement; yet Bond's redeeming grace is that his own work escapes the trap of his reductive public language, that he is a poet whose irra-tionalisms are compelling. Indeed his symbolic imagination—ambiguous, resonant, pre-verbal—is at odds with his publicly expressed belief that the world voids its meaning carelessly. Michel Beaujour has suggested that an hermetic language—a language of poetry, dense, radiant less with clarity of meaning than with mystery—is not adequate to the task of the writer concerned with transformations that should occur not in the internal but the external world. He notes of Saint Paul, attacking the invasion of the Church by glossalia, that, by preferring the language of preaching, he calls into question 'the status and significance of language deprived of meaning,

[32] *Ibid.*, p. 296.
[33] Jacques Ehrmann, p. 11.
[34] Steve Gooch, *Little Red Hen* (1977), n.p.

situated out of society and time', for it is unfit for action, and denies history: 'this prattling moment is a utopia of eternity.' Here, of course, it is not the political idealist who is utopian, but the poet, seeking a timelessness which is both the subject and the context of his work. So, he says, no poet can be revolutionary, because 'poetry is the incarnation of man's permanent aspiration as a speaking being to a *beyond* which only language, whose code is shaken by the poet, can offer him.'[35] The definition may be too severe, but it certainly focuses accurately the problem of the contemporary playwright, on the one hand seeking directness, on the other formal experiment. Indeed the flirtation between political commitment and aesthetic experimentation has always proved difficult: in Russia, the symbiosis ended in effect with the suicides of Esenin and Mayakovsky. For the surrealists it created a series of paradoxes which perplexed that movement over a number of years, as they took turns in excommunicating one another for breaches of aesthetic or political orthodoxy. The risk, which perhaps instinctively places the social revolutionary and the avant-gardist in different camps, is that energy will be deflected into form, that experience will be aestheticized, that the audience will be splintered, that a revolt against language and a sophisticated or ironic apprehension of the real constitutes a threat to a world in which language is presumed to be a precise tool for analysing a reality which stands ready to render itself up completely to the scrupulous analyst. It evades control and as such is suspect. It implies an aristocracy of artists and the existence of an aesthetic world which can escape the axial lines of history and class.

Perhaps this is why some writers resist both the role of artist and the notion of theatre as a formal experience. 'It is not', Steve Gooch insists in an author's note in *Female Transport*, 'a literary piece but primarily a verbal or oral one.'[36] Of *Will Wat? If Not What Will* (1972) he said, 'We weren't presenting a formal theatrical representation of The Peasants Revolt—a "play"—rather it was these ten actors telling and showing the audience what happened to the peasants and artisans in 1381.'[37] One is reminded of Mayakovsky's statement, 'I do not know whether one can call so definitely what I have done a *work*.'[38] For the revolutionary, the status of writer is inherently ambiguous in that it implies a space between him and those he would address; it implies a certain remove from the battle, a degree of objectivity which might be mistaken for lack of total commitment. It should also, however, generate a scepticism about language which is not apparent in the work of a writer like Gooch.

Indeed in some ways the articulateness of the new left drama in Britain is its own downfall. In the context of a tradition forged by Wilde, Shaw, Coward, Rattigan and Stoppard, it inevitably associates itself with its enemy. However, it could perhaps be said to differ from other committed writing in its apparent lack of confidence in its ability to effect change.

[35] Michel Beaujour, 'Flight our of Time', in Jacques Ehrmann, *Literature and Revolution*, p. 47, 48.

[36] Steve Gooch, *Female Transport*, p. 5.

[37] Steve Gooch, *Will Wat* (1975), n.p.

[38] Jacques Ehrmann, p. 179.

McGrath's *Trees in the Wind*, Griffiths's *Bill Brand* television plays, Wesker's *I'm Talking About Jerusalem*, Bond's *Lear* or *Bingo* are obsessively concerned with the failure of political consciousness, the failure to move from language to action (Bond places altogether too much weight on Lear's final act of rebellion in his play). And well they might be, not only because of their awareness of the political realities of late twentieth century Britain, but because of their own situation as writers. They are aware of the danger that language should be seen as a substitute for action, and yet language is their medium. And the process whereby language can survive its own genesis in a corrupt history, its elaboration in a reductive social system, is no more examined than is the survival of the rational mind, the existence of the clear-sighted revolutionary, or the fact of a theatre which declares itself independent of the system which it otherwise wishes to regard as all-pervasive and determining.

Genet suggests that 'If we are clever enough, we can pretend to understand, we can make believe that words are stable, that their meaning is fixed or that it has changed because of us' but concludes, 'As for me, faced with this enraged herd encased in the dictionary, I know that I have said nothing and that I never will: and the words don't give a damn.'[39] However, the idea that language is imprecise and even deceptive, that history and reality are in effect competing fictions, is liable to be seen as a luxury by those on the sharp end of these fictions. As Arthur Miller has said, 'the abrogation of cause and effect was entertaining' only 'so long as one had never felt the effects.'[40] And as Genet himself warned, 'As for language, there is a grammar of action.'[41] The problem for the left, however, was that after ten years of socialist theatre, revolt remained a linguistic rather than a physical fact. Indeed in the course of the 1970s, after a brief hiatus, the country seemed to swing further away from left-wing politics, while some of its more powerful writers publicly declared their disaffection with the kind of socialist theatre which looked for immediate transformation.

The growth of socialist theatre in Britain corresponded with the revival of the Left which took place in the early 1970s. This was a period of wage militancy which led in 1974 to the fall of a Conservative government which chose to challenge union power by taking on the National Union of Mineworkers. It was a deceptive triumph, and never really the conscious challenge to capitalism which it was taken to be by those ever-watchful for the first signs of social revolt. The challenge was in many ways an inadvertent one, and certainly not sought by organized labour. The imagery may have been revolutionary—capital and labour locked in a struggle won eventually by the latter—but the reality was otherwise. In fact a profoundly conservative impulse lay behind much of the union activity of the decade 1968-1978. The social revolt implicit in the 1960s counter-culture had always been vague and in some sense non-ideological. It was anyway diluted

[39] Jean Genet, *Reflections on the Theatre and Other Writings*, trans. Richard Seaver (1972), p. 72.
[40] Arthur Miller, interview with the author, September 1978.
[41] Jean Genet, p. 74.

by the time it reached the working class in the homogenized form of consumer product. The wage militancy of the 1970s, like the deliberate forgoing of that militancy during an extended period of wage restraint from 1975-78, was an indication of the individual's and group's determination not to be excluded from the spectacular society, even in its less spectacular days. Far from sparking revolution, a nearly 30 per cent inflation rate inspired a shocked conservatism which eventually, in 1979, and partly as a consequence of ill-judged, if justified, public-service strikes, even resulted in a Conservative government with the largest majority for a generation and a Cabinet in which only two members had not been to public school.

V

Perhaps the most eloquent justification and critique of the new political theatre of recent years is contained in David Hare's 1978 lecture delivered at King's College, Cambridge. For him theatre is centrally concerned with judgement, as subject and method. The theatre is uniquely suited to revealing the gap between appearance and reality, to dramatizing the lie:

> I would suggest to you crudely that one of the reasons for the theatre's possible authority, for its recent general drift towards politics, is its unique suitability to displaying an age in which men's ideals and men's practice bear no relation to each other; in which the public profession of, for example, socialism has often been reduced by the passage of history to wearying personal fetish, or even chronic personality disorder. The theatre is the best way of showing the gap between what is said and what is seen to be done, and that is why, ragged and gaptoothed as it is, it has still a far healthier potential than some of the other, poorer, abandoned arts.

Thus the health of the theatre in some sense becomes an expression of the disease of society. But the problem for the Marxist writer, as Hare acknowledges, is that, while the urban proletariat are far from ignorant of their plight, and while the country has been through a severe depression and even rampant inflation, there is still no real sign of revolutionary consciousness. For Hare, 'Confronted by this apparent stasis, the English writer is inclined to answer with a stasis of his own.' And he laments,

> Must it always be . . . that Marxist drama set in Europe reflects the state of revolutionary politics with an answering sluggishness of its own? By this I mean, that sinking of the heart when you go to a political play and find that the author really believes that certain questions have been answered even before the play has begun. Why do we so often have to endure the demeaning repetition of slogans which are seen not as transitional aids to understanding, but as ultimate solutions to men's problems? Why the insulting insistence in so much political theatre that a few gimcrack mottoes of the Left will sort out the deep problems of

reaction in modern England? Why the urge to caricature? Why the deadly stiffness of limb?[42]

For him, the reason that 'dramatists have lately taken to brandishing their political credentials as frequently as possible throughout their work and that political theatre groups have indulged in such appalling overkill'[43] is because they are afraid of the volatility, the uncontrollable nature of dramatic performance 'which exists at the moment of interaction with the mind-sensibility of a member of the audience whose experiences and perceptions are not controlled by the dramatist's'. They are afraid, too, of the fact that the real changes in society are perhaps registered in 'the extraordinary intensity of people's personal despair'.[44] He himself writes 'about politics because the challenge of communism, in however debased and ugly a form, is to ask whether the criteria by which we have [been] brought up are right, whether what each of us experiences uniquely really is what makes us valuable.' And so he rejects 'a theatre which is exclusively personal, just a place of private psychology' as 'inclined to self-indulgence'; but, equally reacts against 'a theatre which is just social' as 'inclined to unreality, to . . . impotent blindness'.[45] It is, of course, an analysis which leaves him where we all prefer to locate ourselves in analyses of this kind, irreproachably in the middle, guilty of neither excess. But his is, in fact, a tangential art. The force of his images derives from the fact that they grow out of the sensibility of his individual characters but capture the mood of a culture. The desperate mental fragility of Archie and Anna in *Licking Hitler* (1978), lying for their country in a black propaganda department of British intelligence during the war, and then discovering that this has become the basis for a whole post-war morality, or the unrepressed hysteria of Susan Traherne in *Plenty* (1978), who sees the momentary human solidarity of wartime dissolve in the lies of private and public life, stand as patent symbols of a more general collapse of human values, of a culture built on national self-deceit, an antinomian world of pragmatic ethics. So, too, the protagonist of *Dreams of Leaving* (1980), thankfully relapsing into conformity, oddly grateful to discover that the woman who had urged a sense of moral responsibility on him could finally be dismissed as insane, is offered as an image of a society glad to be relieved of responsibility, released into the redemptive tedium of a routine existence whose primary virtue lies in the fact that it allows no room or time for doubt, for a disturbing attachment to truth and the moral world. Anna, in *Licking Hitler*, observes 'the steady impoverishment of the people's ideals, their loss of faith, the lying, the daily inveterate lying, the thirty-year-old deep corrosive national habit of lying' but herself leads an aimless existence, while her final appeal for confirmation of some redeeming principle is addressed to a man who has sold out to necessity, allowed mendacity to become a basic principle of his art. The final words of the play are, 'He never replied.'[46]

[42] David Hare, 'A Lecture', *Licking Hilter* (1978), pp. 62-3.
[43] *Ibid.*, p. 64.
[44] *Ibid.*, p. 67.
[45] *Ibid.*, p. 69.
[46] *Ibid.*, p. 55.

Susan, in *Plenty*, who, like Anna, tells 'glittering lies' for the advertising industry, observes a world in which those in power, lacking any purpose or principles, believe only that 'Behaviour is all.'[47] For her, too, the war-time acquaintance who was to redeem and justify this collapse of morale and morality proves ineffectual, having sold out to 'a corporate bureaucracy as well'.[48] The play ends ironically. In the final scene, set in 1944, Susan predicts a new world, transformed, infused with a new vital principle. The betrayal of that hope is the play's subject. The graph indicates only continuing decay. The dominant fact is entropy. Language falls apart, as does character. Social cohesion collapses along with the sustaining myths of the past. And neither of these plays indicates any way of breaking out of this process. That is left to *Fanshen* (1975), his earlier play, and I doubt if Hare realizes just how chilling a portrait that play draws of the collective spirit which he was then tempted to peddle as his own solution to western decadence.

David Hare is a poet of disintegration. His plays are extended metaphors of collapse. In *Slag* (1970) it is the slow decline of a girl's school; in *The Great Exhibition* (1972) the end of a marriage; in *Teeth 'n' Smiles* (1975) the accelerating attrition of a rock band. A central image in *Teeth 'n' Smiles*, indeed, is of a bomb explosion in the Café de Paris, full, at the time, of the rich, studiously declaring their supposed immunity from the war. As they lie dead and wounded so two anonymous figures move among them, stealing their money and jewels. The scene is in essence repeated in present time as a member of the rock band sets fire to a tent as they perform at Cambridge University, while the other members of the group steal the college silver. The apocalypse is no longer deferred; it has arrived. But everyone is 'on' something—drugs, alcohol, pursuit of career, money; they all ignore the evidence of disintegration and decay. And their ability to ignore it is adduced as further proof of its reality.

The England whose alternative history David Hare has been writing, from *Brassneck* to *Plenty*, is a country whose energy is spasmodic, nervous, artificial. It is a country in which private despair is the constant. There are no models of an alternative system, no calls for working-class solidarity, only a clear-eyed analysis of moral entropy, the failure of public myths and private values. And as such, I suspect, he is responding more directly to a national sense of failed purpose and moral attrition than those writers for whom a simple shift in the distribution of wealth and power constitutes a clear solution to problems which are perceived as primarily a product of late capitalism. He does insist that moral collapse is related to public values, and that the individual cannot sustain a moral self in such a context. But his own self-doubts are as apparent; the power of the theatre to detect a lie extends even to his own desperate belief in a socialist alternative.

There is indeed a self-irony expressed by one of David Hare's characters which might be applied equally to several other highly educated middle-class socialist playwrights. 'I went into socialism', explains the socialist MP in *The Great Exhibition*, 'like other people go into medicine or the law.

[47] David Hare, *Plenty* (1978), p. 72.
[48] *Ibid.*, p. 84.

It was a profession. Half out of eloquence, half out of guilt. And as the eloquence got greater so did the guilt. I could cut my tongue off.'[49] It is a real dilemma. Indeed the central image of that play is the socialist as 'flasher', as exhibitionist. The fear is that commitment to public change is rooted in a fear of insufficiency, in a profound self-doubt extended to include the revolution coyly flaunted because not fully believed in. The greater the evidence of social inequity, the greater 'the weight of knowledge of what *ought* to happen',[50] the more impossible seems the ideal which so stubbornly resists translation into social fact. The very obviousness becomes the source of despair. And Hare felt profoundly disillusioned by the pragmatism of contemporary politics: 'The only political experience I had had was believing passionately in the Labour Government of 1964, and watching that government sell everything down the river.'[51] Deprived of that animating conviction, he was left with the feeling, expressed in the Ortonesque *Knuckle* (1974), that contemporary English society—the society of property millionaires and political accommodation—was morally corrosive, the more so because it was wilful. Unlike Joe Orton he identifies the need for a moral world but can find no way of dramatizing it within the context of a destructive social system. But in 1975 he confessed to being 'sick to death with writing about England—about this decadent corner of the globe'. As a consequence, his next play, *Fanshen*, was set in revolutionary China and was about a society and a period of time 'in which one felt that people's lives were being materially and spiritually improved, in a culture that was completely different to anything we knew'. It was the result of a desire to 'write a positive work using positive material'.[52]

But by 1980, he had, anyway, moved away from his concern with dramatizing a public world, with offering himself as pedagogue. In describing the shift in his work, which led to the television play *Dreams of Leaving* (1980), he is reported to have said;

> If you've written a long time about social and political things you're aware that the question of who sleeps with whom is of more interest and daily currency than the state of the economy or the decline of the West. . . . I wanted to write something which a mass audience would recognize as a situation in which they'd been. And to deal with the impact of sex on people's lives. . . . I'm trying to push aside the business of being a teacher or a moralist because that is a trap for a writer. The longer I've been at it, the more I've felt it's silly telling people what to do. They've not taken any notice. And one's own life isn't so wonderful that one has the right to preach. That's why in *Dreams of Leaving* there are no big speeches or bursts of rhetoric . . . it's not a didactic work. At the end I'll be happy if people think to themselves 'It may not say anything but it's true.'[53]

[49] David Hare, *The Great Exhibition* (1972), p. 30.

[50] *Ibid.*, p. 52.

[51] David Hare, 'From Portable Theatre to Joint Stock . . . via Shaftesbury Avenue', *Theatre Quarterly*, V, xx (1975), p. 112.

[52] *Ibid.*, p. 114.

[53] *Radio Times*, January 12-18, p. 17.

Hare's real power is, indeed, as a writer concerned with pressing towards this sense of truth, with elaborating painful images of decline rather than with mobilizing a revolt against a class and economic system which may itself be a symptom rather than the cause of disease. And in this respect he is close kin to Howard Brenton, to Stephen Poliakov, to Steve Berkoff and Barrie Keefe. Indeed in *Sore Throats* (1979) Howard Brenton moves into essentially the same territory as that mapped out in *Dreams of Leaving*, presenting a drama of personal, sexual disintegration in a country which has 'abandoned you' and in a city which is 'just a tank, rusty old sludge tank, storing you for nothing'.[54] Howard Brenton's achievement lies partly in his stylistic subtlety, which goes beyond simple eclecticism, and partly in a self-doubt which leads him to dramatize characters themselves uncertain of the realities which they claim to serve. His own social background makes him an unlikely revolutionary, but in a play like *Magnificence* (1973) that becomes his subject as he dramatizes the unexamined assumptions of revolutionary and reactionary alike. He takes as his epigraph three lines from Brecht's *Die Massnahme*, 'Sink into the mire/Embrace the butcher/But change the world',[55] but disinters the hypocrisy of those who choose to substitute slogans for truth. Revolutionary and ruler are equally trapped within their private worlds, distorting the real, creating false dramas tangential to an external world of genuine suffering. They remain blind to the sheer beauty of existence, trapped in a banality which their own histrionics are designed to evade but not to cure. Lacking real understanding they sink into the mire and embrace the butcher but, failing to perceive the reality of the world, fail equally to change it.

And the nature of that reality is made apparent in *The Churchill Play* (1974), which offers what Brenton sees as a logical extension of social and political processes already under way. Like Amiri Baraka's *S-1*, in the United States, it projects a world in which personal freedom has been proscribed by law. A group of internees act a play for a visiting parliamentary select committee as they are imprisoned in the Churchill Internment Camp. The play, which features Winston Churchill risen obscenely from the dead, is in effect an attempt to trace the origins of a class presumption and a capitalist brutality of which the present imprisonment is merely a natural consequence. As one of the characters remarks, 'Never noticed. Ten years the country sliding down. Through the nineteen-seventies. Guns. Barbed wire . . . Journalist I were. Good story that. But I never noticed.'[56] Another character's repeated observation that 'I don't want the future to be like this' is eventually disrupted by the advance of soldiers who are to punish their apparently futile rebellion.

Brenton began his career on the fringe. Although an early play, *Revenge* (1969), a surreal assertion of the shared values of criminals and police, was produced at the Royal Court Theatre, he subsequently worked with groups like the Brighton Combination and the Portable Theatre. He responded to

[54] Howard Brenton, *Sore Throats* (1979), p. 20.
[55] Howard Brenton, *Magnificence* (1973), p. 7.
[56] Howard Brenton, *The Churchill Play* (1974), p. 88.

both the aggressive experimentalism of the groups and their community orientation. Indeed the collapsed physical space of such theatres, and particularly the enforced proximity of actors and audience, became 'an almost moral force in the writing and in the presentation' and from that 'you begin to want to write about how people conduct themselves in life as groups, as classes, as interests.'[57] Political engagement, in other words, was generated out of what was in origin a theatrical necessity, but which became in time a metaphor. But for Brenton there was no virtue in denying himself access to the facilities and the sheer professionalism of the conventional theatre. Indeed by 1975 he was convinced that the fringe had failed:

> Its failure was that of the whole dream of an 'alternative culture'—the notion that within society as it exists you can grow another way of life, which, like a beneficient and desirable cancer, will in the end grow throughout the western world, and change it. What happens is that the 'alternative society' gets hermetically sealed, and surrounded. . . . Utopian generosity becomes paranoia.

Hence one engages reality with the only set of tools available, 'bloody and stained but realistic. I mean communist tools. Not pleasant.'[58]

A similar ambiguity invades the work of Trevor Griffiths, and in *Comedians* he sets the humanist and the revolutionary traditions side by side. Indeed his work, like Hare's and Brenton's, shows him more committed to the former than he might care to admit. Thus the crux of his television play *Through the Night* (1975), about the casual indifference to human suffering of those—the hospital specialists—whose task is to obviate it, lies in a speech by a young doctor who believes 'we have lost all idea of you as a whole, human being, with a past, a personality, dependents, needs, hopes, wishes. . . . We invite you to behave as the sum of your *symptoms*.' It is a criticism that can be levelled at the committed playwright himself, as at Marxism. Yet, despite this, Griffiths defends his own position. When the doctor quotes Hippocrates on medicine:

> Whoever treats of this art should treat of things which are familiar to the common people. For of nothing else will such a one have to enquire or treat, but of the diseases under which the common people have laboured, which diseases and the causes of their origin and departure, their increase and decline, unlettered persons cannot easily find out for themselves, but still it is easy for them to understand things when discovered and expounded by others. . . . For whoever does not reach the capacity of the common people and fails to make them listen to him, misses his mark.[59]

Griffiths is clearly the socialist playwright asserting a defence of his art.

Similar problems exist in the work of Stephen Poliakov. When, in his 1978 lecture, David Hare lamented a student generation 'who seem to have

---

[57] Howard Brenton, 'Petrol Bombs Through the Proscenium Arch', p. 10.

[58] *Ibid.*, pp. 10-11.

[59] Trevor Griffiths, *Through the Night* and *Such Impossibilities* (1977), pp. 63-4.

given up on the possibility of change, who seem to think that most of the experiments you could make with the human spirit are likely to be doomed or at any rate highly embarrassing', adding 'There is an almost demeaning nostalgia for the radicalism of the late 1960s',[60] he could well have been one of the characters of Poliakov's *Hitting Town* (1975), who asks: 'Why are students now all so grey and defeated, and miserable and can't do anything?'[61] The play likewise attacks the nostalgia for a period which in fact simply ushered in the nerveless and disintegrative world of the 1970s. And Hare's and Poliakov's works offer an implicit answer to the question in their characters' desperate preference for a world of unreality, and beyond that a world which has seen the collapse of successive models of revolutionary liberation. Poliakov's entropic images, however, lack Hare's implied political momentum, and his characters can barely suppress an incipient hysteria as they alternate between catatonic indifference and neurotic collapse. They move through a contemporary world without social or moral purpose, deliberately pressing experience to extremes in the hope that it will render up some kind of meaning. Poliakov is a moralist who forbears to offer a model of the society in which his characters could move with freedom and dignity. His plays can, to be sure, be seen simply as exposing the alienating nature of capitalism, the spiritual corrosion consequent upon a world in which consumption is made a primary value. And he is indeed concerned with the moral lobotomy effectuated by materialism and sustained by the media. But the perspective is not overtly a Marxist one. What he primarily laments is the loss of individual identity, the collapse of transcendence. The society which he observes lacks any clarity of outline. It is amorphous, viscous. It is a world which is never silent. The blank television screens flicker through the night. The air is full of bland popular music. The immediate environment is either brutally anonymous—concrete walkways, blank walls—or disturbingly plastic, the artificial setting of Wimpy bars or modernized pubs. His characters are constantly consuming junk food or nothing at all. There is no substance to them or to their surroundings. The sub-text of all the messages projected by the public world of signs is submission and conformity. Under this pressure identity dislocates, a neurotic intensity is substituted for that public meaning which can only emerge from the confrontation of selfhood with hard-edged reality. His characters, like Hare's, tend to exist on the brink of madness, profoundly disturbed by the contingency of the urban world, shocked, by the constant possibility of terrorism and the brutalism of their environment, into a numbing indifference.

In *Hitting Town* Ralph and Clare try to neutralize its power with an answering anarchy, displacing the battle into a sexual context by committing incest (Freud's image of anarchy). But nothing makes an impression on a plastic world. The struggle is an unequal one, perfectly symbolized by Ralph putting his hand over the flame of a cigarette lighter as he listens to the corrosive banalities from the radio. As he observes, 'He's made of plastic

---

[60] David Hare, 'A Lecture', p. 70.
[61] Stephen Poliakov, *Hitting Town* and *City Sugar* (1976), p. 26.

and if I light this under him, he'll bubble and melt into a long black sticky line and flow completely away—taking all the rest with him.'[62] And the power of that world lies in particular in its ability to destroy language itself and through language genuine feeling which can now only express itself through frenzied spasms of destructiveness. In *City Sugar* (1975), he focuses directly on a local radio station and its DJ, Leonard Brazil, who keeps up a narcotizing flow of words, night and day. Brazil, once a teacher, now broadcasts bad music to people whom he holds in contempt. Its social function is underlined by the occasional messages which he broadcasts on behalf of the police, appeals for conformist behaviour which alternate with commercials. Reality only intrudes in the form of the news, but this is easily absorbed into the general atmosphere. It consists, anyway, mostly of sensational items and has, finally, to defer to the unreality of its context, being cut off in the interests of a pointless competition organized by the radio station. Both acts end with a self-revealing flood of language, as he describes his function, which is to 'use words so sumptuously for your pleasure . . . we're the new jokers of the pack, we're the new clowns, we tell it how it should be . . . . We're going to make it aren't we, get through "to the other side", of course we are—and if you've just seen some horrible things, on the television, bomb blasts, unemployment, politicians and all that part of our good old England, and you've switched it off to listen to me, sensibly! then remember, no need to fear. . . .'[63] And so the language flows on, offering to cauterize real wounds, to pull together random experiences, to give form to the shapeless, to fill the silence with words which dislocate and dissolve.

American Days (1979) tracks the virus to its source and elaborates an image of a society constructed purely of externals. The play stands as a paradigm of a consumerism in which individuals exist only in so far as they may momentarily serve the interests of fashion. Set in the headquarters of an international record company, which promotes and depends upon a homogenized world, it dramatizes the plight of three would-be pop stars who endure abuse and humiliation in order to receive the momentary privilege of personal attention. In order to secure that attention they have to contort their appearance, establish their significance through gratuitous violence, allow themselves to be moulded to meet the arbitrary and momentary needs of a public which is itself the victim of manipulation. At the heart of this enterprise there is no ideology, no independent mind bending the world to its pattern. The chief executive confesses, 'I have no prejudices, no politics, no allegiances.'[64] It is a world without conviction, without purpose, without values, without shape. The alienation at the heart of Poliakov's work is profound, as again in his later *Bloody Kids* (1980), perhaps the more so because it is not contained by any ideological framework.

This air of bafflement, stunted hopes, betrayed ideals, and spiritual capitulation is a strong note in the later 1970s, present again in Barrie Keefe's trilogy *Gimme Shelter* (1975-77) and his *Frozen Assets* (1978). The trilogy is

[62] *Ibid.*, p. 32.
[63] *Ibid.*, p. 56.
[64] Stephen Poliakov, *American Days* (1979), p. 36.

essentially concerned with that section of the population 'educated to be disillusioned'. On the one hand, there are those 'interested in decency and endeavour—order', representing authority, money and power, and on the other those who represent disorder, and rebel in brief spasms of violence before submitting to a system that seems part of the natural process; both groups are equally bewildered. Neither control their own lives or sustain any commitment beyond themselves. The humour they deploy is mostly destructive—a defensive gesture or a homeopathic response to pain. Rebellion is pointless: the final line of the play, 'We've won . . . again', is wholly ironic. Keefe's is a world without victory. Describing, in *Frozen Assets*, a magistrate's advice to 'Be optimistic', Sammy, an alcoholic ex-boxer, offers an elegy on the working class which the play's action deliberately undermines:

> Be optimistic he said. Optimistic. I sat on park swings in the twenties, thirties in the depression. I saw bare-footed kids running wild in the streets with rickets in their legs and scars of malnutrition . . . I see them. I see them in the slums and I say . . . I've seen deprivation and poverty and seen rats chewing babies in slum rooms. But I ain't a pessimist. Smash down the manor, rip it up, smash it down, fuck up decent people's lives but—the tribe lives on. . . . Never give in, never surrender. Do what the fuck you like to us mister. Can't destroy the heart. It's in the blood. Never kill that. Never.[65]

The play is contemptuous equally of a callow sentimentality and a self-deceiving people.

VI

> Moralists have always wondered haplessly why Poe's morbid tales had to be written. They need to be written because old things need to die and disintegrate, because the old white psyche has to be broken down before anything else can come to pass.[66]

Drained of its mysticism, this comment on Poe, by D.H. Lawrence (quoted, incidentally, by Steven Berkoff in the introduction to his play, *The Fall of the House of Usher*), captures something of the spirit of English drama of the last quarter of a century. It has, by and large, been concerned with elaborating a pathology of English society, with identifying the collapse of social and moral forms, the dislocation of language and the slow depletion of energy. For many younger writers this is primarily a symptom of capitalist society—an inevitable stage in an historical development which will lead towards a redemptive socialist future. For others it is simply evidence of a more profound collapse of personal and public meaning, consequent upon the growth of consumerism and the loss of liberal ideals of selfhood and social responsibility. For Stoppard, indeed, that latter process is seen at its most chilling precisely in those socialist countries for whom the voice of the

---

[65] Barry Keefe, *Frozen Assets* (1978), p. 48.
[66] Steven Berkoff, *East, Agamemnon, The Fall of the House of Usher* (1978), p. 86.

artist is likely to be the first to be silenced if it chooses to appeal to models of private and social morality temporarily laid aside in the name of unchallenged social process. For him the arrest of Vraclav Havel was symptomatic.

Either way, the theatre is seen as an ethical instrument, a clinical tool laying bare diseased tissue. Either way the social nature of theatre is seized upon as a justification for engaging realities which surface in a social form but which are rooted, too, in a sense of dislocation which is presented in some degree, as a product of modernity. And the dominant images of these new playwrights tend to be those of disintegration (Brenton, Hare, Keefe), alienation (Poliakov), the contingency (Stoppard) and even destructively deceptive (Hare) nature of language. The fixed points are no longer secure, either socially (Bond) or metaphysically (Pinter). Such energy as is identified tends, and not always for political reasons (Berkoff), to be seen as a working-class prerogative. The middle and upper classes move in a social and metaphysical world whose crust is paper thin. Their public confidence is fragile. And since those classes effectively define the nature of public reality, the forms and institutions, the language and symbols of cultural life, this fragility becomes a social and cultural reality. But, in fact, for Poliakov and Berkoff, indeed at moments for Edgar and Keefe no less than for Stoppard, this barely suppressed hysteria infects everyone. The world which they picture is under extreme pressure. There is no space for moral values to operate. Nonetheless the urgent necessity for a moralized existence is implied in everything they write. Indeed the act of writing itself is offered as a desperate and tentative but urgently willed attempt to arrest further decay.

Nor were these images without their basis in fact. The truth was that when Britain was not stagnating it was in decline. The Gross Domestic Product rose only eighteen points in the decade 1968-78 and actually declined between 1973 and 1975, only returning to the 1973 level in 1978 before once more declining. Industrial production was even worse, remaining stagnant from 1969 to 1971 and then declining from 1973 until 1978. Unemployment rose steadily and under the pressure of these economic realities the political parties lost their ideological distinctiveness, shoring up the system with incomes policies and desperately hoping to be bailed out by North Sea oil. Salvation was presumed to lie in an ideologically neutral technology so that when that vision began to collapse there was no enabling ideology, no transcending myth to turn to. The Labour Party, returned to power at the bottom of the slump, devoted its energy to sustaining a system to which in theory it was unalterably opposed, using methods indistinguishable from those employed by Conservative governments. Political, economic and moral stasis did not simply invade popular imagery, it had its basis in fact. And if the period from 1968 to the mid 1970s saw the rise of a politically committed theatre, the period which followed was increasingly typified by a defection from the barricades, by the creation of baffled images of personal disintegration, social entropy and spiritual aridity deployed equally by socialist and liberal writers. Articulate, frequently witty, though seldom theatrically innovative, the theatre of the 1960s and 1970s reflected more directly than, I suspect, did poetry or the novel, the writer's doubts not only about his society, in a state of genuine crisis, but about the function of art, the nature and power of language and the role of the writer, presumed to be so completely a product of the social and cultural system which he observes but with which he is nonetheless in unceasing conflict.

Note

Life and Writing

John Osborne was born in London in 1929. He was educated at Belmont College, Devon and at the time of his first success was an actor. He is the recipient of a number of awards, including an Academy Award, a Tony Award and a New York Drama Critics Circle Award. He is a prolific writer whose work covers a wide range. His hatred of drama critics is legendary.

His first play, *Look Back in Anger*, which appeared in 1956, though it opened to somewhat mixed reviews, was hailed by Kenneth Tynan as a crucial breakthrough for the English theatre. Though the passage of time has inevitably blunted some of its effect Tynan was clearly right in identifying the play as marking some kind of shift in the emphasis of English drama. It also helped to establish the importance of the Royal Court Theatre as the base for much of the important work of the next decade and more.

The present essay deals with Osborne's later work and references in the text are to the following editions, all of which are published by Faber and Faber: *Time Present* and *Hotel in Amsterdam* (1968), *The Right Prospectus* (1970), *Very Like a Whale* (1971), *West of Suez* (1971), *The Gift of Friendship* (1972), *Hedda Gabler*(1972), *A Sense of Detachment* (1973), *A Place Calling Itself Rome* (1973), *The Picture of Dorian Gray* (1973), *The End of Me Old Cigar* and *Jill and Jack* (1975), *Watch it Come Down* (1975), *You're Not Watching Me Mummy* and *Try a Little Tenderness* (1978).

Criticism

Simon Trussler's *The Plays of John Osborne* (1969) remains the best study of his plays up to and including *The Hotel in Amsterdam*. Terry Browne's *Playwright's Theatre* (1975) is a brief account of the English Stage Company at the Royal Court. Irving Wardle's *The Theatres of George Devine* (1978) is also useful although Mr Osborne's refusal to help in compiling it makes it less so for our purpose. Michael Anderson's *Anger and Detachment* (1976) has a chapter on Osborne up to *The End of Me Old Cigar* and there are useful hints in Katherine J Worth's *Revolutions in Modern English Drama* (1972), Chapter V, and John Elsomé's *Post-War British Theatre* (1976, rev. 1979).

II

Whatever Happened to John Osborne?

ARNOLD P. HINCHLIFFE

I

My question is prompted by an invitation to write an essay on John Osborne which would concentrate on his work of the last decade. For, apart from not much liking *West of Suez* (1971) or *Watch It Come Down* (1976), I could not recall that anything much *had* happened to him. In 1974, one recalls, his favourite play was *Pyjama Tops*; he was divorced in the August of 1977; in October of that year he was leading fellow playwrights into battle against the theatre critics. Yet it is never safe to dismiss Osborne. In fact, since *The Hotel in Amsterdam* (1968), he has published thirteen plays. His work has always been controversial, and his talent uncertain, though undeniable. The revival of *Inadmissable Evidence* in 1978 confirmed the force of the earlier work, even making allowance for the remarkable part played by Nicol Williamson in the role of Maitland. But, as Simon Trussler reasonably points out in his book on Osborne, he is and has always been 'an ad hoc playwright with no predetermined sense of direction',[1] and his work seems to repel criticism, much as he says he is repelled by the critics. If we were asked to choose a paradigmatic Osborne play, we would have difficulty in choosing one. He exhibits a great variety and virtuosity, but the variety often seems to derive from restlessness. He is so constantly experimenting that we have to ask what he is experimenting *for*. He is a playwright of clear social concern, yet again and again we are likely to be disconcerted by the haphazard way in which he treats his social themes.

Nevertheless, *Look Back in Anger* (1956) was indeed, in John Russell Taylor's much-quoted phrase, 'a breakthrough,' and one can still appreciate Kenneth Tynan's flamboyant declaration that he could not love anyone who did not wish to see this 'best young play of its decade'. Osborne, typically, confused the issue by calling it 'a formal, rather old-fashioned play . . . that . . . broke out by its use of language', a remark he has since confessed was misguided,[2] for it was an innovation, as was all his early work. That play still, in fact, exhibits the strengths and weaknesses of all Osborne's writing.

---

[1] Simon Trussler, *The Plays of John Osborne* (1969), p. 14.

[2] 'In fact I took a lot of daring risks. For instance, it was almost a rule when I first started working in the theatre at all that you never discussed anyone on the stage who never appeared because it worried the audience. That's putting it at its crudest level. In *Look Back in Anger* there are about 27 people referred to and only five of them actually appear. I knew it was going to be difficult and everybody pointed it out to me at the time. So in that sense there was innovation. . . .' *The Sunday Times*, 24 November, 1974.

Harold Hobson rightly detected in it at the time two plays: one of them was 'ordinary and noisy, and Mr Osborne has written it with some wit but more prolixity', and the other was quiet and 'superbly played, in long passages of pain and silence, by Miss Mary Ure'.[3] Some critics have preferred one part, or one Osborne, to the other; in fact Osborne's success has always depended on his ability to fuse the two parts—the public and the private—in the feeling exhibited by a central character who takes on a Marlovian stature. There are successes and failures: *The World of Paul Slickey* (1975) failed because both of these plots are left essentially on the same public level, and Jack Oakham is too pallid to keep them in counterpoint. The unifying element in a successful Osborne play is always a large character whose feelings connect the public and private layers. The private layer is passionate, angry, caring and anti-intellectual; but the public layer is satiric, and, therefore, intellectual. The social comment is never of first importance, though Osborne frequently allows himself to be seduced by the merely topical. Basically, however, he is interested in the suffering hero, and the sense of failure, and his plays illuminate that suffering rather than explore causes or offer solutions. This concentration on the feelings of a hero has encouraged his tendency to rhetoric and tirade and discouraged conversation. It also makes his work intensely subjective, whereas a satirist must be objective. Social comment in Osborne is often funny and accurate, but it tells us more about the character speaking than the object under attack.

That Osborne does care about society is obvious. He cares about the state of the nation, the state of the theatre, and the state of language. Words are, he feels, our last link with God,[4] and in the last scene of *A Subject of Scandal and Concern* (1960) he protested that theatregoers seemed to want a play to provide a solution—'like a motto in a Christmas cracker. For those who seek information, it has been put before you. If it is meaning you are looking for, then you must start collecting for yourself.' (p. 46) But too often, thinking about an Osborne play afterwards, we do not have a very clear idea of what it was that moved us in the theatre—apart from memorable performances from actors like Olivier, Albert Finney, Richard Burton, Nicol Williamson, Paul Scofield and Ralph Richardson.

But as Laurie, who surely speaks for Osborne, observes in *The Hotel in Amsterdam*: 'I work my drawers off and get written off twice a year as not fulfilling my early promise by some Philistine squirt drumming up copy.' (p. 99) And, however uncertain or undefinable his talent, Osborne's continuing importance is, in fact, clear. He has provided major acting roles, destroyed many inhibitions about plays, acting and language, and kept the English Stage Society solvent—and therefore able to encourage other new dramatists—for many years. And he remains a great entertainer. John Elsom may be correct in seeing 1966 as a turning point in his career, with the death of George Devine.[5] Afterwards there was *A Bond Honoured* for Tynan as

---

[3] Hobson's review for *The Sunday Times* is reprinted in the *Casebook* edited by John Russell Taylor (1968), p. 47 ff.

[4] See the *Observer*, 24 May, 1968.

[5] John Elsom, *Post-War British Theatre* (1976), p. 79.

dramaturge at the National Theatre, and this, certainly, was hardly success-ful. But Osborne also began to move in the direction of the ensemble play, organized around, but not completely focused on, one character, which critics had said that Osborne could not write. If something of the great Osborne period, when it was hard to think of English theatre without think-ing first of him, was over, a significant stream of work went on.

II

Time Present and *The Hotel in Amsterdam,* which were both performed at the Royal Court in 1968, are the first strong signals of this later develop-ment. They are plays for the meantime, or for a mean time. And, together with *West of Suez,* performed at the Royal Court in 1971, they can be seen as a trilogy. For all three plays deal with a group of people in a particular situa-tion linked to an older or more powerful figure who dies during the action of the play. In all three the characters are, like their creator, older, wealthier and more 'successful' than before, and the most articulate character is con-cerned with the values of civilized life rather than being an anti-social rebel. That Osborne has a zest for life and style can be seen from the film script for *Tom Jones* (1964), but today's hero cannot easily be assimilated into a conventional happy ending. Critics who were alarmed that the rebel had apparently become conservative should have remembered that Osborne had always had a capacity for nostalgia, and that, like Fielding, had sought to improve society by attacking those who distort its values. This paradox is less striking if we can accept Esther's definitions of 'rebel' and 'revolution-ary' in Arnold Wesker's *The Friends:*

> Rabble-rousers frighten me, they're only rebels, not revolutionaries. My brother's a rebel, Macey, I—am a revolutionary. He talks about leaders of our time, I see a need for men who belong to the end of a long line of all time. He's obsessed with our responsibility to the twentieth century, I'm obsessed with our responsibility to an accumulation of twenty centuries of sensibility. My brother is a rebel because he hates the past, I'm a revolutionary because I see the past as too rich with human suffering and achievement to be dismissed.[6]

If we call Osborne a revolutionary under this definition we can incorporate rebellion and nostalgia. But it is also obvious that, as Osborne has grown older, and himself more successful, the emphasis has shifted. For him, today, grace, style and breeding belong only to a dying class. What makes his treatment of the subject more poignant is that the possessors of such virtues are the losers, so that sympathy for them must be balanced with the angry recognition that the vulgar and the compromisers are successful and happy.

As if to emphasize the break with his past work, Osborne chose to make the first of these new-style losers a woman—although the fact that the role was played by his wife, Jill Bennett, is not without significance. The central character of *Time Present,* Pamela, is about 34, was born in India and is

---

[6] Arnold Wesker, *The Friends* (1970), p. 46.

staying, for the moment, with a woman MP, Constance, whose flat, because it is close to the hospital where Pamela's father is dying, is being used as a kind of waiting room. Trussler has objected to the clumsiness of the exposition, calling much of it 'extraneous'[7] but he overlooks the context. Waiting for a death is a situation that brings together people who could otherwise stay apart, and it brings them together constantly. It is amazing how well and how badly people behave in such circumstances and Osborne, it seems to me, captures that edgy situation exactly. As Pamela says when Edith and Pauline finally go:

> Thank God! They've gone! We must be *going*. Why didn't she *go*? Instead of drinking champagne and going on about it, being so busy looking tired and distressed. (p. 26)

Pamela is, basically, just another Osborne outsider. Devoted to her father, Gideon Orme, she feels adrift in the world represented by her step-sister, and, in the theatre, by Abigail. She cannot adjust to this world as Edith and Constance have done. Far from striding into the 1970s, she cannot manage to hobble about in the 1960s and, when Constance rebukes her for making fun of those who plan for the future, she replies:

> But what about the meantime? We've got to get through that, haven't we? I don't know about striding off anywhere. I seem to be stuck here for the moment. (p. 33)

Pauline puts her finger on the problem in terms of the theatre (though it also applies to the wider context of life) when she observes that Pamela is 'a bit special' and that 'you don't know what to *do* with her.' Through Pamela, Osborne attacks two kinds of theatre: the happening ('sort of about leaving nude girls in plastic bags at railway stations. Non-verbal, you understand, no old words, just the maximum in participation') and the 'finely wrought and blessedly well constructed play' which, as Pamela tartly remarks, means that it is like a travelling clock ('You can see all the works. That way you know it must keep the right time'). (p. 46, 70) But Pamela admits that however fashionable and shallow Abigail is, she isn't wooden, she has life; whereas, by the end of the play, Pamela, who has conceived life for the first time, is planning an abortion, leaving Constance (returning her lover to her), and will eventually stay in her little house alone, waiting for the telephone to ring. And if it doesn't ring *she* will ring someone—if they're in. The play ends with Constance telephoning her lover, and life goes on. Pamela may have carried the grace of detachment too far, but she is, or she is intended to be, like Bill Maitland, more interesting in failure than those around her who have adjusted to the present time.

   The Hotel in Amsterdam went a stage further in ensemble playing by making the group more homogeneous. In *Time Present* the focus was on a Pamela alienated from the rest of the characters; here it is on Laurie, who is the centre of a group of friends and who would come to life without

---

[7] See Trussler, Chapter ll.

the services of Paul Scofield but who, nevertheless, is not allowed to dominate the play. The three couples, Laurie and Margaret (who is pregnant), Gus and Annie, Dan and Amy, are all around forty but 'pretty flash and vigorous looking'. They are all escaping for a weekend from their employer, the film director, KL. In Act I they arrive and in Act II they prepare to depart. Meanwhile they have explored relationships within the group and their curious friendship:

> How often do you get six people as different as we all are still all together all friends and who all love each other. After all the things that have happened to us. Like success to some extent, making money—some of us. (p. 98)

The only action that disturbs the talk is the arrival, towards the end of Act 2, of Margaret's hysterical sister who has told KL where they all are. But he has killed himself—with their telephone number on his desk pad, fulfilling Laurie's curse in Act I.[8] Laurie's declaration of love for Annie, however moving, changes nothing; life goes on. They will not come to this hotel or even Amsterdam again, but, as Laurie says at the end of the play, '. . . I expect we might go somewhere else. . . .'

Osborne, in fact, sends them *West of Suez*. Wyatt Gillman and his family are spending Christmas on an unnamed tropical island, a former British colony, that is neither Africa nor Europe 'but some of both, also less of both'. Again there is little to do but talk and drink and again the group is reasonably at ease with itself. Once more the central character is a writer and the play ends with an unexpected death. The problem in bringing your great man on stage, however, is that the portrayal of genius is difficult, even for Ralph Richardson. Osborne throws in names like Yeats and George Moore for verisimilitude, but it is obviously easier to present a writer like Lamb who is the successful author of best-sellers and has, we are told, invented tax havens! The daughters, and indeed most of the group, were born in Imperial places like Kandy and Kuala Lumpur, though one of the husbands, Robert, has to make do with the Royal Infirmary, Hastings. The talk is interrupted by a local reporter (female) who interviews Gillman, a truculent American, Jed, and the natives who dash on and shoot Gillman at the end of the play. All this talk, and particularly the interview, allows Osborne to range through his usual repertoire—nostalgia, language, despair, the English imagination—but for this group of people, now, life can be summed up in the phrase: shit, blood, vanity and a certain prowess. This is a bleak combination. Both Gillman and Jed have an unsatisfying hate, but whereas Jed's is negative (he reduces 'love' to 'fuck' and 'life' to 'shit') Wyatt's hate comes to suggest something more. He becomes representative, in theatrical terms, of that ability to talk, use words, grasp concepts and be witty which Jed so despises. The interview, perhaps, is too much of a set-piece and the shift to the representative value of Gillman and his family is a shade contrived. Early reviewers compared the play with Chekhov, and particularly with

---

[8] This recalls the device used in *Look Back in Anger* where Jimmy hopes certain things will happen to Alison and they do.

Shaw's *Heartbreak House,* and, indeed, the similarities with this play are strong: an ageing inventor, his daughters, their husbands and their friends in a house which symbolizes cultured England about to drift on to the rocks. But Osborne seems to be using the similarity in counterpoint. Those critics who disliked the play for what it said missed this and concentrated only on content. Benedict Nightingale complained, in the *New Statesman,* that it was as if Jimmy Porter had accepted his knighthood and become joint master of the Quorn. Stranger things have happened in life. Mary Holland objected to the High Tory Osborne—'his increasingly maudlin chauvinism, his petty resentings against the young, the un-British, journalists'—and complained that he lacked the wide humanity of Chekhov, who could sympathize with the dispossessed while recognizing the aspirations of those knocking at the gates: 'When violence erupts on the stage it is casual, irrelevant, without meaning. One experiences no sense of shock when Wyatt Gillmann is shot by revolutionaries.'[9]

The idea that violence can be meaningful is interesting. But Osborne cannot, like Shaw, spare his voluptuaries because the time will no longer allow it. And the wide sympathy available to Chekhov and Shaw is more difficult when the future is represented by Jed. The shooting is meaningless because only another 'heroic' time would try to make murder meaningful, and the ending is not tragic, only bad manners (and bad manners only to a very small class of people at that): but, Osborne suggests, this is all that today offers. Nevertheless some critics saw the play as an advance. J.W. Lambert described it as 'a great bound forward'[10] and Helen Dawson as 'a brave and loving play'[11], while Michael Billington saw Osborne standing on the threshold of greatness and about to enter his richest period as a dramatist.[12]

His next play, *A Sense of Detachment,* performed at the Royal Court in 1972, was certainly different, and can be seen either as 'a reaching out, a development of talent . . . a seminal point in Osborne's career'[13] or a mischievous experiment in audience participation. Unfortunately the play seems to reflect Jed's hate rather than that of Gillman. It is about the awful business of living in this century and ends with the phrase: God rot you. It is Osborne's most radical experiment, abandoning plot and characters in favour of a parody of contemporary theatre forms and language. The actors sit on the stage as actors, while two more actors disguised as a beer-swilling football fan in a box and a disapproving Tory who moves from stalls to circle and back encourage the audience to contribute their share of insult and interruption to what is happening on the stage. There the actors discuss theatrical alternatives to a play, the critics and audiences and then, in Act 2, if the audience has returned, practically anything that angers Osborne. Thus the second act is really an anthology of contrasts between Past and Present, excerpts from a pornographic catalogue juxtaposed with Elizabethan love

[9] *Plays and Players,* October 1971.
[10] *The Sunday Times,* 22 August, 1971
[11] The *Observer,* 22 August, 1971.
[12] Michael Billington, *The Modern Actor* (1973), p. 171.
[13] Terry Browne, *Playwrights' Theatre* (1975), p. 99.

lyrics, and music by Mozart, Elgar and Strauss. The 'play' may owe something to Handke's *Publikumsbeschimpfung* but, obviously, insulting an audience is a two-edged weapon. And, though the sight of Rachel Kempson fastidiously reading out descriptions of pornographic films is not easily forgotten, the joke goes on much too long. Towards the end the GIRL sums up life now: 'We are not language. We are lingua. We do not love, eat or cherish. We *exchange*. Oh yes; we talk. We have words, rather: environment; pollution; problems; *issues.* . . .' (p. 58)

Ronald Bryden described it as Osborne's *Waste Land,* and lamented that the paranoia was no longer kept in balance by comic irony. Certainly Osborne hardly seems to have achieved that grace of detachment both Pamela and Frederica so admired. At any rate he returned to a story and characters in *The End of Me Old Cigar* which opened at the Greenwich Theatre on January 16, 1975. The title, apparently, comes from an old music-hall song (or Kipling?). Unfortunately, as in *Under Plain Cover*, Act 2 moves in a direction that undercuts Act 1. An aggressive, satiric and very funny first act is followed by a sentimental second act. Osborne called it 'a modern comedy of modern manners' and has written a first act in the manner of a Restoration romp in which a group of women set out to end male domination by catching important men with their trousers down. A Jewish girl from Hackney has become, by marriage, Lady Regine Frimley, and is now the presiding madame of a house of pleasure which welcomes millionaires, MPs and pop stars who are serviced by a carefully chosen band of Women's Libbers, including a journalist and an American feminist. The trouble is that the person who films their activities is, implausibly, a man and in the end he sells them down the river. The second act, however, does not continue the themes of orgy and revolution but looks at a love affair between Isobel and Len (played by Jill Bennett and Keith Barron) who are characters unlikely to be in such a situation, and whose simple love is supposed to contrast with Lady Frimley's unscrupulous manipulation of human beings and prevent the nation from falling into anarchy. England, an old music hall in *The Entertainer,* is now a brothel run by female militants bent on exposing male corruption. Apart from the creaky plot, what is difficult to accept here is not that our masters are corrupt but that anyone, even in 1975, could be either surprised or shocked by such a revelation, particularly as the brothel is such a high-class establishment. Act I is really a peg on which to hang caricatures of society figures—the pleasure lies mainly in knowing who they are—while Act 2 is maudlin and clumsy, because Osborne is using the relationship rather than exploring it. It is, in the first act, often rich and lively, but it is more a revue than a play, and was written, apparently, while Osborne was working on another play. Harold Hobson thought it was 'a finely conceived play' in which there was a gleam of hope—though for whom is not clear.[14]

The other play was, presumably, *Watch It Come Down,* published in 1975 and performed at the National Theatre in 1976. With this play Osborne

[14] *The Sunday Times,* 19 January, 1975.

returned not merely to plot and characters but to the plot of the trilogy: a
man and his dependants in a particular situation, with a few deaths at the
end. Ben Prosser, a film-director in his mid-forties, has retired to the country with his wife, Sally (who is supposed to be a novelist), a dying homosexual, Glen, a lesbian, Jo (who is in love with Glen), Sally's sister (who
paints), Raymond, the homosexual boy-of-all-work, and a large bitch. The
location is a converted railway station through which, once a week, a goods
train still passes. The pastoral idyll has proved an illusion. While the group
inside the station seethe with passion and resentments, the countryside
around them is in the same hectic condition. By the end of Act I Ben has
beaten his wife up and the bitch has been shot by the revolting peasants after
multiple rape by their dogs. In Act II the insiders are joined by Ben's ex-
wife, Glen dies, Jo throws herself under the weekly train, Ben has been
wounded by gunshot from the local people and is almost dead (or in a coma),
and the station is under siege and falling down around their ears. The village
doctor observes that they lead odd sorts of lives as police sirens herald the
arrival of law and order. In the interstices conversation takes place. The play
is as ramshackle as the set (but then a set that has to collapse every night can
hardly be well-made) and it is difficult to believe in or get interested in this
group of people. Those critics who disliked the High Tory Osborne could
take comfort from the attack mounted here on the Home Counties. England
is not 'green much and rarely pleasant' and the barbarians who storm the
gates are no longer vague black natives nor even Americans but English
country folk.

III

Apart from the four stage plays since *The Hotel in Amsterdam* (1968)
Osborne's output has been in unexpected places: three adaptations and six
plays for television.

Osborne's previous experience in adaptation, *A Bond Honoured*, had not
been a particularly happy one. However, *Hedda Gabler* was performed at the
Royal Court in 1972, and in 1973 Osborne published *A Place Calling Itself
Rome* and *The Picture of Dorian Gray* (subsequently staged at the Greenwich
Theatre in 1975). *Hedda Gabler* is a play that fascinates Osborne, and
obviously provided a splendid role for his wife, Jill Bennett. All three main
characters in these plays—Hedda, Coriolanus and Dorian Gray—are at odds
with society in one way or another, and therefore congenial to Osborne, but
the art of adaptation or translation raises too many problems of judgement
for discussion here. The plays for television were surprising in view of
Osborne's frequently stated contempt for that medium and those who run it.
In 1961 he complained that it '*reduces* life and the human spirit.'[15] For a
dramatist who wants to make people feel, television is not the happiest of
means. *A Subject of Scandal and Concern* was finally transmitted by BBC TV
on 6 November, 1960 with Richard Burton in the main part. When Osborne
published the script, he did so as a three-act play, though he retained the

[15] See 'That Awful Museum' reprinted in the *Casebook*, p. 66.

directions for television. (It was staged in New York in 1965.) There is no sign that Osborne is any happier with television as a medium—except that he has written six plays for it.

The Right Prospectus was transmitted by BBCI on 22 October, 1970. A young-to-middle-aged but childless couple, the Newbolds (played by George Cole and Evi Hale), are looking at various schools and, having chosen the right one, enrol themselves. From here on everything is solid, matter-of-fact and yet, obviously, unreal. The author's instruction is that no one takes any notice of their age, sex or relationship: they are simply new boys. The Newbolds want to take advantage of the time offered by school: time to grow, to think and be free. The experiment does not work, at least for the working-class husband, though his middle-class wife has a splendid time and finds no difficulty in fitting in. Through the head boy, Heffer, Osborne is able to attack society and the privileged middle classes in fine caustic terms. The tone is bitter-sweet, and the material is organized by the point-of-view technique reminiscent of *Gulliver's Travels* or *The Way of All Flesh*. The same technique of unusual point-of-view is also used in *Jill and Jack,* transmitted by Yorkshire TV on 11 September, 1974. Here the social roles have become confused 'if not completely reversed': the women perform what are usually considered male functions in society while the men act out the role of girl friends without—Osborne instructs the actors—the slightest suggestion that either Jack or Mark 'are remotely "gay" to use the fashionable cant word'. (64-5)

The other four plays look at Osborne's England in more conventional form. Osborne's England, as Michael Anderson has observed, is 'a landscape of the imagination rather than of historical reality'.[16] It is a kind of club whose members have a capacity for suffering and telling the world about their suffering. Tolerance is not a requirement and, as time passes, club members grow increasingly alienated from a society where feeling and the language to articulate that feeling are degenerating. The young were condemned in *Inadmissable Evidence* and *Time Present,* a condemnation that leads to Jed who is, significantly, American. This alienation of the 'hero' continues in the next two plays, *Very Like a Whale* (1971) and *The Gift of Friendship* (1972), intensified by disillusion and the passing of time. Bill Maitland and Pamela were failures but Jock Mellor, in *Very Like a Whale,* has, at 44, all the trappings of success. At the beginning of the play he is knighted for services to exports, but during the action of the play we see him unsatisfied at work and at home, out of touch with his second wife and daughter, his first wife and son, his sister, his father (who prefers a dog and television) and even his old school chum, moving inexorably to collapse and death. How, he asks, does one avoid cruelty and survive in the present time, which is, as the allusion to *Hamlet* suggests, out of joint? The theme of success as failure reminds us of Pinter's *Tea Party* (1965) though Osborne lacks Pinter's opaqueness and terror. Osborne's hero, like Hedda, is just bored and disgusted with today's society.

[16] Michael Anderson, *Anger and Detachment* (1976), p. 29.

The same disquiet is reflected in *A Gift of Friendship*. Jocelyn Broome, an eminent writer in his early fifties, invites Bill Wakeley, a successful writer (i.e. 'a literary commercial traveller'), to dinner after six years of estrangement. When Bill arrives at Broome's 'rather grand but discreet Palladian house' he discovers that Broome wants him, as the only person he can trust, to be his literary executor. After Broome's death he is surprised to find that his friend hated him. Broome sees life today as Hell and America (or the United States and Despair), and reminds Wakeley that 'Times does NOT make ancient good uncouth.' What is significant about this play is that none of the characters is contemptible. Madge, Wakeley's wife, who is rather shrill at the beginning of the play, emerges as a person with insights and a neat way of putting things, while Wakeley survives the knowledge of how Broome felt and is the better for it. The absence of asperity and easy caricature was hopeful, and the balanced tone continued into two plays published in 1978: *You're Not Watching Me, Mummy* and *Try a Little Tenderness*.

You're Not Watching Me, Mummy was to have been transmitted by Yorkshire Television on 30 July, 1979 but a strike prevented this—an irony Osborne would appreciate. The play opens on Shaftesbury Avenue awash with the 'moving garbage of tourism' while a voice drones on about no man being an island and that what counts in these harsh times is money. The scene then shifts to an actress's dressing room where Jemima (who, as so often, was born abroad, in Nairobi, in 1932) and her homosexual dresser, Leslie, prepare to entertain the hordes who come backstage after the show. This gives Osborne a splendid opportunity to parade all his favorite dislikes: the Marxist-Women's Lib author, the critic, the research student (from Seattle), an old school chum and her husband (who refer to one another as 'Boot' and 'Petal'), and the second wife of Jemima's ex-husband who is celebrating her divorce and many more, there for the champagne. In fact all Jemima wants to do after, as she puts it, 'you've knocked your arse off for two and a half hours' is to go home, have a cup of Ovaltine and go to bed, which she does, leaving Leslie to close the bar. Her departure either goes unnoticed or is unimportant. This is a situation which suits Osborne, but he also seems to like his main characters and thus if he shoots down the familiar targets the treatment sparkles with wit and humour. And this healthy tone appears in *Try a Little Tenderness* too.

Try a Little Tenderness recalls *Watch It Come Down*. Ted Shilling, a writer in his fifties, has retired from London to the country with his wife, her mother, her friends, his son and his son's friends, who are squatting in a part of the house, and his dog Colditz. Ted is not particularly welcome in the village, but he organizes it to fight back when the village learns that it is about to be invaded by a Pop Festival. Ted, however, if not a patient man, knows how to wait and when to strike and this is the time. Having organized the village to resist the Pop Festival, he goes home where he slams a chocolate cake into the face of his wife's friend, announces that he is having an affair with his son's girl friend, plants drugs on the squatters and then walks out with his son's girl friend to watch as the squatters are arrested, and the village descends on the Pop Festival with sheep, cows and finally the Hunt while the church bells ring furiously. The Battle of Arkley soon ceases to be funny and turns into bloody carnage but, when Ted is asked if he is satisfied, he replies quietly: 'No, but I never expected to be.' Told that he must stand up and be counted Ted's response is: 'who with?'

The tone of these last two plays suggests that Osborne is alive and growing better. It has always been dangerous to write Osborne off, as critics who did so after *Plays for England* soon learned. John Whiting suggested that Osborne had 'the universal appeal of misanthropy,'[17] but I think not. He does not hate mankind; only those who give it a bad name (usually with four letters). Born in 1929, he passed his childhood in an adult-dominated world, and his adolescence in the austerities of wartime, and he came of age just when the idolatry of youth took over, fostered by an alarming growth in what we call the media. It is not that he has never had it so good as that he has never had it—though his present life-style suggests that irony and humour ought not to be too difficult. But he cannot temperamentally be a good satirist and nowadays, when there is no centre, it is difficult to mock the eccentric. His anger, therefore, recalls the disgust of Swift rather than the temper of Juvenal. But he cares too much to be driven into the final refuge of silence. He is still at his best an entertainer; and more than ever, perhaps, do we need his voice crying in our wilderness: O tempora! O mores!

[17] John Whiting, 'At Ease in a Bright Red Tie', reprinted in *The Encore Reader* (1965), edited by Charles Marowitz, Tom Milne and Owen Hale, p. 107.

Note

Life and Writing

Born in 1932 in London's East End of immigrant Jewish parents, early involved in left-wing politics under his mother's influence, Arnold Wesker left school at 16. From 1948 to 1956 he worked as farm labourer and bookseller's assistant in London and Norfolk, with 2 years' National Service in the Air Force, before becoming a pastry cook in London and Paris for two years. He saved enough money to enter the London School of Film Technique; hence the cinematic element in *The Kitchen* (1956). Then, as a result of seeing John Osborne's *Look Back in Anger*, he wrote *Chicken Soup With Barley* (1957). Both plays were seen by director Lindsay Anderson and sent to George Devine at the Royal Court, where *Chicken Soup* was performed after being produced at the Belgrade Theatre, Coventry. *Roots* (1959) was followed by *I'm Talking About Jerusalem* (1960), which was produced with revivals of the previous two plays as *The Wesker Trilogy*. This was Wesker's most successful period, with the film of *The Kitchen* in 1961 and *Chips With Everything* voted the best play of 1962. However, *The Four Seasons* (1965) was poorly received, and *Their Very Own and Golden City*, though it had won the Italian Premio Marzotto prize in 1964, had a poor London opening in 1966.

During the 1960s Wesker directed Centre 42, a project with trade-union involvement for making the arts more widely accessible. This led to the purchase of the Roundhouse, a huge disused engine-shed in London, for conversion to a theatre, but there were financial and administrative difficulties. In 1970, after producing his *The Friends* there, Wesker resigned and persuaded Centre 42's Council to dissolve. Conflict and frustration also dogged his plays: *The Old Ones* (1972) passed from the National Theatre to the Royal Court due to a managerial revolution; *The Journalists* (1974) was abandoned by the Royal Shakespeare Company, apparently because of actors' pressure, and has remained in limbo; *The Wedding Feast* (1977) opened to excellent notices in Leeds but never transferred to London; *The Merchant* (1978) lost its lead actor Zero Mostel, who died on the pre-Broadway tour, and after an unsuccessful New York opening had only provincial production in Britain.

Wesker's plays up to and including *The Friends* are published by Jonathan Cape, *The Wesker Trilogy* as one volume, the others individually, and I have referred to these editions. References to the later plays are taken from Penguin's complete four volume edition of Wesker's plays, *The Old Ones* from Volume Three, and *The Journalists*, *The Wedding Feast* and *The Merchant* from Volume Four.

Wesker has also written short stories and essays: main collections are *Six Sundays in January* (1971), *Said the Old Man to the Young Man* (1978); and *Fears of Fragmentation* (1970).

Criticism

The only full-length study is Glenda Leeming and Simon Trussler, *The Plays of Arnold Wesker: An Assessment* (1971), on his work up to 1970. Glenda Leeming, *Arnold Wesker* (1972) is a shorter introduction: Harold U. Ribalow, *Arnold Wesker* (New York, 1965) and Ronald Hayman, *Arnold Wesker* (1970) discuss earlier plays— also considered in Laurence Kitchen, *Mid-Century Drama* (1962) and W.A. Armstrong (ed.), *Experimental Drama* (1963). Gary O'Connor, 'Production Casebook No. 2: Arnold Wesker's *The Friends*', *Theatre Quarterly*, I,2 (1971), 78-92 offers important background; also see Wesker's interviews in Charles Marowitz and Simon Trussler (ed.), *Theatre at Work* (London, 1967/New York, 1968) and in *Theatre Quarterly*, VII, 28 (1977), 5-24.

Articulacy and Awareness: The Modulation of Familiar Themes in Wesker's Plays in the Seventies

GLENDA LEEMING

I

At first sight, the plays by Arnold Wesker that appeared in the 1970s are not radically different from those that made his name in the previous dozen years. For if the plays of the late 1950s and 1960s fall mainly into two groups—the social and family relationship plots of the trilogy; and the work-oriented worlds of *The Kitchen, Chips With Everything* and *Their Very Own and Golden City*—then after 1970 the same two broad areas of interest reappear. *The Old Ones* (1972) and *The Wedding Feast* (1977) return to the trilogy's East End or Norfolk settings respectively, and *The Journalists* (1974) and *The Merchant* (1978), as the titles suggest, pursue further the fate of the individual personality being shaped by the economic pressures of society.

But beneath this recognizable consistency there is change; and what perhaps has changed is the emphasis. To say, as Wesker does, that *The Friends* in 1970 was an attempt to confront the idea of death, and 'Not only death, but a sense of one's mistakes'[1] indicates broadly what could be called the interiorizing of his themes. Of course, in the earlier plays social pressures are also focused through their psychological effect on Ronnie, Beatie, the Simmonds and others; but in *The Friends* and *The Merchant*, particularly, the psychology of the characters, aware and conscious of their sufferings, becomes in itself the arena of the drama. The comedies of this period, *The Old Ones* and *The Wedding Feast*, are slighter in ambition and, though their corrective, satiric purpose is evident, the brushstrokes of this genre are comparatively simple; they have lost the complexity for which the more leisurely development of, say, the trilogy allows scope. These two comedies, then, stand apart from the mainstream of Wesker's less formally comic writing; a more recognizable example of continuity appears in *The Journalists*, which turns to the working life of a group of Sunday newspaper journalists, in a detailed reconstruction reminiscent of Wesker's first play, *The Kitchen*.

It is the different approach to the subject matter, then, rather than its appearance after some years' silence at the turn of a decade, that qualifies *The Friends* as a watershed in Wesker's career. The 'friends' of the title *are* friends—not the extended family of the trilogy, nor the chance collection of workmates of *The Kitchen*. One might say that *The Friends* in fact is less a

---

[1] 'A Sense of What Should Follow' *Theatre Quarterly*, VII, 28 (1977), p. 6.

watershed than a confluence of usually divergent elements in Wesker's work
—his growing concern with 'private pain', and his interest in juxtaposing
a number of different characters. The relationships of the characters have
a new importance, because each is seen as aware of his own sufferings as
part of the common predicament. Certainly, many of the earlier plays have
large casts, but there is the traditional division between major and minor
characters, the latter tending to illustrate various social tendencies—the
interior life of someone like Monty Blatt in *Chicken Soup With Barley*, for
instance, is hinted at, but it plays no part in the main plot. The seven
characters in *The Friends*, on the other hand, are all major characters and
have an equal importance. They are united not only by friendship but by
their work, though significantly that work—the chain of shops they own,
selling the interior design products they create—is slipping away from them,
unheeded and unregretted. Macey, the shop manager, tries to make the six
friends react to the threat of bankruptcy. They ignore him: now in their late
thirties, they are losing both youthful arrogance and their sense of endlessly
available time; and they are the more pressingly aware of their mortality
because Esther, the dominant personality of the six, is dying of leukaemia
there in the house where they have gathered. For all her strength of mind,
Esther herself shouts:

> MACEY! I want to go on living! ROLAND! I *don't* want to die. MAN-
> FRED, SIMONE, TESSA! All of you. I-do-not-want-to-die. (p. 31)

and, after apologizing, goes on

> Do you know anybody who was prepared to die? Despite all the suffering
> and the knowledge of suffering and man's inhumanity, everyone wants to
> go on living—for ever and ever, gloriously. (p. 31)

There is no solution to this. So, where the causes of despair and disillusion in
Chips, Golden City and the trilogy might be removed by human endeavour
and a better state of society, the inevitability of death and its impact on the
characters cannot be explained away. This is private pain at its most intense,
and Roland, Esther's lover, is most affected by sheer animal terror of death
—he becomes speechless, literally dumb with fear. Manfred, her brother,
is stricken with a despair that reflects on the rest of his life: ageing and
the approach of death take away the flavour from all endeavour. Similarly
this realization of death illuminates for all the friends the uncertainties and
insufficiencies of their achievements so far. Manfred speaks for them when
he says:

> It's not because we've forgotten about injustices and the pursuit of
> happiness, it's because of little damages we've done to each other and a
> terrible sense of defeat and time passing and appetites fading and intellect
> softening. Our mess is not only made of Esther's dying, but the know-
> ledge that this is a once and only life more than half over, and if you want
> to thrash the gloom from us then you'd have to give us back youth and the
> strength not to despise ourselves. (pp. 69-70)

And to a great extent he is right. Where Ronnie Kahn or even Pip in *Chips* had been defeated by something outside themselves that has affected their character—the behaviour of other people, the temptations of the system as it exists—here the friends are faced with one of the insoluble problems of being alive at all. The only alleviation of their anguish must be an adjustment within themselves. Therefore Simone, her task made the more difficult because she is the odd one out, the upper-class scapegoat among the other North country, working-class friends, urges them to an acceptance of life (and therfore of death) by asserting the values she at least finds in life. Assurance of values, she says, will give them the necessary feeling that their lives have had worth, have even had some meaning.

Not understanding this, Tessa protests 'But she's talking about order and nobility and Esther's lying there dead and it's all irrelevant.' (p. 66) As in *Roots*, the friends have to be thrust into a sudden realization that life is worth living, not by argument alone but by an emotional whipcrack: Simone appeals to the testimony of the now dead Esther and, grotesquely and touchingly, she moves Esther's body to the centre of the friends' circle. Forcefully, she directs their attention from the loss of Esther's life to what her life has meant: 'She wanted to *live* . . . . *She* wanted to live.' (p. 70)

This final sequence between Simone and the rest develops without a break from the more personal bitchiness of a general quarrel. Structurally, the whole play is shaped into a series of movements, sometimes overlapping in Wesker's favourite device of counterpointed monologues, each with its own mood and rhythm. Thus in Act I, scene 2 the mood is consistently dark, as they wait for Esther's approaching death, but varies from shade to shade of misery. At first Macey and Simone discuss Simone's position in subdued tones, until Manfred comes forward half asleep trying to tell them about his depression, his contempt for 'the Englishman'; his insistent gloom is followed by Roland's more febrile entry, burning pound notes in an exhibitionist but futile gesture. He too subsides, then Crispin bursts in, raising the temperature to the third and highest peak by his fury at Simone's overemotional letters to him; he taunts her with her unrequited love for him, reading her note aloud, until his anger gradually gives way as he recognizes her unattractive sincerity. The scene concludes with 'a tableau of misery and silence'. In this sequence, the incidents are separate from each other but motivated by the same shared feelings; their demonstration of the group's demoralization, and the different way this affects its members, is orchestrated to the climax of the 'tableau'.

The continuous evolution of the dramatic movement through alterations in tone and mood—rather than through decisive twists of plot—formally corresponds to the subject matter: *how* the friends' personalities colour their views is the substance of the play, which is not concerned with external circumstances, confrontation with outside characters, exposition as such. One can find a similarly free-flowing structure, based on mood, as far back as *Roots*, where there are several sequences of busy and meditative passages reflecting the unfolding of Beatie's character, but a chronologically nearer correspondence can be found in *The Four Seasons*, which not only develops in a series of mood movements, as does *The Friends*, but is an earlier attempt to dramatize private pain.

To me, this attempt does not seem successful, for all the apparent similarities with *The Friends*. *The Four Seasons* shows its protagonists, Adam and Beatrice, experiencing a love affair which is at first soured then destroyed by a will to failure. Both have a self-fulfilling expectation of defeat that is very much the same as Manfred's, Crispin's or Tessa's. But because of the way that the expectations are first hinted at, then inexorably fulfilled, and because the characters echo each other's experience of failure in the past as they duplicate it during the course of the play, all this reinforced by the cyclical framework of the four seasons, the message is one of psychological fatalism. The first false step predestines all steps thereafter to bend the same way. This is perhaps a tenable opinion, but as dramatized here there is paradoxically no conflict, although the action between the characters consists almost entirely *of* conflict. The action is set as nebulously nowhere and anywhere as that of *Godot*, but its substance, the characters' psychological determinism, is a condition of the contingent everyday world. In short, the form protests too much. *The Friends*, on the other hand, allows full play to the complexity of character and influences upon it so that at the end one is satisfied to accept the friends' choice.

It is interesting to compare with *The Friends* and *The Four Seasons* the short play *Love Letters on Blue Paper*, although perhaps it should not be discussed on the same terms as the other plays, having been written originally as a short story and then adapted for television (later it was adapted for the stage and produced at the National Theatre). It traces the slow sinking into death—again of leukaemia—of Victor Marsden, his conversation with a younger friend, Maurice, expressing his memories and fears. These, in turn, are counterpointed by the letters that his outwardly dour, practical wife has started writing to him. As Victor tries to work out, explicitly and through discussion, some suitable way of meeting his death, Sonia, in letters which recall moments of their life together—cherished, trivial or puzzling—is obliquely doing for him what Simone was seeking to do for the friends: affirming the value his life has had, so that he has a sense of achievement, not of waste, to support his final weeks. The relationship between Victor's diminished physical world and the world outside, including the experiences of the past, is convincing and unforced; there is no oppressive universalizing. Here Wesker is expressing his concern with private pain in its simplest and most economical form (the brevity of a short story and the conciseness required for a television play perhaps promoting this economy of effect). It seems that this theme could hardly be pared down further without losing the balance of interior and exterior worlds.

II

After the step forward in *The Friends*, *The Old Ones* is something of a step backwards in its nostalgic return to the area of *Chicken Soup*. In subject matter at least, there is such a strong continuity with Wesker's early work that the play might well be considered as making the trilogy into a quartet. Moreover, Wesker says that 'You can imagine that all the old ones in all the plays are the same people.'[2] For instance among the 'old ones' is Sarah, at seventy years old the central point in a network of friends and relations, mostly in their late sixties and seventies, and this Sarah has the same personality as well as the same name as the dominant Sarah in *Chicken Soup*. Sarah's two brothers are the instruments for setting out the tension between optimism and pessimism prevalent in all Wesker's plays. The tension is schematized in a running battle of quotations between the optimist, Emanuel (Manny), and the pessimist, Boomy. They challenge each other, sometimes in the middle of conversations, sometimes apropos of nothing, sometimes in voice-over at the end of scenes involving other characters: their respectively optimistic and pessimistic quotations from great writers seek to pose an unanswerable comment on human nature or to cap the opponent's offering with a conclusive refutation on the same subject.

Wilful and childish, this contest is both fantastic and credible, the sort of eccentric ritual generated by deep-rooted animosities peculiar to family relationships. And although the dialectical form, as well as the time-hallowed content, is different, there is an obvious link with Beatie Bryant's habit of quoting her absent fiancé, Ronnie, in *Roots*. She quotes not to support her point of view but because she hasn't *got* a point of view of her own, and is uneasily resentful of her own confusion. It will be remembered that, in the denouement of *Roots*, Wesker perceptively shows the emotional shock of being jilted triggering Beatie's sudden comprehension of what it means to be exploited, used, ignored. Some critics, overlooking the fact that it is this comprehension that is all-important, have objected that Beatie was still using Ronnie's terms rather than her own: the conclusion of *The Old Ones*, on the other hand, shows Manny's and Boomy's contest moving on to a new plane when Manny's final and quite impressive retort to *Ecclesiastes* is expressed in his own words. Just as Beatie's sister-in-law accuses her of 'quotin' all the time', (p. 140) so Manny's wife Gerda complains 'You've been having quarrels through other people's books for years now. Yell at him in your own voice for a change.' (p. 150) So it is not that Manny's manufactured 'quotation' is superior to *Ecclesiastes,* or that it wins game set and match by its pertinacity: the important thing is that, like Beatie, Manny has broken through a barrier. Boomy, however, retreats to *Ecclesiastes*, and the last words of the play are 'There is no man that hath power over the spirit to retain the spirit, neither hath he power in the day of death. . . .' (p. 194) The conflict between the brothers is not resolved; each has intensified his own position, positive or negative.

The deadlock tends to be overlooked, on stage especially. The final confrontation takes place at Sarah's party to celebrate the Jewish feast of Succoth, and the spectacular, bouncy, semi-nude performance of the last speech by Manny overshadows Boomy's unregenerate resistance; the supervening party atmosphere, the singing, dancing and clapping, works in favour of Manny, optimism and human contact. Wesker says 'I had envisaged . . . a triangle of tensions between a group singing in the background and a brother who is hurling quotations of doom from Ecclesiastes and the brother he is hurling them at, who is laughing.'[3] This is similar to the final tableau of *Roots*, where Beatie's triumphant speech eclipses the stolidity of her family, the silent majority, who will never make the leap to understanding. But the solitary radicalization of Beatie has been prepared by the whole play; in *The Old Ones* it is the illusion of Manny's victory (over Boomy; his victory over himself is no illusion) that has been prepared for. The tendency of the material of the play is towards resolution and happy ending, and the character of Sarah is partly responsible for this.

Sarah moves in calmer waters than her beleaguered namesake in the trilogy: although she is too old to have to go out to work, her health and energy seem as yet unimpaired, so that she has attention for her family and neighbours, which in turn means that she is seen in action administering sympathy and advice to a stream of visitors, and, unlike some of them, is herself untroubled by the loneliness of old age. Her methods vary from direct argument to uncritical reassurance: her friend Teressa's reference to the young thugs of 'your working class' is met with a long argument reminiscent of the other Sarah's 'electric light' speech in *Chips*, ending 'Everywhere you look—new buildings, new roads, new cities—who puts them there? So leave me alone about my working class.' (p. 160) Her daughter Rosa's despair of ever communicating with the unruly schoolchildren she is supposed to advise about careers is consoled with the observation that 'You'll try again. . . . With another lot, you'll learn. . . . Who knows about things in the beginning?' (p. 172) She does not condemn her neighbour Jack's account of ill-treating his wife and children, does not even comment on it, except by an anecdote about her own guilty pleasure in scoring off her superior son-in-law. This positive attitude is of course an attribute of Sarah as a character within the play, but the play as a whole is behind her—Teressa's sniping *is* a mere façade, for, we learn, 'half her pension she sends to left-wing charities'. (p. 160) Rosa does try again with the children, and, productively or not, makes a strong impression on them. Jack starts visiting Sarah's friend, Milly, who is slipping into senility, and this encourages her to talk to him instead of only to herself.

Certainly there is suffering in the play to fuel Boomy's despair. A bitter scene of recrimination takes place between Boomy and his son Martin, who at twenty-eight is still dangerously involved in student politics and likely to go to gaol, and has left his wife and baby; his appeals for money, understanding and sympathy are all rejected by Boomy. Gerda is beaten up by three youths who have already threatened Milly, and although Sarah, almost in self-parody, says 'I'm glad it happened . . . she'll be more careful in future' (p. 167), Gerda is not inclined to forgive and forget. But Martin is absent from the final scene, and though this is apparently because he has in fact been imprisoned, his absence is not strongly felt. Gerda lies bandaged on the

[3] Ibid p. 12

sofa throughout the party, but in the background, saying little.

Thus the action of the play seems to support Sarah's practical and Manny's theoretical optimism; but after the gaiety of the conclusion there is a feeling that perhaps Boomy's, Gerda's, Martin's protests (not to mention Carlyle's and Voltaire's) are being given less weight than one might expect. On the other hand this feeling may be unfair or inappropriate to the kind of play that *The Old Ones* is: it is a comedy, where the similar trilogy plays, for all their incidental humour, are not. The comic form requires that questions raised should mostly be resolved, and *The Old Ones* can reasonably be seen as a comedy with a sting in its tail, rather than a drama diluted with too much comedy.

III

The same distinction can be applied to *The Wedding Feast*, which followed the intervening play, *The Journalists*. *The Wedding Feast* derives by way of an unproduced filmscript from an adaptation of Dostoevsky's short story *An Unpleasant Predicament*. But Wesker's play is set in Norfolk, and his central character is Louis Litvanov, a paternalistic, socially conscious, rich Jewish shoe manufacturer. Louis's earnest wish to behave well and be on terms of equality with his employees (while retaining his profits, power and control as their employer) inspires him to arrive unannounced at Knocker White's wedding reception. Here his ambivalent social expectations produce alternating frozen embarrassment and excessive familiarity from the disoriented wedding guests, so that the feast (unlike the conclusion of *The Old Ones*) is very far from uniting the participants in harmony, let alone social unity. Kate, who is Louis's secretary and Knocker's sister, spells out the message after Louis has mercifully passed out:

> Just give them the rate for the work and the sweet sweet *illusion* that they're equal to any man. Stop pretending it's a reality. (*Pause*) And don't be kind or ashamed or apologetic for your money. You go around behaving like that how shall we be able to hit you when the time comes, bor? (pp. 178-9)

and Louis's last words as he shuffles out the following morning after,—'Yes, that's the way it has to be'—indicate that he has accepted this class division.

Again, then, there is a sting in the tail of the play, but again the comic effect is different from the sting of a straight drama. The difference can be illustrated from a comparison with the problems of the would-be crosser of class barriers in *Chips With Everything*. Pip, like Louis, also begins with apparently idealistic motives, then finds in his own character and upbringing the will to power and position that he cannot bring himself to give up. Therefore he promotes mutiny as long as he is in a dominant position—the classic revolutionary trap, of substituting one hierarchical system for another—but cannot tolerate an equality that will make him, too, merely equal. Much the same applies to Louis who does not contemplate relinquishing his position. But the earlier play adds to its many comic scenes a greater proportion of potentially tragic conflict, and not only demonstrates a typical and recurrent situation of confrontation, but raises further complex questions about motivation, conditioning, and failures of communication.

The Wedding Feast is a comedy with a fair amount of slapstick—Louis falls into the blancmange twice, and the newly-married couple's wedding couch collapses under them—and although the party includes a menacing Pinter-esque sequence in the 'shoe game', in which the blindfolded Louis is beaten with shoes, at first in fun, then with increasing hostility, nonetheless the moments of discouragement and conflict rise only to submerge in the flow of comic incident. The implications and complications are not pressed further. No pause for a 'tableau of misery' here. So, while *The Wedding Feast* succeeds within its own terms as a socially satiric comedy, it is unable, because of the limitations of the comic form, to develop the introspective subject matter that Wesker had elaborated in *The Friends*.

This is not the case in *The Journalists*, which, for all the number of jokes and anecdotes swapped by the characters during the action, is not to be seen as a comedy. Moreover, for all its return to the work environment of *The Kitchen* or *Chips*, *The Journalists* is not concerned with the 'effects of work' theme in quite the same way as the earlier plays. As Wesker says in his intro-duction to the text: '*The Kitchen* is not about cooking, it's about man and his relationship to work. *The Journalists* is not about journalism, it is about the poisonous human need to cut better men down to our size, from which we all suffer in varying degrees.'[4] But because this poisonous human need is here embodied in the journalistic profession, *The Journalists* is also a work-relationship play, as the effects on the characters show. Almost all the action takes place in the offices of the fictional *Sunday Paper*, and the physical environment is stressed with all its multiplicity of different pressures and influences. The offices are represented on stage by small, possibly raised, areas around the stage, and the scenes, which are on average shorter than in Wesker's other plays, shift from area to area, the action being plotted to move the audience's attention across the widest possible area of the stage. At the same time as a scene is taking place in one area, the characters in all the other offices are to continue unobtrusively busy, so that individuals are always seen in relation to the rest of the newspaper team.

From this point of view it becomes clear that the characters are, as one would expect, affected by their daily work, some more than others: Tamara's coverage of wars and massacres for foreign news assignments is pushing her to the verge of a nervous breakdown, a photographer is becom-ing more and more obsessed with the gruesome scenes he is required, and increasingly prefers, to photograph. More subtly, the dominant character Mary Mortimer, a star columnist, has a professionally destructive approach to topics and people, which is at odds with her own liberal and tolerant, even idealistic, beliefs. Mary's obsession is with cutting people down to size, puncturing pretences; her grown-up children say she has 'elevated the gutter question "who does he think he is?" to a respected art form.' (p. 90)

[4] *The Journalists* (1975) Introduction p. 5

In dramatic terms, Mary's 'lilliputianizing' is worked out through her one-sided feud with an off-stage Member of Parliament, Morton King, who, like Ronnie in *Roots*, never appears in person. She attacks him, it seems, for his widely expressed ideals, which she finds pretentious, patronizing, and immodest. Yet these ideals appear, for the most part, identical with her own: her words of self-defence, provoked at the end of a row with her children, echo those of her enemy's latest speech—as her children again point out. And when she is about to reveal Morgan King's active leadership of a Robin Hood style secret society (which robs banks to finance deserving strikers), unknown to her, her youngest son is found to be one of King's criminal band. She is fighting against herself, as her daughter Agnes puts it, in more ways than one.

Though this development is thematically appropriate, the melodramatic element is not entirely convincing. This is not because of the spectacular nature of the society's 'guerrilla' activities, which fits in with the theme of increasing violence reiterated by several news stories in the play; it is rather that the 'secret plot' aspect conflicts with the intended status of the nebulous Morgan King as one of the 'better men' who ought to be listened to, and removes him to the fringe of lunatic or criminal politicians who are from time to time involved in well-earned scandals. If Wesker had made King the purely *unintentional* inspirer of the secret society, his ideals being over-enthusiastically misapplied, the irresponsible destructiveness of Mary's attitude—which embodies the lilliputianizing theme of the play—would be clearer. As it is, her suspicions seem not unjustified by events.

Mary's indiscriminately suspicious attitude, her refusal to be impressed, is obviously destructive of the exchange of ideas between people, but it is also one manifestation of the general levelling off of the flow of news as it is received and absorbed by the journalists. Tamara's reactions to her horrific material is an exception; the contrast is the more striking given everyone else's matter-of-fact acceptance of these horrors—this callousness being a more common effect of this particular work situation. When a massacre of intellectuals in Bangladesh proves the final straw for her strained nerves, her colleague Gordon admonishes, 'For Christ's sake, you're a journalist. Is this any worse than your reports on the Eichman trial?' and adds briskly 'Don't be a bloody fool. Men have been slaughtering their thinkers for centuries.' (p. 101) And this tends to be the effect on the reader too. As another journalist, Cynthia, remarks:

Don't you ever feel uneasy, sometimes, as a journalist? We inundate people with depressing information and they become concerned. Then we offer more information and they become confused. And then we pile on more and more until they feel impotent but we offer them no help. No way out of their feelings of impotence. Don't you ever feel guilty? (p. 43)

And apart from the feelings of impotence, there is the bewilderment of not knowing which piece of news is more significant than another.

The absolute need for a system of values but the confusion, the sense of being overwhelmed by the outside world, when no such system of values is in operation, is, in fact, a recurrent theme of Wesker's plays. What Cynthia says about the information that comes through journalistic channels presents the same problem that Manfred in *The Friends* expresses: '. . . each fresh discovery of a fact or an idea doesn't replace, it undermines the last; it's got no measurement by which to judge itself, no perspective by which to evaluate its truth or its worth.' (p. 18) and to go back further, this is the same uncertainly that means Beatie Bryant can't answer the question 'What make that [song] third rate, and them frilly bits of opera and concert first rate?' (p. 115) In *The Journalists* there is an inevitable levelling of values by the methods and demands of presentation, and 'lilliputianizing' is a manifestation of this virtual denial of values.

However, though *The Journalists* pursues its theme to considerable depth and does not simplify the conflicting points of view involved, it is true that the plot moves in the public rather than the private sphere (deliberately so, it seems, as Wesker changed the title to the plural from a singular which would have given individual importance to Mary Mortimer) and, as such, is to be grouped with *Chips with Everything* and *Their Very Own And Golden City*, which it resembles in its episodic form as well as in subject and seriousness, rather than with *The Friends*.

IV

However, Wesker's later play, *The Merchant* (1978), both fully explores its chosen issues and places strong emphasis on the interior worlds of its main characters. Here, as in *The Kitchen*, the pressures of society curtail the individual's scope for development and distort human relationships. Based, as the title suggests, on Shakespeare's *The Merchant of Venice*, the play retains most of the familiar names from Shakespeare, but the characters have rather different personalities and this, in turn, contributes to different themes and emphases. Beginning from the premise that, in the trial scene, when Shylock loses his claim to a pound of Antonio's flesh, 'the kind of Jew I know would stand up and say, "Thank God" ',[5] Wesker extends this idea further and makes Shylock and Antonio close friends, so that the course of the play shows the social pressures that turn a joke into near murder. Shakespeare's Shylock is motivated by racial hatred in requiring the pound of flesh from Antonio if his debt is unpaid: Wesker's Shylock makes the same condition as an irritable joke against the anti-semitic laws of Venice that insist on a bond—ridiculous laws, he considers, forcing the formality of a legal contract between friends, when he would prefer to *give* the money or, if Antonio will not permit that, at least to lend without interest.

The point made here is the central one of the play: no free trust, or any other relationship, is allowed between the Jews and Gentiles in Renaissance Venice, because the fragility of mutual tolerance, like the fragility of verbal promises in business, is undermined by anti-semitic theory—the Jews deserve no trust, they are exempt from the common duties of humanity. Only the written Venetian laws, then, however irksome, protect the Jews

<hr>

[5] 'A Sense of What Should Follow' p. 21

from self-righteous exploitation. Therefore, inexorably, when the debt is not paid, the bond *must* be fulfilled—any waiving and consequent weakening of the law might be used next time as a precedent against the Jews. Shylock has involved himself not as an individual, a friend, but as 'the Jew', the representative of his race. After the trial, when Wesker's Portia intervenes as Shakespeare's does (and Wesker's Shylock *does* cry 'Thank God!'), the court takes the opportunity to confiscate Shylock's goods, including his precious books, and he, embittered and impoverished, banishes himself to Jerusalem. Antonio, who had counted his friendship as the blessing of his life, finds that blessing withdrawn. A brave human relationship ends in defeat; it is not unlike the conclusion of E.M. Forster's *A Passage to India*, where the Englishman and the Indian discuss friendship: ' "Why can't we be friends now? . . . It's what I want. It's what you want" ' but the circumstances, the surroundings even of inanimate nature, the temples, the birds, the countryside, 'said in their hundred voices, "No, not yet," and the sky said, "No, not here." '[6] For Wesker, characteristically, the responsibility is not mystically placed on the alien landscape, but on the men who make up a divisive society, of Venice or elsewhere.

Again, the continuity of *The Merchant* with the previous half dozen plays appears in other characteristic themes: Shylock himself draws together the concerns of several earlier characters; his contempt—'I am sometimes horrified by the passion of my contempt for men' (p. 247)—mirrors Manfred's contempt for the Englishman, but his naïve enthusiasm is like Louis Litvanov's, and he unites the complementary sides of the brothers in *The Old Ones*, manic Manny and gloomy Boomy, concluding his 'contempt' speech with the words 'Take those books, one by one, place on one side those which record man's terrible deeds, and on the other their magnificence. Do it! Deed for deed! Healing beside slaughter, building beside destruction, truth beside lie. Do it! Do it!' (p. 247) And Shylock is a strongly enough drawn character to sustain the weight of these Weskerian complexities, and carries the momentum of the play by his driving energy.

Less convincing is the character of Portia, who declares herself the 'new woman' who can 'spin, weave, sew,' and reads 'Plato and Aristotle, Ovid and Catullus, all in the original!' and, moreover, 'conversed with liberal minds on the nature of the soul, the efficacy of religious freedom, the very existence of God!' (p. 197) She is not, however, given much opportunity to live up to this awesome catalogue within the play. In short, she is perfect, and has little to do but comment on the imperfections of others until it is time for her to intervene at the climax of the trial scene. It seems that Portia's experience should parallel Shylock's, since she also has to suffer the attentions of fools—particularly her complacent and opportunist suitor Bassanio —while, thematically, her surviving confidence at the end ('Bassanio will come to know his place, accept'it, or leave it') (p. 265) is a positive balance to Shylock's defeated exile. This theme is not, however, fleshed out dramatically, and when Portia finally admits to Antonio that 'something in me has

[6] E.M. Forster, *A Passage to India* (Penguin 1936) p. 287

died struggling to grow up' (p. 265) (though we have noticed her critical reactions to Bassanio) the inward development of this disillusion has to be taken on trust.

Shylock's daughter Jessica, on the other hand, is a fully realized major character. Having given Shylock a sympathetic personality, Wesker has to re-motivate Jessica's elopement with a gentile, which in Shakespeare's play was an understandable escape from a miserly and obviously repulsive, if affectionate, tyrant. The father-daughter love-hate relationship admirably supplies this motivation, in that Shylock's very pride and love make him, too, an affectionate tyrant, here a sympathetic trait but intolerable to the similarly proud and self-willed Jessica.

The Merchant, then, has the plot mechanics of elopement, courtship, and trial scene inherited from Shakespeare's play, which means that there is far more classic, eventful, plot development than in any other Wesker play. But for all this *The Merchant*, just as much as *The Friends*, is mainly concerned with the developing awareness of the characters. Antonio, Jessica, Shylock himself, are unsuccessfully trying to force their ideas upon resisting circumstances, and learning and suffering as a result. Shylock is crushed by what he knew, intellectually, already, but would not accept emotionally; Jessica finds that her romance has been mere romancing; and Antonio endures, lonely, picking up the pieces of Shylock's catastrophe. Compared with them Beatie Bryant, whose character is also examined in depth, and who learns from experience, is for most of her appearance bewildered and not really conscious of the issues confronting her. Shylock, Antonio, Jessica and even Portia, on the other hand, are fully aware of what is involved in their defiance of circumstances, though they also make mistakes. Antonio looks back with regret on the life he has been part of: 'Those books. Look at them. How they remind me what I am, what I've done. Nothing! A merchant!' (p. 194). (It could be Manfred or Tessa speaking.) And when Shylock's exuberance breaks out in his long set-piece speech on 'the scheme of things' and the immortality of knowledge, he is still aware of the narrow-mindedness of Renaissance man, as he reaches for his compulsory and humiliating yellow hat, symbol of other, greater persecutions; he 'shrugs sadly, as though the hat is evidence to refute all he's said. And yet . . . he defiantly places it on his head . . .' (p. 233) Both Shylock and Antonio taste the full bitterness of the situation when Antonio's ships are lost and the joke bond becomes deadly earnest. They rehearse the elements of the trap that has closed on them:

Antonio	We shall both be put to death.
Shylock	I know.
Antonio	I by you. You by them.
Shylock	I know.
Antonio	For the foreigner who takes the life of a Venetian—
Shylock	I know, I know!
Antonio	We know, we know. We keep saying we know so much.
	pp. (246-7)

And they do *know*—they understand not only the immediate facts, but all the implications of being a Jew and a gentile in sixteenth-century Venice. They appreciate the scheme of things, as Shylock would say.

V

Five plays in some ten years is a reasonable rate of production, roughly that of Wesker's contemporaries among the 1950s 'New Wave' dramatists, Osborne, Pinter, and Arden. Again, like his contemporaries, Wesker's later plays have had mixed theatrical success, though the hazards of theatrical production and audience reaction are no real guide to the value of the works. In the event, the comedies were the best received, but it is the other plays— *The Friends, The Journalists, The Merchant*—that show a consistent advance in carrying themes familiar from the previous decade, themes of disillusion, the need for values, the interrelation of character and work, into situations where the conditions are more complex and the characters more articulate and aware. The characters in *The Friends* and *The Merchant* are self-analytic and intelligently speculative—as indeed they are in *The Journalists*, though the nature of that play precludes any full-length study of a single individual. Thus, after the digression of *The Four Seasons*, which explores private pain for its own sake in something of a vacuum, we find Wesker including the dimension of individual suffering, not for the first time (for it has provided the crisis point of all the earlier plays) but as a far more weighty and influential element in the 'pattern' that his characters are trying to make of their lives.

Note

Life and Writing

Harold Pinter was born in Hackney, London, in 1930. Educated at Hackney Downs Grammar School from 1941-7 he entered the Royal Academy of Dramatic Art in 1948 and was thereafter a professional actor. He was a conscientious objector and did no military service. His first play, *The Room,* was produced in 1957. He has received a number of awards including the Italia Prize, the Screenwriters Guild Award, the New York Film Critics Award, a British Film Academy Award, a Tony Award and a New York Drama Critics Circle Award. In 1966 he was made a Companion of the Order of the British Empire.

The most easily available edition of Pinter's plays up to *Silence,* is the three-volume Master Playwrights series of Eyre Methuen (vol 1, 1976; vol 2, 1977; vol 3, 1978). The later plays are also available from Eyre Methuen: *Old Times* (1971), *No Man's Land* (1975), *Betrayal* (1978). *Monologue* was published in a limited edition by Covent Garden Press (London, 1973). The film scripts are publish as *Five Screenplays* by Methuen (London, 1973) and *The Proust Screenplay: 'A la recherche du temps perdu'* (with the collaboration of Joseph Losey and Barbara Bray) by Grove Press (New York, 1977). The poems are published as *Poems* (1968) and *Poems and Prose, 1949-1977* (Methuen, London, 1978).

His main writings and interviews about the theatre are available in 'Between the Lines', *The Sunday Times,* London, 4 March, 1962; 'Writing for Myself ', *Twentieth Century,* 168, February 1967, pp. 34-6; 'Writing for the Theatre', *Evergreen Review,* August-September, 1964, pp. 80-82 (reprinted in H. Popkin, *Modern British Drama* (1964); 'Interview with Lawrence M. Bensky', *The Paris Review,* 39, 1966 (reprinted in *Writers at Work: The Paris Review Interviews,* Third Series, New York, 1967; London, 1968; also reprinted in *Theatre at Work,* Methuen, London, 1967).

Criticism

The most useful critical works on Pinter are, Martin Esslin, *The Peopled Wound: The Plays of Harold Pinter* (1970); John and Anthea Lahr, eds., *A Casebook on Harold Pinter's The Homecoming* (New York, 1971), reprinted by Davis Poynter (1974) in an edition which is used in the following article. Arthur Ganz ed., *Pinter: A Collection of Critical Essays,* (Englewood Cliffs, 1972); Steven H. Gale, *Butter's Going Up: A Critical Analysis of Harold Pinter's Work* (Durham, North Carolina, 1977). This contains a useful annotated bibliography; a chronology of Pinter's writings and of first performances with casts and directors; a list of productions directed and of roles acted by Pinter; a list of awards; selected reviews or Pinter's plays and films, interviews etc.

Harold Pinter's Idiom of Lies

GUIDO ALMANSI

I

Were I to trace with the firm hand of a surveyor or an accountant the graph of Harold Pinter's progress, or regress, or dramatic itinerary, from the early works to his latest plays, a few trends would emerge: a progressive baring of the symbolic superstructure; new disguises of a violence which becomes purely verbal or goes underground; monologues spreading, following some Beckettian suggestions, while stichomythia, which reached its apex with the interrogation of Stanley in *The Birthday Party*, recedes; intensification of pauses and silences, becoming the natural repositories of meaning (for instance in *The Basement, Landscape* and *Silence*, respectively of 1967, 1968 and 1969). But the fundamental element, language, has hardly changed. From *The Room* (written in 1957) to *Betrayal* (performed in 1978), Pinter has systematically forced his characters to use a perverse, deviant language to conceal or ignore the truth. In twenty years of playwriting he has never stooped to use the degraded language of honesty, sincerity, or innocence which has contaminated the theatre for so long. Nor did Pinter have to wait for his own maturity as a dramatist before he acquired the language of deceit and meretriciousness (as often happens with writers who only reach a strategic idiom after a first juvenile production of free-wheeling expressionism). His language was never chaste, but corrupt from birth. In his plays, even the virginal page protected by its candour is polluted, for the blank space conveys evil intentions and vile meanings. Pinter's idiom is essentially human because it is an idiom of lies.

Irving Wardle in a celebrated article[1] suggested that Pinter's characters ought to be analysed from an ethological perspective, as humanized animals fighting for territory (the room in *The Room, The Caretaker, The Basement*; the boarding house in *The Birthday Party*; the old house of *The Homecoming*; the flat of *No Man's Land*) rather than for sex, or power, or pleasure, or glory, or immortality.[2] But although the Pinterian hero is often as inarticulate as a pig, stumbling pathetically on every word, covering a pitifully narrow area of meaning with his utterances, blathering through his life, he does not, like any honest animal, seem to whine or grunt or giggle or grumble to give an outlet to his instincts, desires, passions or fears. He

---

[1] 'The Territorial Struggle' in Lahr (See Note for bibliographical details), pp. 37-44.
[2] The same idea reappears in self-conscious form with other critics. See for instance Ronald Hayman, *Harold Pinter*, 1975 (especially the *Conclusion* where the animal comparison is taken so literally as to become ludicrous).

grunts in order to hide something else. Even when he grunts ('Oh, I see. Well, that's handy. Well, that's . . . I tell you what, I might do that . . . just till I get myself sorted out.'[3]), his grunt is a lie. Pinter's characters are often abject, stupid, vile, aggressive: but they are always intelligent enough in their capacity as conscientious and persistent liars, whether lying to others or to themselves, to hide the truth if they know truth's truthful abode. They are too cunning in their cowardice to be compared to noble animals. They are perverted in their actions and speech: hence human.

On the traditional stage, characters use dialogue for their underhand strategy, but reveal their true selves in monologues. This is not true of Pinter's plays, where both dialogue and monologue follow a fool-proof technique of deviance. You can trust his characters neither when they are talking to others nor when they are talking to themselves: this is what makes *Landscape, Old Times, No Man's Land* such difficult plays. Characters shift position crab-like, move forward like knights on a chess-board,[4] an oblique tentative step rather than a bold progress. In Pinter's games players do not advance towards their goal (except for the kill, as in Spooner's final speech in *No Man's Land*): they dribble. This requires a picklock-language, used askew, whose crooked insinuation—penetrating between the reality of the *thing* and the reality of the *word*[5]—mocks the straight approach of the honest key.

With Pinter, expression is no longer the specular reflection of an emotion nor the *word* of a *thing*: the mirror is slanted, and the expression therefore does not reflect the opposite and apposite emotion but the adjacent one, so that each sound and image is systematically distorted (Robert to Emma: 'I've always liked Jerry. To be honest, I've always liked him rather more than I've liked you. Maybe I should have had an affair with him myself. (*Silence*) Tell me, are you looking forward to our trip to Torcello?' (p. 87)) The stage—and the post-Shavian English stage in particular—was used to a perpendicular language, reflecting the inner world of mind and heart with geometric inevitability. Pinter replaced the right angle by an obtuse angle, so that repartees do not rebound directly: this is his special effect which gives the odd ring to his conversations. Not the language of thinking robots, like Shaw's; not the language of men aping apes, like Artaud's; not the language of hysterical clowns, like Ionesco's; not the language of existential preoccupations, like Beckett's: his is a language of hide-and-seek, human/inhuman ('*inhuman*: the characteristic quality of the human race', Ambrose Bierce[6]). Pinter's world is plausible and understandable in so far as everyone attempts not to be understood.

---

[3] All quotations from the early plays are from the three volume Eyre Methuen edition, and will be incorporated in the text. This quotation is from II, 25. Where no volume number is given, references are to the editions cited in the Note.

[4] 'Knight-move' is the title of a celebrated article by V. Sklovsky about literary strategies.

[5] I use the terms of Michel Foucault in his classical study, *Les mots et les choses*, Paris, Gallimard, 1966 (English edition, *The order of things: an archeology of the human sciences*, Tavistock Press, 1970).

[6] Ambrose Bierce, *The Enlarged Devil's Dictionary*, Penguin, 1971.

Yet, in a sense, Pinter's characters do behave like beasts. Their language articulates the three basic survival techniques of animals: fight, flight and mimetism. Stanley, Davies, Teddy, Spooner, Jerry use language either to attack, or to retreat, or to disguise what they are (and what they are is neither here nor there, to crack the wind of a poor pun). In some often quoted statements from early speeches and interviews, Pinter attempted to distinguish himself from the Absurdist tradition by shifting the issue from the difficulty of communication to the danger of communication:

> I think we communicate only too well, in our silence, in what is unsaid, and that what takes place is continual evasion, desperate rearguard attempts to keep ourselves to ourselves. Communication is too alarming. To enter into someone else's life is too frightening. to disclose to others the poverty within us is too fearsome a possibility.[7]

Sincerity, honesty, linguistic generosity, openness, are diabolical inventions that must be shunned because they create chaos. Survival is based on a policy of reciprocal misunderstanding and misinformation. If we were to chose a straightforward approach, we would be at the mercy of others, or of language itself; or even worse: of ourselves, that part of ourselves we do everything to ignore—and this drive towards self-ignorance is the one intellectual enterprise in which we excel. Nothing is more frightening than making Yakov Petrovitch Golyadkin's ordeal of meeting his doppelgänger on the Fontanka Quay close to the Ismailovsky Bridge[8] into a daily routine. Mirrors are 'deceptive' says Bill in *The Collection* (III, 146), and this is our salvation.

In *Uno, Nessuno e Centomila* (*One, No One and One Hundred Thousand*) by Luigi Pirandello,[9] Vitangelo Moscarda, shaving in the morning, realizes for the first time in his life that his nose is crooked. This means that mirrors are 'deceptive': they have either deceived him in the past, when he was thinking of himself as a straight-nosed individual, or they are deceiving him now, as he discovers the crooked nature of his trump. Vitangelo creates a breathing space for himself in the antagonism between his two alter-egos (the straight-nosed Cleopatra of history facing the crooked-nosed Cleopatra of hypothesis), and eventually finds solace and comfort in the serene harbour of madness where all opposites are reconciled. Rimbaud's frightening 'Je est un autre' ('I *is* another one')[10], or Lacan's ironical 'L'inconscient, c'est le discours de l'autre' ('The unconscious is the discourse of the Other')[11] require intellectual heroes. Like us, Pinter's characters lack this boldness and continue to pretend to be themselves with thorough and impudent bad faith (think of the supreme bad faith of Deeley in *Old Times*) because they are aware that their secrets are so well hidden that they themselves have

---

[7] *Sunday Times* (London), 3 March 1962.
[8] I am referring to the scene in Dostoevsky's *The Double* when the protagonist crosses his double in the street.
[9] The first edition was 1926 (I use the recent Oscar Mondadori edition, Milan, 1979).
[10] Letter to Georges Izambard, 13 May 1871.
[11] J. Lacan, 'Le seminaire sur *La Lettre Volée*', in *Ecrits I*, Paris, 1966, p. 24.

forgotten where they are. No one is likely to dig them out: not Goldberg or McCann, who must resort to real violence to *get* at Stanley; not Mick with Davies, or Lenny with Ruth, or Anna with Deeley; not Foster and Biggs either, who are defeated by Spooner's proteanism. 'Now-a-days to be intelligible is to be found out', says Lord Darlington in *Lady Windermere's Fan*.[12] But, as usual, Wilde is at his best when he does not really know what he is saying. Pinter, whose style abhors the paradoxical truisms *à la Wilde* (the reference to mirrors in *The Collection* is almost a slip), seems to know what he is doing; he wants characters who are *born* liars, and an audience who mistrust them.

In spite of this, critics seem to refuse their new roles as unbelievers. No matter how improbable the statement, implausible the situation, extravagant the motivation, tall the story, honourable critics ponderously assess and discuss the declarations of the Pinterian character as if they were reliable. Spooner 'is acquainted with the impeccably aristocratic Lord Lancer. He is able to organize a poetry reading for Hirst that will include . . . a dinner party at a fine Indian restaurant. . . .'[13] Mick dreams 'of seeing the derelict house as a luxurious penthouse'.[14] 'It is made quite clear by Ruth that when Teddy met and married her she was a nude photographic model —and this is widely known as a euphemism for a prostitute.'[15] When Davies is invited by Aston to stay, 'Mick's jealousy is instantly aroused.'[16] 'In his anger Mick picks up and smashes the figure of the Buddha which is one of Aston's favourite pieces in the room.'[17] 'Now there is a serious question as to whether Lenny really did this (belting the old lady in the nose, and kicking her to finish the job). . . at all, much less with such terrifying indifference.'[18] 'Mick had believed Davies to be an interior decorator . . .' (!?!)[19] In all these instances, critics give the Pinterian hero a credit that he does not deserve and does not require. I don't think we are supposed to believe that Spooner is acquainted with Lord Lancer; that Mick is jealous and angry; that Ruth was a prostitute; that Lenny met a woman who made him 'a certain proposal' and beat her, or that he had kicked the old lady who wanted the mangle removed. Least of all are we expected to believe that Mick believed that Davies was an interior decorator. All we know is that there are characters who are making these statements: not that these statements are valid. The Pinterian hero lies as he breathes: consistently and uncompromisingly. Not

[12] Act 1. Wilde's witticism is quoted by Arthur Ganz in his interesting introduction to a collection of essays on Pinter.

[13] Lucina Paquet Gabbard, *The Dream Structure of Pinter's Plays*, Associated University Press, 1976, p. 260.

[14] Esslin, p. 99.

[15] Ibid, p. 151.

[16] John Russell Taylor, *Anger and After. A Guide to the New British Drama*, Methuen, 1962, p. 247.

[17] Esslin, p. 100.

[18] Bert O. States, 'Pinter's *Homecoming*: The Shock of Nonrecognition', in *The Hudson Review*, xii, 3, Autumn 1968, pp. 474-86. The quotation is from p. 482.

[19] Nigel Alexander, 'Past, Present and Pinter', in *Essays and Studies 1974*, edited by Kenneth Muir for the English Association, 1974. The quotation is on p. 10.

to lie is as inconceivable to him as to 'eat a crocodile'[20] or make love to a
spider. Goldberg, Mick, Edward, Ben, Lenny, Spooner, are not just occa-
sionally unreliable: they are untrustworthy by definition, since their words
only bear witness to their capacity for speech, not to their past or present
experience. Pinter's opus, like Pirandello's, is a long disquisition on the
masks[21] of the liar: the liar as the man who panics (Davies, Edward, Stanley,
Hirst); the liar as the man who conceals his panic (Mick, Ben, Lenny,
Spooner, Robert); the liar as the man who chats ('I talked too much. That
was my mistake.' says Aston in *The Caretaker* (II, 63); but these words
would fit Gus, Duff, Foster). In Pinter mendacity is avoidance of identity:
the existential equivalent of our daily avoidance of responsibility.

In a sense this is something new in the western theatre. Traditionally the
liar is an identifiable character who can be recognized by his mendacious
habits. Maskwell, in Congreve's *The Double Dealer*, Don Garcia, in
Alarcon's *La Verdad Sospechosa*, Dorante, in Corneille's *Le Menteur*, Lelio,
in Goldoni's *Il Bugiardo*, are typological liars, as distinct in their psychological habit as the Spanish braggart, the old dotard, the sententious scholar
(or the vamp with a two-foot long cigarette holder). They come on stage and
introduce themselves as liars, in the same way as other characters are presented as merchants, seamen or carpenters. Some are good, experienced,
well-trained, professional liars; and among them the best and most heroic is
Dorante, a giant among his fellow word-forgers, who is even willing to
switch his sentimental allegiance in the last scene of the play in order to be
able to tell a further lie. Dorante lies to himself, about his own feelings
towards two possible beloved women, Clarice and Lucrèce,[22] so as to lie to
others, since his commitment to his art as a liar is greater than his commitment to his heart as a lover.

Pinter's liars are not of the same ilk: since everyone lies, the genuine
liar no longer exists. Yet the social and emotional survival of characters
still depends on speed: how fast they succeed in running away from themselves (once again we come across Golyadkin who 'looked as though he
wanted to hide from himself, as though he were trying to run away from
himself').[23] I remember an old 1920s comic film in which an actor, frightened by his own shadow, was running—literally like a horse—in order to
escape from the incumbent menace. In Pinter's plays people do not sell their
shadow like Peter Schlemihl:[24] they give it away because they are frightened
by it, and there is no real desire to get it back. Papers are left in distant
Sidcup—surely as memorable a literary location by now as Bartleby's Dead
Letter Office at Washington—and Davies, unwilling to recover them until
the weather breaks, cannot even face the remembrance of his birthplace: 'I
was . . . uh . . . oh, it's a bit hard, like, to get your mind back . . . so what I

---

[20] *Hamlet*, V, i, 264.
[21] Pirandello's theatrical works are in fact collected under the general title of *Maschere Nude*
= *Naked Masks*.
[22] Dorante falls in love with Clarice, believing that her name was Lucrèce.
[23] F. Dostoevsky, *The Eternal Husband and other stories*, Heinemann, 1956, p. 173.
[24] Adalbert von Chamisso, *Peter Schlemihls wundersame Geschichte*, Leipzig, 1834.

mean . . . going back . . . a good way . . . lose a bit of track, like . . . you know . . .' (II, 34)

The past is either unknowable, or modifiable at will. In *No Man's Land* Hirst and Spooner attempt to control each other through a manipulation of the past. The rich and the poor, the successful man of letters (is he?) and the unsuccessful poet, the parched dipsomaniac and the thirsty beggar, fight for two hours, creating and destroying plausible and implausible backgrounds, inventing different versions of the past in which they had met or not met; known or not known each other; seduced or not seduced their respective wives or lady-friends. The factual truth of these fanciful reconstructions is demoted since what matters is the game of pressures and counterpressures. The recollection or the invention of a second wife, of a different mistress, of a new experience, of another life-style, of different war-years (Hirst: 'You did say you had a good war, didn't you?' Spooner: 'A rather good one, yes.' (p. 71)), are gambits in the social game. Autobiography becomes subservient to the necessity of survival, to the requirements of polemics. The character has been married, or fought a war, or belonged to a Club, or turned into a homosexual or a voyeur, if this item of information can be used to humiliate the opponent. This does not exclude the immediate material advantages that are at stake. In *No Man's Land*, Spooner—not unlike Davies in *The Care-taker*—needs settling down, and is available to any moral, social, or sexual prostitution which will solve his problem. But the density and pungency of the dialogue distract us from the drama of the two men (destitution and squalor for Spooner; for Hirst 'the last lap of a race . . . [he] . . . had long forgotten to run' (p. 52)) and focuses on the brilliance of the verbal duel rather than on the revelations of anguish and despair. The play is a compromise between the linguistic idiosyncrasy of the characters (especially in the case of Spooner, the aged bohemian whose speech is an exquisite florilegium of revolting clichés) and their personal drama built on psychological emptiness. Spooner and Hirst are linguistic shells made of words words words, but there is nothing inside since a man with two lives has no life of his own; a man with several pasts has no past which belongs to him.

It may be interesting to compare the two major productions of *No Man's Land*: Peter Hall's at the *National Theatre* in London, in 1975, and Roger Planchon's at the *Théâtre de l'Athénée* in Paris, in 1979. Hall insisted on the Pinterian theme of the outsider coming in and the insider going out (as in *A Slight Ache* and *The Basement*). On the one hand, Spooner hopes to find a haven of security in the close space of Hirst's residence (hence the emphasis laid on the luxury of the flat); on the other hand, Hirst dreams of escaping into a land of lakes and waterfalls, which turns into 'no man's land' when he is awake: a place 'which never moves, which never changes, which never grows older, but which remains forever, icy and silent' (p. 95). Hall's quasi-naturalistic approach is somewhat at variance with the last scene of the play, when litanies, incantations, logical and linguistic games prevail. For instance, when Hirst proposes 'to change subject . . . for the last time' (p. 91), the three other character's ritualistic elaboration on the ulterior meaning of this proposal ('But what does . . . [for the last time] . . . mean?'

(p. 91)) imposes a symbolic pattern upon the play which is alien to Peter Hall's interpretation. Similarly, John Gielgud's impressive crawling across the stage towards a bottle of whisky or a box of cigarettes does not really fit with his final role as a guru, leading Hirst to his glacial abode. Peter Hall, peerless in the tit-for-tat exchanges and in the parodic treatment of the comedy of manners and sexual innuendoes ('Stella?' 'You can't have forgotten.' 'Stella who?' 'Stella Winstansley.' 'Winstansley?' 'Bunty Winstansley's sister.' 'Oh, Bunty. No, I never see her.' (pp. 72-3)) is ultimately defeated by his own ability.

Roger Planchon takes almost the opposite approach, stressing the logical/illogical games/galimatias over the flights of fancy and psychological infightings. His whole production concentrates on Spooner, the tempter, the ambiguous manipulator of symbols, who is not quite a drunken Charon but a soused tourist-guide to no man's land. The different ways in which the two main actors in the Paris production drink their liquor is revealing. Hirst downs his drinks with sharp nervous determination, whereas Spooner obscenely lets his whisky linger for a while in his puffed-up cheeks, and seems to find inspiration for the next twist in his yarn from the internal fumes of alcohol, like a drugged oracle. Planchon lays great emphasis on the Bolsover Street passage, which turns into a description of a second-class hell, a dead-end suitable for unimaginative citizens, while the protagonists fight elsewhere on the border of dream, madness and death:

Briggs   He . . . Foster . . . asked me the way to Bolsover Street. I told him Bolsover Street was in the middle of an intricate one-way system. It was a one-way system easy enough to get into. The only trouble was that, once in, you couldn't get out. I told him his best bet, if he really wanted to get to Bolsover Street, was to take the first left, first right, second right, third on the left, keep his eye open for a hardware shop, go right round the square, keeping to the inside lane, take the second mews on the right and then stop. He will find himself facing a very tall office block, with a crescent courtyard. He can take advantage of this office block. He can go round the crescent, come out the other way, follow the arrows, go past two sets of traffic lights and take the next left indicated by the first green filter he comes across. He's got the Post Office Tower in his vision the whole time. All he's got to do is to reverse into the underground car park, change gear, go straight on, and he'll find himself in Bolsover Street with no trouble at all. I did warn him, though, that he'll still be faced with the problem, having found Bolsover Street, of losing it. I told him I knew one or two people who'd been wandering up and down Bolsover Street for years. They'd wasted their bloody youth there. The people who live there, their faces are grey, they're in a state of despair, but nobody pays any attention, you see. All people are worried about is their illgotten gains. I wrote to *The Times* about it. Life at A Dead End, I called it. (p. 62)

Properly done, the speech is hilarious and terrifying, with the sudden irruption of the irrational (of the metaphysical?) into the realm of the most banal quotidian preoccupation (how to deliver a parcel in Bolsover Street, London W.1.). For Planchon the key moments of the play were these ritualized speeches: the evocation of the scene in Amsterdam, for example, which Spooner wants to immortalize in a painting (an absurdist 'spot of time'); or the stupendous cricket metaphor, which must sound even better in Paris in front of an audience unacquainted with the extravagance of the technical vocabulary of that sport.

> *Spooner* Tell me then about your wife?
> *Hirst*   What wife?
> *Spooner* How beautiful she was, how tender and how true. Tell me with what speed she swung in the air, with what velocity she came off the wicket, whether she was responsive to finger spin, whether you could bowl a shooter with her, or an offbreak with a leg-break action. In other words, did she googlie? (p. 30)

The fact that the names of the four characters, Hirst, Spooner, Foster and Briggs, belong to four well-known cricketers of the turn of the century[25] is clearly central to the play, but only an English-born critic could venture into this dark domain. Foreigners like Planchon, and myself, have to bow in awe when faced by the mystery of the universe. Planchon's is a darker *No Man's Land*, since the director stressed the areas of obfuscation, whereas Hall preferred the areas of illumination. As a spectator, I preferred the London production; as a reader, I am more tempted by Planchon's interpretation.

II

No matter how determined the playwright is to stamp out the world of intimate thoughts, memories and desires, it always perversely re-emerges. Behind the skin there is the skull, and inside the skull there are ideas, emotions, feelings, amorous longings. In other words, people continue against all evidence and all decency to be 'a bit inner'. Pinter is the only writer who has transformed psychological depth and inwardness into an insult. Here are Albert's close friends, in *A Night Out*, talking about his 'inner life':

> *Kedge* He's a bit deep, really, isn't he?
> *Seeley* Yes, he's a bit deep. (*Pause*)
> *Kedge* Secretive.
> *Seeley* (*irritably*) What do you mean, secretive? What are you talking about?
> *Kedge* I was just saying he was secretive.
> *Seeley* What are you talking about? What do you mean, he's secretive?
> *Kedge* You said yourself he was deep.
> *Seeley* I said he was deep. I didn't say he was secretive. [I. 214]

[25] D.A. Cairns, 'Batting for Pinter', in *The Times*, 7 June 1975.

But the sworn enemy of any form of *internal* life is Lenny in *The Home-coming*, who wants to know whether Ruth's *proposal* is a *proposal*, leaving no margin for unexpressed desires or intentions. In the tense exchange with Teddy ('taking the piss' out of him, in Peter Hall's apt definition of the mood of the play),[26] Lenny accuses his brother of the ultimate sin: having a life inside. 'Mind you, I will say you do seem to have grown a bit sulky during the last six years. A bit sulky. *A bit inner*. A bit less forthcoming.' (III, 80. My italics) The adjective *inner* becomes truly offensive, since *innerness* is a defiance against the unwritten laws of common decency which requires one should never say or think anything related to the *inner* life. The 'hidden imposthume'[27] is no longer located in a special point of the rotten body of the individual or of society: it becomes equivalent to the totality of *inner* life. Characters are superficial and unfathomable in their superficiality.[28] In his cruel exchange with Max about his own conception, Lenny mocks the fact that there could be an emotional or sentimental background—an *inner* motion—behind the copulative act which generated him: 'That night . . . you know . . . the night you got me . . . that night with Mum, what was it like? Eh? When I was just a glint in your eye. What was it like? What was the background to it? I mean, I want to know the real facts about my back-ground. I mean, for instance, is it a fact that you had me in mind all the time, or is it a fact that I was the last thing you had in mind?' (III, 52) Even if Lenny, because of his own bastardy, was just mocking his presumed father, as some critics have suggested,[29] the main target of his speech remains the *inner* life. Pinter's characters long for a world without conscience, not out of fear that it will 'make cowards of us all', but out of laziness. Thought and feeling are tiresome and demanding.

I have emphasized the novelty of Pinter's exploitation of man's supreme cultural gift: mendacity. Yet the reference to Hamlet reminds us that, in another sense, Pinter's use of a beguiling language is not new in the western theatre. On the contrary, the language of lies may be innate with the theatrical phenomenon. For Martin Esslin, who has been the sensible and reasonable chronicler of the unreasonable Absurd, there is a main line of development in European theatre, 'from Sophocles to Shakespeare to Rattigan',[30] where people on the stage have 'always spoken more clearly, more directly, more to the purpose than they would ever have done in real life.'[31] Then dramatists like Strindberg and Wedekind started to introduce 'a certain defectiveness of communication between characters—who talk past each other rather than to each other . . .'[32] Finally we get to Chekhov, who

[26] See Lahr, p. 14.

[27] 'The hidden imposthume', from *Hamlet*, IV, iv, 27, is the key to the Shakespearian play according to Frances Fergusson, *The Idea of a Theatre*, Princeton, N.J., 1949, p. 110.

[28] 'Nichts ist unergründlicher als die Oberflächlichkeit des Weibes', Karl Kraus, *Beim Wort Genommen*, Munich, 1955, p. 14.

[29] For instance both John Lahr and Steven M.L. Aronson in Lahr, pp. 3 and 69.

[30] Esslin, p. 194.

[31] Ibid.

[32] Esslin, p. 195.

inaugurates *The Theatre of Chatting*, in Alberto Moravia's felicitous formulation.[33] Esslin singles out the mortuary promise of peace and serenity that Sonia makes to her uncle in the last scene of *Uncle Vanya*[34] as the point of compromise between a rhetorical tradition, that wants Sonia's speech more eloquent than it would have been in real life, and the exigency of obliqueness, so that she pretends to believe what she does not believe, though aware that no one believes that she believes what she says she believes (a Dantesque conundrum). Esslin's is a brilliant re-invention of three thousand years of theatre history from discourse to chat, from an open game to a closed game, from the language of confession (characters in Greek drama are like Quakers forced to confess their sins in public) to the language of strategy.

Yet this interpretation ignores irony (the author's, the character's, the spectator's ironies) without which drama is merely a vulgar metaphor. If we take into consideration the role and function of irony in western theatre, then theatrical language has always been strategical. Is it necessary to remind ourselves of the 'antic disposition', which is a blue-print for deceit and a licence for self-deceit, or of Shakespeare as the supreme ironist in Kierkegaard's paradoxical definition (for Heine the supreme ironist was God; for Kierkegaard Shakespeare)?[35] If we look at the past history of the theatre from another perspective than the one taken by Martin Esslin, the stage becomes a territory dominated by strategic preoccupations, and its language a language of manoeuvres, not of confrontation. Words have been uttered on the stage with a certain purpose in mind, and it would be wrong to believe that the aim has always been clarification and not obfuscation. I am well aware that before Freud and Heidegger people were stupid and ignorant about obfuscations, since they had not read *Traumdeutung* and *Sein und Zeit*; but even our ancestors had their own occult means of distinguishing between clarity and darkness.

III

If a character in a play says 'Mother, give me the sun!', this utterance can be frightening because it is indicative of a deranged mind. Pinter has succeeded in transfering the frightening effect from the extravagance of madness to the banality of normality. He knows how to exploit the disgust of worn-out expressions, making us feel that only a deranged mind would dare to use them. The first hero of repulsive chichés is Goldberg in *The Birthday Party*. His complacent self-satisfied articulation of rotting fragments from a language of null feeling and null sensibility succeeds in creating a full-fledged character, obscene because he uses language at its most common denominator. 'Culture? Don't talk to me about culture. He was an all-round man, what do you mean? He was a cosmopolitan.' (I, 38) 'School? Don't talk to me about school. Top in all subjects. And for why? Because I'm telling

---

[33] Alberto Moravia 'The Theatre of Chatting', in *The London Magazine*, July-August 1969, pp. 94-109.

[34] Anton Chekhov, *Plays*, 1960, p. 245.

[35] Quoted in Harry Levin, *The Question of Hamlet*, 1970, p. 75.

you, I'm telling you, follow my line? Follow my mental? Learn by heart. Never write down a thing.' (I 87) Only Max, in *The Homecoming*, reminiscing about his family life, can create such a feeling of revulsion for the utter emptiness of his speech. We laugh at chat, small talk, gabble, because their revelations would be too awesome if we took them seriously (Heidegger is the modern thinker who has dared to contemplate the abyss of Gerede,[36] chatting, and Pinter is his representative on the stage). In *A Night Out*, a much under-rated play, conversation viscidly crawls from one pool of slime to the next. The exchanges between the old man and Albert's young friends at the coffee-stall, the dialogue between the two office girls at the party, are a magnificent display of linguistic horrors. There are bubbles of empty speech which explode with dismal dampening effect when Kedge and Seeley comment about a football match:

Kedge   What's the good of him playing his normal game? He's a left half, he's not a left back.

Seeley   Yes, but he's a defensive left half, isn't he? That's why I told him to play his normal game. You don't want to worry about Connor, I said, he's a good ballplayer but he's not all that good.

Kedge   Oh, he's good, though.

Seeley   No one's denying he's good. But he's not all that good. I mean, he's not tip-top. You know what I mean?

Kedge   He's fast.

Seeley   He's fast, but he's not all that fast, is he?

Kedge   (*doubtfully*) Well, not all that fast . . .

Seeley   What about Levy? Was Levy fast? (I, 210-11)

Am I the only reader who finds this fragment of conversation hurtful in its vacuity? Empty chatting possesses an existential fullness, when a comment upon the weather, or about the routine of daily life, is the disguise of a fundamental question: 'Do you know that I exist?' or 'I do exist. What about you?'[37] Kedge and Seeley are beyond that pale. They fulfill the ultimate structuralist dream: a language that speaks us instead of a language that is spoken by us. The *koine* of the tribe ensnares the characters into a deceptive *distinguo*. The difference between 'good' and 'all that good', 'fast' and 'all that fast', gives the speakers the illusion of free will and freedom of speech and choice. They believe that they are in control while they are being controlled. They are the puppets of language: their *parole* is utterly subservient to the *langue*, which is perversely vacuous and futile.

In normal life language ranges from a full sensual enjoyment of the phonetic articulation in our mouth, the voicing process in our throat, the mechanics in our brain and nervous system to a purely repetitive production of alien sounds and alien concept,[38] as if the vocal apparatus were

[36] See Martin Heidegger, *Being and Time*, 1962, pp. 211-214.

[37] See Harold Pinter's sketch *Request Stop* (II, 243, 245).

[38] 'I have mixed feelings about words. . . . Moving among them, sorting them out, watching them appear on the page, from this I derive a considerable pleasure. But at the same time I have another strong feeling about words which amounts to nothing less than nausea.' Pinter in the *Sunday Times*, 4 March, 1962 (quoted by Esslin, p. 44).

merely the loudspeaker of a cheap Hi Fi system. At the one end we have the language evoked by William Gass: '. . . the use of a language like a lover . . . not the language of love, but the love of language, not matter but meaning, not what the tongue touches, but what it forms, not lips and nipples, but nouns and verbs.'[39] Or by Jean Genet: 'The word balls has a roundness in my mouth.'[40] On the other end we chew over and over the language of dead people.[41] It is like the range of salivas in Salvador Dali's celebrated metaphor: 'la bave immonde, antigéométrique du chien' ('the lurid, anti-geometrical spittle of the dog') vs. 'la bave quintessentielle de l'araignée' ('the quintessential spittle of the spider').[42] Kedge's and Seeley's phonation resembles a form of articulatory rumination. In their mouth they masticate the dessiccated saliva which was once in the mouth of an idiot who first *coined* these sentences: and the words of the idiot signify nothing. The two boys' destiny is the triumph of fatuousness: hence it is a tragic destiny. They cannot enjoy their football because they have been denied the linguistic capacity to utter their personal appreciation.[43]Pinter refuses—rightly in my view—to give voice to their inarticulate sounds in the old populist manner: but he gives them an audience.

In the early plays Pinter had been the virtuoso of phonomimesis: a 'super-realist', in the sense the word has acquired in the modern art scene. He used to exploit the stammerer: either the phonetic stammerer, or the conceptual stammerer, piling up debris of words, stumps of phrases, truncated fragments of meaningful expressions to barricade the entrance to the nearest burrow where, in a cowardly way, they hid themselves. Martin Esslin effectively sums up the novelty of Pinter's elegant and spectacular illiteracy: '. . . inarticulate, incoherent, tautological and nonsensical speech might be as dramatic as verbal brilliance when it could be treated simply as an element of action . . .'[44] Davies, in *The Caretaker*, was the expert in the art of stuttering acrobatics, interspersed with *Pindaric* flights of stupendous *bad grammar*: 'What about them shoes I come all the way to get I hear you was giving away?' (II, 24) These are linguistic *tours-de-force*, as difficult and as artificial as the sketch of the master skater who pretends to be a clown who pretends not to know how to skate. In the latest plays, however, the treatment of inarticulacy tends to disappear, whilst the texts still manipulate the inane components of small talk as the weaponry of pusillanimous characters (Deeley in *Old Times*, Duff in *Landscape*, Jerry in *Betrayal*). Two new mannerisms come to light: the mannerism of the hard-of-hearing, and the

---

[39] William Howard Gass, *On Being Blue: a Philosophical Inquiry*, Boston, Mass. 1976, p. 11.

[40] 'Le mot couilles a une rondeur dans ma bouche . . .', Jean Genet, *Journal du Voleur*, Paris, 1949, pp. 261-2.

[41] 'You will repeat the same words that have always been uttered. Do you believe that you are living? You are just chewing over the life of dead people.' L. Pirandello, *Henry the Fourth*, Act II.

[42] Catalogue of the Dali exhibition at Beaubourg, Paris, 1979.

[43] 'It's one more thing we do to the poor, the deprived: cut out their tongues . . . allow them a language as lousy as their lives . . .' W.H. Gass quoted, p. 25.

[44] Esslin, p. 199.

mannerism of the hard-of-understanding.
    Hard of hearing:

Emma   It's Torcello tomorrow, isn't it?
Robert   What?
Emma   We've going to Torcello tomorrow, aren't we? (II. 75)

And in *No Man's Land*:

Hirst   What was he drinking?
Spooner What?
Hirst   What was he drinking?
Spooner Pernod. (pp. 24-5)

Hard of understanding:

Robert   I thought you knew.
Jerry   Knew what?
Robert   That I knew. That I've known for years. I thought you knew.
Jerry   You thought I knew? (p. 38)

And in *Old Times*:

Kate   Yes, I quite like those kind of things, doing it.
Anna   What kind of things?
Deeley   Do you mean cooking?
Kate   All that thing. (p. 21)

Pinter is a maestro in orchestrating not small but minute talk: the almost unnoticeable curves in an evasive conversation (well, all conversations are evasive in Pinter). He successfully strives to create meaning in the most unpromising areas of signification: casual remarks, perfunctory exchanges, usage and abusage of worn-out phrases, absurd observations, gossip, the grating sound of blathering and blabbering, the tittle-tattle of quotidian verbiage.

In the area of the absurd nothing can rival the intimate aggression of the opening line of a text which lures the reader into a territory whose conventions, location, rules, time-scale and habits he ignores. By definition the *incipit* must be shocking and alienating, since it forces us to enter into a dark room, without knowing what and whom to expect there. 'Who's there?' 'Nay, answer me; stand and unfold yourself'[45] is no mean example of initial shock. The unsurpassed master in opening gambits in the twentieth century was Ernest Hemingway. Take the initial strategy of *The Light of The World*: 'When he saw us come in the door the bartender looked up and then reached over and put the glass covers on the two free lunch bowls.' This seems to me supreme: a sense of tactical manoeuvering which is unmatched in modern literature. But since Hemingway's death the insignia of the foremost expert in opening theory—where the author tries to defeat the reader on the chessboard of the text—have been passed on to Harold Pinter. His late plays present a stunning range of dramatic entrances:

[45] *Hamlet*, I, i, 1.

The Lover   *Richard* (*amiably*)   Is your lover coming today?
                     Sarah   Mmnn.
                     Richard   What time? (II, 161)

Old Times   *Kate* (*reflectively*)   Dark.
                     Deeley   Fat or thin?
                     Kate   Fuller than me, I think. (p. 7)

No Man's Land   *Hirst*   As it is?
                     Spooner   As it is, yes please, absolutely as it is. (p.15)

This last exchange is *absolutely* untranslatable. Hirst pours a glass of whisky in the *Théatre de l'Athénée* saying 'Tel quel?'. And Spooner: 'Tel quel. Absolument tel quel.' That's not it. And 'absolument' is miles away from 'absolutely'. Gone is the ritual, lost is the effect.

The Pinterian speech often opens with a statement which sounds familiar and yet is already lost, irrevocably alien. Like Freud, Pinter makes the insignificant significant; unlike Freud, Pinter refuses to explain and expand on the forces which govern these transformations. Ruth's 'Oh, I was thirsty', after draining a glass of water in *The Homecoming*, is pregnant with signification, and yet is impregnable in its mystery. It suggests an avenue of meaning, but declines to open or illuminate it. In other words, Pinter is generous with his reader, contrary to current belief. He allows him to think, and puzzle, and struggle with his own emotional and intellectual incompetence. Beyond that lies another territory which is more frightening, mysterious and unfathomable: where feelings are uttered, ideas debated, emotions expressed. As Karl Kraus put it, 'Nothing is more incomprehensible than the discourse of a person for whom language is only used to make himself understood.'[46] This is the ultimate horror, which is the preserve of artists of a different ilk. But Pinter is no Lawrence, is no Conrad. He provides us with the oblique tools to come to terms with our own inadequacy, accept our moral and intellectual cowardice, understand our misunderstanding. He is the unreliable guide to a land of unreliance: hence within his terms of reference he is consistent, persuasive and ultimately trustworthy. Elsewhere one finds the *agents provocateurs* who promise feelings, emotions, passions, desires or even ideas.

[46] Kraus quoted, p. 66.

Note

Life and Writing

Joe Orton was born in Leicester in 1933. After studying shorthand and typing, he went in 1951 to the Royal Academy of Dramatic Art. In that year he moved in with Kenneth Halliwell, a fellow student at RADA, and they began collaborating, without success, on a number of novels. In 1961 both were sentenced to six months in prison for malicious damage of library books. In 1963 Orton was commissioned to write a radio play for the BBC, performed in 1964; in that year too *Entertaining Mr Sloane* opened in London, going to New York the following year. In 1965 *Loot* was tried provincially, but did not reach London until the new production of 1966. In 1967, *Crimes of Passion*—a double bill consisting of stage adaptations of his radio play *The Ruffian on the Stair* (1964) and his television play *The Erpingham Camp* (1966)—opened at the Royal Court. On the 9 August, 1967, Orton was battered to death in his sleep by Halliwell, who killed himself with sleeping pills after the murder. In 1968 *Funeral Games* (written 1966) was televised, and the next year *What the Butler Saw* opened in London.

Orton's works have been published as follows:
Plays: The Ruffian on the Stair in *New Radio Drama* (1966); *Entertaining Mr Sloane* (1964 and 1973); *Loot* (1967); *Crimes of Passion* (1967); *Funeral Games and The Good and Faithful Servant* (1970); *What the Butler Saw* (1969). These, except fot the radio version of *The Ruffian on the Stair*, are collected in John Lahr (introd.), *The Complete Plays of Joe Orton* (Methuen, 1976: page references refer to this text, Orton's incomplete novel, *Head to Toe*, was published posthumously (1971); so was the film-script of *Up Against It*, originally intended for the Beatles (1979).

Criticism

John Lahr's *Prick Up Your Ears* (1978) is a vigorous biography. Main critical discussions are John Russell Taylor, in *The Second Wave* (1971), and Simon Trussler, in James Vinson (ed.), *Contemporary Dramatists* (1977).

Joe Orton: The Comedy of (Ill) Manners

MARTIN ESSLIN

I

Joe Orton's first play to be accepted for performance, *The Boy Hairdresser* (later re-titled *The Ruffian on the Stair*), arrived at the BBC's radio drama department in 1963 in a brown envelope marked 'H M Prisons'. He was still serving his sentence for defacing public library books by removing plates from art books, replacing illustrations by pasting in somewhat porno-graphic substitute pictures and inserting scurrilous or obscene material. Having in this way damaged, it was alleged, 83 books and stolen 1,653 plates, Orton and his flat-mate Kenneth Halliwell gleefully used to watch old ladies in the Public Library, enjoying their shock and indignation. Orton's work as a playwright might well, in some of its aspects, be regarded as a continuation of the same pursuit by other and more widely effective means. Cocking a snook at the stuffed shirts, shocking the *bien-pensants* bourgeois, certainly was among his main aims in life. Behind it one can discern a violent desire to hurt their feelings, to revenge himself on society, to transgress its rules—even in cases when the stuffed shirts did not realize that the rules had been transgressed—merely for the elation of having got away with it.

The Ruffian on the Stair (1964) is a case in point. The plot of the play revolves around a young man whose brother was run down by a van and killed (probably in the course of a vendetta among gangsters). So the young man, Wilson, decides to revenge himself on the murderer by pretending to be making love to the murderer's mistress, so that the jealous brute will kill him; in this way he can fulfill his two objectives simultaneously: to commit suicide and to have his brother's murderer hanged. In short, on the surface, the plot seems to belong to the genre of the sentimental gangster melodrama, well known from innumerable B-pictures produced under the Hays code. But after this play had been accepted and broadcast by the BBC, Orton was jubilant that he had put one over on the prim bourgeois broadcasting organization, 'Auntie BBC'. They had not even suspected, he boasted, that the play was, in fact, about a sexual perversion so outrageous that not even the Irish had a name for it, namely 'homosexual incest'. In the original, radio version, the only indication in the text is in the lines:

His fiancée won't mind. She's off already with another man. . . . I was more intimate with him than she was. I used to base my life round him . . .[1]

---

[1] *The Ruffian on the Stair* in *New Radio Drama*, BBC Publications, 1966, p. 219.

In the version he made for the stage performance of the play in 1967, Orton felt able to come out into the open:

> Wilson: ... We were happy, though. We were young. I was seventeen. He was twenty-three. You can't do better for yourself than that, can you? We were bosom friends. I've never told anyone that before. I hope I haven't shocked you.
>
> Mike: As close as that?
>
> Wilson: We had separate beds—he was a stickler for convention, but that's as far as it went. We spent every night in each other's company. It was the reason we never got any work done.
>
> Mike: There's no word in the Irish language for what you were doing.
>
> Wilson: In Lapland they have no word for snow (pp. 49-50)

This desire to shock at all costs, allied with a streak of extreme violence that runs through all of his work, springs from a *saeva indignatio* of great intensity; however, unlike that of Swift and most other satirists, Orton's rage is purely negative, it is unrelated to any positive creed, philosophy or programme of social reform. And it is this aspect of it, which, in my opinion, makes Orton's *oeuvre* so significant for an understanding of the social situation in Britain, and no doubt many other countries, in his lifetime and up to the present: for he articulates, in a form of astonishing elegance and eloquence, the same rage and helpless resentment which manifests itself in the wrecked trains of football supporters, the mangled and vandalized telephone kiosks and the obscene graffitti on lavatory walls. Orton, one might say, gives the inarticulate outcries of football hooligans the polished form of Wildean aphorisms. While thus Orton's writings have, quite apart from the sheer brilliance of his dialogue and plotting, considerable importance as manifestations of a whole society, the story of his life, which could well be the perfect specimen of the plot of one of Orton's plays, constitutes a cautionary tale of the first order, almost too apposite to be true, as though it had been invented by one of the moralizing philistines he so much detested.

II

Born on New Year's Day 1933 in Leicester, the son of a gardener and a charwoman, Orton failed his 'eleven plus' and was sent by his socially ambitious mother to Clark's College, in the mistaken assumption that that institution was an academic one, when in fact it merely taught the skills needed by secretaries and clerks, mainly shorthand and typing. Drifting in and out of a succession of clerical jobs in Leicester, Orton tried to inject some excitement and romance into a dreary existence by joining an amateur dramatic company. He developed ambitions to become an actor, took elocution lessons to eliminate a lisp, and, to everybody's astonishment, was accepted by the Royal Academy of Dramatic Art and received a local authority grant to finance his studies. In May 1951 Orton started his studies at RADA, met Kenneth Halliwell and a month later moved in with him.

Halliwell, seven years older than Orton, came from a middle-class background and had received a classical education. He became to Orton what Wilson's older brother was to him in *The Ruffian on the Stair*: admired model, mentor and teacher as well as lover. Neither Orton nor Halliwell was successful at RADA. Orton spent some time at the Ipswich Repertory Theatre, but after his return to London he and Halliwell embarked on a collaborative writing career. It was only after 1957 that Orton began to write independently. Halliwell's taste was a mixture of the camp and the classical: on the one hand Euripides and Aristophanes; on the other Oscar Wilde and Ronald Firbank. Orton's *oeuvre* bears the imprint of this combination. To give but one instance: the end of *What the Butler Saw* clearly derives both from *The Importance of Being Earnest*, with the discovery that Nick and Geraldine were conceived by Mrs Prentice in the linen cupboard at the Station Hotel; and from Euripidean tragedy with the descent of Sergeant Match, wearing a leopard skin, from the skylight as the *deus ex machina*.

When, after a decade of rejections and disappointments, Orton finally broke through to success, Halliwell, who felt the senior partner in their alliance, the teacher and thus the true begetter of Orton as a writer, became obsessed with envy and frustration. When it looked as though Orton had at last decided to move out of their one-room flat in a working-class neighbourhood and to acquire a house of his own Halliwell, in a panic that he might be abandoned, smashed Orton's skull with a hammer and then killed himself with an overdose of sleeping pills. Thus, on 9 August 1967, Orton's career as a writer came to a sudden end. In the five years between the acceptance of *The Ruffian on the Stair* (1963) and his demise in 1967 Orton had produced three full-length plays—*Entertaining Mr Sloane* (1964), *Loot* (1964-65) and *What the Butler Saw* (1967)—as well as three television plays—*The Good and Faithful Servant* (1964), *The Erpingham Camp* (1966) and *Funeral Games* (1966/7)—and a film script, originally intended for the Beatles: *Up Against It* (1967). Of the novels which Orton wrote before his breakthrough as a playwright, together with Halliwell or by himself, only one, unfinished, specimen has been published posthumously: *Head to Toe* (original title: *The Vision of Gombold Proval*) (1961).

That Orton had considerable talent as a playwright is beyond doubt; equally, the extravagant claims made for him by his biographer, John Lahr, who regards him as a major dramatist, seem to me to have to be taken with a grain of salt. Orton's earliest efforts were clearly derivative from Harold Pinter: the opening of the original (radio) version of *The Ruffian on the Stair* is an obvious imitation of the breakfast scenes in *The Room* and *The Birthday Party*:

Joyce: Did you enjoy your breakfast?
Mike: What?
Joyce: Did you enjoy your breakfast? The egg was nice wasn't it? The eggs are perfect now I have the timer. Have you noticed? (Pause) The marmalade was nice. Did it go down well?
Mike: The egg was nice. (p. 197)

Similarly the basic situation of the play repeats that of *The Room*: a visitor who claims that there is a room to let, while the woman in the house neither has such a room nor wants to let one. It is the formula of the 'comedy of menace' almost mechanically applied. There are distinct echoes, too, of *The Dumb Waiter* in the setting up of Wilson's revenge by having himself murdered.

In the second (stage) version of *The Ruffian on the Stair* the Pinteresque breakfast dialogue has been omitted. A much more characteristically Ortonian note has been added. Now the play opens with:

> *Joyce:* Have you got an appointment today?
> *Mike:* Yes. I'm to be at Kings Cross station at eleven. I'm meeting a man in the toilet.
> *Joyce:* You always go to such interesting places. (p. 31)

The last of these lines, held over from the earlier version, thus gains a typically Ortonian flavour and becomes part of something like Orton's version of the Wildean paradoxical epigram. Altogether, a comparison between the radio and the stage version of the play (Orton prepared it for the double bill at the Royal Court which opened almost two months to the day before he was murdered, under the title *Crimes of Passion*) clearly shows the playwright's development. The plot line has been strengthened and the ending given a characteristically ironic twist. In the earlier version of the last lines Mike accepts that he is going to be hanged for shooting Wilson:

> *Joyce:* This has brought us together.
> *Mike:* Yes.
> *Joyce:* You agree with me.
> *Mike:* What does it matter whether I agree with you or not?
> *Joyce:* This is a happy ending we are having. (Pause) Isn't it. (p. 233)

In the stage version Mike and Joyce agree that they will tell the police that Wilson assaulted Joyce and that Mike was acting in self-defence. Wilson's revenge will thus, no doubt, have been frustrated:

> *Joyce:* Go to the telephone box. Dial 999. I'll tell them I was assaulted.
> *Mike:* *(horrified)*: It'll be in the papers.
> *Joyce:* Well, perhaps not assaulted. Not completely. You came in just in time.
> *Mike:* You'll stick by me, Joycie?
> *Joyce:* Of course, dear. (*She kisses him*) I love you. (*she sees the shattered goldfish bowl*)
> Oh, Look, Michael! (*bursting into tears*) My goldfish! (*she picks up a fish*).
> *Mike:* One of the bullets must've hit the bowl.
> *Joyce:* They're dead. Poor things. And I reared them so carefully. (*she sobs. MIKE puts his arms round her and leads her to the settee. She sits*).
> *Mike:* Sit down. I'll fetch the police. This has been a crime of passion. They'll understand. They have wives and goldfish of their own.

(*JOYCE is too heartbroken to answer. She buries her face in
MIKE'S shoulder. He holds her close.*) CURTAIN. (p. 61)

The mature revised version of *The Ruffian on the Stair* thus also includes the
very characteristically Ortonian *motif* of a 'good' ending brought about by
the happy collusion of the guilty bourgeois and the police, also found in
Entertaining Mr Sloane (at least in so far as all concerned agree to conceal
Sloane's murder from the police), *Loot* and *What the Butler Saw:*

Prentice: Well, Sergeant, we have been instrumental in uncovering a
          number of remarkable peccadilloes today. I'm sure you'll
          cooperate in keeping them out of the papers?
Match: I will, sir.
Rance: I'm glad you don't despise tradition. . . . (p. 448)

In *Entertaining Mr Sloane* (1964) Orton's view of society as a conspiracy of
the wealthy, designed to conceal crime and facilitate their lusts, had
hardened. The suggestion that love could be the ruling passion motivating a
play, which still informed *The Ruffian on the Stair*, has disappeared; it never
showed itself in any of Orton's further dramatic efforts. Yet, in this first full-
length play of Orton's, the Pinter influence can still be discerned in the basic
situation: an intruder who enters a household and disrupts it. Just as Aston
offered shelter to Davies in *The Caretaker*, Kath has picked up Sloane 'in the
library' and taken him to her home because 'he was having trouble. With his
rent . . . His landlady was unscrupulous'. Sloane, a young man 'with very
smooth skin', has murdered a photographer who had taken some porno-
graphic nude pictures of him. Kemp, Kath's old father, happens to have
been employed by that photographer and recognizes Sloane. Ed, Kath's
wealthy businessman brother, is a homosexual who is attracted by Sloane.
Sloane, who sleeps with Kath and has become Ed's chauffeur and prospective catamite, seems set for a successful exploitation of both. But when
Kemp threatens to reveal Sloane's past crime to the police, Sloane kills him.
This enables Ed and Kath to blackmail him into an arrangement which con-
demns him to remain bound to them indefinitely while they share his
favours equally: six months with Kath, six months with Ed each year. Thus,
as in *The Caretaker*, the play revolves around an intruder who, at first, seems
to dominate two unequal and seemingly hostile members of the household,
only to have the tables turned on him and to be dominated by an alliance of
both insiders.

But, whereas in *The Caretaker* the situation is invested with genuine
pathos, both in Aston's need for a companion and in Davies's for a home, so
that there is a real feeling of human suffering and tragedy behind even the
most grotesquely deprived and ludicrously incompetent characters, the
atmosphere of *Entertaining Mr Sloane* is totally heartless. And while in *The
Caretaker* the real action lies in a rich texture of subtext, in *Entertaining Mr
Sloane* everything is on the surface. From the very start sexual bargains are
openly and explicitly negotiated. Kath takes Sloane's trousers off to bandage
his leg; later she appears in a negligée of extreme transparency: 'I blame it on

the manufacturers. They make garments so thin nowadays you'd think they intended to provoke a rape' (p. 93), while Ed, engaging Sloane as his 'chauffeur', asks for assurances that he is not 'vaginalatrous', having been assured by Sloane that he is an all-rounder, and not only in sport: 'Yes. Yes. I'm an all rounder. A great all rounder. In anything you care to mention. Even in life.' (p. 86)

This absence of a sub-text reduces the chatacters to fully conscious person-ifications of their basic instincts: it is characteristic of Orton's fully devel-oped style. While *Entertaining Mr Sloane* is still, outwardly, structured like a comedy, the mechanical nature of its characters and the explicitness of its language already clearly assign it to the realm of farce, even though it lacks the plot mechanisms of that genre (complications heaped upon complica-tions or numerous doors opening with split-second precision). In *Loot* and *What the Butler Saw* Orton finally found the plot structure to match his vision of humanity and the style of his dialogue.

The television play *The Good and Faithful Servant*, written in 1964, before *Loot*, but not broadcast till 1967, still shows Orton groping towards his own style. Written for television mainly to make money, the play obviously represents an attempt to conform to the the vogue for 'social' drama on the medium at that time. It is a simple tale about an old man who has served his firm faithfully as a doorkeeper for fifty years and is retired, having been presented with a toaster and electric clock as parting gifts. On his last day on the job he runs into an old woman, a cleaner in the firm, who has also been there for fifty years and turns out to have been the only woman in his life: their brief chance meeting, it now turns out, made her pregnant and pro-duced twins who died in the war. But a grandson, Raymond, has remained behind as living proof of that single amorous episode in Buchanan's life. Raymond in turn has made a girl in the firm pregnant; he himself is a work-shy youth. But Debbie's pregnancy induces him to take a job with the firm: there is a double wedding: Buchanan marries Edith, Raymond Debbie and the cycle of empty and meaningless lives obviously starts up again, as Buchanan, having smashed his useless retirement presents with a hammer, dies. The proceedings are watched over and stagemanaged by Mrs Vealfoy, the firm's grotesquely hearty personnel officer.

On the face of it, this would be material for a touching little play, however hackneyed the theme. But again, in a story calling for at least some emotion and sympathy with the characters, Orton remains unwilling, or unable, to make his characters into more than mechanical functions of a schematic plot. Again there is no sub-text, no suggestion that the people of the play have any life outside the actual lines they are speaking. We are left to believe that in the fifty years between his one amorous encounter (which lasted only one afternoon) and his retirement literally nothing happened to Buchanan. Nobody in the firm knows him; he cannot remember anything that occured during that time; similarly, Raymond fathered his child on Debbie with complete casualness (she knows neither his name nor his address when she informs Mrs Vealfoy of her predicament); and yet, when mildly prodded by Mrs Vealfoy, he takes a job with the firm and marries her without demur.

The total passivity and acquiescence of those characters who are presented as victims of society thus not only deprives them of credibility as human beings but also renders them quite unsympathetic. The format of the play is that of realistic social drama with a touch of satire in the caricatured personnel officer, but the central characters are puppets who have strayed into this realistic world from the mechanical universe of farce.

III

In *Loot* (1965), at last, Orton had found own voice and his own style. The plot is characteristically complex. Two delinquent young men, Hal and Dennis, have robbed a bank. Mrs McLeavy, Hal's mother, has died, and to escape detection by the police officer, Truscott, who is roaming through the house, Hall and Dennis remove the corpse from its coffin and hide the money there, stowing the corpse in the cupboard. Fay, the nurse who has been looking after Mrs McLeavy in her last illness (and has, in fact, murdered her in order to marry Mr McLeavy and add his fortune to the large sums she has amassed by murdering a long list of previous patients as well as men she had married after disposing of their wives) has had an affair with Dennis. After many macabre incidents involving the corpse, Dennis, Hal, the nurse and the policeman agree to share the loot from the bank robbery. The bereaved husband, old Mr McLeavy, the only character in the play not involved in a crime, is arrested and will have to be removed:

McLeavy: I'm innocent! I'm innocent! (*at the door, pause, a last wail*). Oh what a terrible thing to happen to a man who's been kissed by the Pope.
              (*Meadows goes off with McLeavy*)
Dennis: What will you charge him with, Inspector?
Truscott: Oh, anything will do.
Fay: Can an accidental death be arranged?
Truscott: Anything can be arranged in prison.
Hal: Except pregnancy.
Truscott: Well, of course, the chaperon system defeats us there. (p. 274)

This, then is the farcical universe with a vengeance and at its blackest: the world of Harry Graham's *Ruthless Rhymes for Heartless Homes* rather than that of Labiche, Feydeau, Courteline or Ben Travers, who still had compassion for the characters they whipped through preposterous situations. Here the onslaught on the values of the *bien-pensants* has become total: religion, death, the police, law and order, as well as all human emotion are under attack. What Orton is saying is that behind a façade of respectability there is literally *nothing*. Having been assured that the police will murder his father, Hal merely remarks about the corrupt policeman:

Hal: (*with a sigh*). He is a nice man. Self-effacing in his way.
Dennis: He has an open mind. In direct contrast to the usual run of civil servant.

Hal:	It's comforting to know that the police can still be relied upon when we're in trouble. (*They stand beside the coffin, Fay in the middle*)
Fay:	We'll bury your father with your mother. That will be nice for him, won't it?
	(*She lifts the rosary and bows her head in prayer*)
Hal:	(*pause, to Dennis*): You can kip here, baby. Plenty of room now. Bring your bags over tonight. (*Fay looks up*)
Fay:	(*sharply*): When Dennis and I are married we'd have to move out.
Hal:	Why?
Fay:	People would talk. We must keep up appearances. (p. 275)

This certainly is satire with a truly Swiftian acerbity and savage irony, even though there is no indication of a positive viewpoint from which society is being criticized. The tone is one of contempt and derision throughout, directed against all the characters equally. They all take it for granted that murder is an acceptable way of gaining one's ends—which, invariably, amount to no more than sensual gratification, sheer greed. And all this is expressed in language of studied and stylized elegance. There is no suggestion of a realist's concern for the vernacular, for class or regional differences. The lowliest characters express themselves in an eloquent standard English. This has led to Orton being compared to Restoration dramatists. And there certainly is something in this comparison with the traditional English high comedy of manners, except that Orton's best work might better be described as 'high comedy of ill-manners'. Yet the motivation for Orton's use of this style is different from that of the Restoration playwrights, who wanted to express the speech of elegant people in an elegant manner. Orton's aim was to achieve comic effects through the contrast between the coarseness of the subject matter and the refinement of its expression. John Lahr quotes a passage from Orton's private diary, in which he discusses Genet's *Querelle de Brest*:

> I find a sentence like: 'They (the homosexuals of Brest) are peace-loving citizens of irreproachable outward appearance, even though, the long day through, they may perhaps suffer from a rather timid itch for a bit of cock' irresistibly funny. A combination of elegance and crudity is always ridiculous.[2]

This particular combination of crudity and elegance, doubtlessly, arises from the style of the translation rather than that of Genet's original text, but it certainly exhibits the characteristics of Orton's own comic technique. It is a device which has a long tradition in one of the minor bye-ways of literature: parody. We all know those Shakespeare parodies in which dustmen speak in the tones of Hamlet or Coriolanus. In exactly the same way Orton, in *Entertaining Mr Sloane*, uses mock-Biblical language to convey a banal sentiment. Thus a lack of total sexual commitment is rendered as follows:

[2] John Lahr, *Prick Up Your Ears*, London, 1978, p. 163.

Even if he thee worshipped with his body, his mind would be elsewhere. (p. 148)

The television play *The Erpingham Camp* (1966) (later adapted for the stage as part of the double bill of *Crimes of Passion*) is a case in point. Orton spoke of it as his version, or recreation, of *The Bacchae* of Euripides, but, in fact, it is hardly more than a parody of that play on the lines mentioned above. The transposition of the plot into a British holiday camp—a favourite target of topical satire at the time—yields neither a contemporary reinterpretation of the theme of *The Bacchae* nor illuminating variations on its meaning: it merely lowers its social level and trivializes the plot. While Euripides deals with profound tensions in human nature, Orton is merely describing the inmates of a holiday camp getting out of hand through the incompetence of an entertainments manager who is too inexperienced or clumsy to control the evening's floor show. Thus the Dionysus of the play, Chief Redcoat Riley, is no God, no personification of primeval forces, while its Pentheus, Erpingham, is no more than a slightly authoritarian lay-figure, given to mouthing an occasional patriotic cliché. Even in terms of mere parody the parallels are extremely feebly drawn: the raging maenads amount to hardly more than a pregnant lady, who claims that she has been insulted, and her feebly protesting husband. And Erpingham dies not under any assault by orgiastic, unchained revellers, but merely because the floorboards of his office give way so that he drops down among the dancers on the ballroom floor. The final scene of his burial, in a parody of a sanctimoniously conducted patriotic state funeral, has no organic justification and seems merely tacked on to make another hackneyed parodistic point. The suggestion that the holiday camp might be a symbol for contemporary Britain, with Erpingham as the embodiment of the establishment (the monarchy, the government), would, if it represented the author's intention, merely underline the shallowness of the concept. Orton himself had a high opinion of the play: but that simply confirms the absence in him of any serious thought about the society he was not so much attacking as 'cocking a snook at'. *The Erpingham Camp* is hardly more than an extended, and rather feeble, cabaret sketch.

Orton's last television play, written in 1966, but not broadcast till a year after his death, *Funeral Games*, reverts to the style of black farce that had been so successful in *Loot*. Again the satire is directed against sanctimoniousness and religious zeal; again there is a corpse at the centre of the action. Pringle, the leader of a religious sect, suspects his wife, Tessa, of adultery and has announced to his flock that he will kill her. McCorquodale, a defrocked priest, whom Tessa has been frequenting because she is trying to find a lost woman friend of hers who was reputed to have been married to him, has in fact killed his wife, the self-same Valerie, and has hidden her in the cellar under a pile of coal. Pringle confronts Tessa at McCorquodale's lodgings but fails to kill her. Having proclaimed his determination to root out adultery he would lose all credibility with his flock if it were known that his wife is still alive, so it is decided that Tessa will disappear and live with McCorquodale as his wife, while a hand severed from the body of that murdered woman is produced to satisfy Pringle's flock—and the popular press—that he really has had the moral fervour necessary to murder his adulterous spouse. When Tessa, recognizing the dead Valerie's wrist watch as belonging to her long-lost friend, discovers that, in fact, McCorquodale had killed *her* because she had committed adultery with Pringle, all becomes clear. Pringle is McCorquodale's hated enemy, the bishop, who at one time had defrocked him. In the end, unusually for Orton, the police catch up with both of them. Yet, even here, the suggestion that it will be possible to get round the police by bribery or social influence remains. The play ends with Pringle saying:

> Let us go to prison. Some angel will release us from our place of confinement. Do not weep. Everything works out in accordance with the divine will. (p. 360)

The language in which this preposterous tale (it formed part of an ITV series on 'The Seven Deadly Virtues' and was to represent 'Charity') is told is even more baroque than that of *Loot*; it exploits not only all opportunities to mix low subject matter with a biblically elevated phraseology, but, also—and above all—capitalizes on the opportunities for *double entendres* which this combination offers:

> *McCorquodale:* . . . Oh, my Lord Bishop, you should never have taken on that extra female penitent.
> *Pringle:* You should've kept your evil temper under control.
> *McCorquodale:* You were teaching her tricks not even a grandmother should know.
> *Tessa:* Was he misbehaving with Val?
> *McCorquodale:* He was making a breach in the seventh commandment and my wife. (To PRINGLE) That's foul churching, Bishop.
> *Tessa:* (to *Pringle*): How long had it been going on?
> *Pringle:* The spirit of the Brotherhood entered Valerie about a year prior to her death. . . . (p. 357-8)

And so on. The part of the embalmer's glass eye that is kicked around with such gruesome comic effect in *Loot* is here taken by the murdered Valerie's severed hand, which, moreover, is, at the end, replaced by a faked one which enables the playwright to achieve another shock comic effect, when one of its fingers is broken off 'with a sharp crack' before we are informed that the gruesome article is not the real thing but a rubber one of the kind obtainable in joke shops. Indulgence in disgusting detail and baroque black humour are here driven to such extreme lengths that *Funeral Games* does achieve something like a superlative of inverted grandeur, and becomes a kind of Albert Memorial of mannerist preposterousness and execrable taste.

IV

Orton's last play, completely shortly before he was murdered and generally regarded as his 'masterpiece', is *What the Butler Saw* (1969). It is a farce plotted in the style of Feydeau, and carries an epigraph from *The Revenger's Tragedy*: 'Surely we're all mad people, and they, whom we think are, are not'. It is accordingly set in a lunatic asylum and its central character is a psychiatrist, Dr Prentice. The starting point for a chain of cleverly contrived farcical complications is Dr Prentice's interview with a young woman, Geraldine Barclay, who has applied for a secretarial position in Dr Prentice's clinic. Dr Prentice, of course, would not engage a secretary without first having had carnal knowledge of her, so he orders her to undress. While she is lying naked on the couch behind a curtain in the surgery, Mrs Prentice, whom he believed to be out of town, reappears. The rest of the play consists of attempts to conceal the naked girl behind the curtain, to find clothes for her, to explain, when the only clothes that could be procured are those of a male bell-boy from the Station Hotel who has been carrying Mrs Prentice's luggage, that she is, or is not a boy, that Nick, the bell boy is, or is not a girl, and so on in ever more complex permutations and contortions. Others involved in the proceedings are Dr Rance, another psychiatrist charged with investigating the clinic, and the policeman, Sergeant Match, who appears when exasperation and confusion have reached a first climax. The chief comic effects of the extremely cleverly constructed plot derive from both transvestitism and nudity. The basic idea is that Geraldine and Nick, the bell-boy, are in fact twins conceived by Mrs Prentice in the linen cupboard of the Station Hotel during a post-war power cut so that the man involved has remained unknown to her. He was, it turns out, none other than Dr Prentice himself. Geraldine, with whom Dr Prentice was caught *in flagranti* on his couch, and Nick, who was seduced by Mrs Prentice when she was staying at the Station Hotel recently, are thus the couple's children and, what is more, have had incestuous relations with their respective mother and father. Dr Rance, the inspecting psychiatrist, is overjoyed by this news, as a case of double incest will make his new book on mental illness a bestseller. The pattern of the basic structure of the plot is thus—in the light of Orton's classical education acquired through Kenneth Halliwell—quite deliberately that of the classical Plautean comedy of the separated twins, while the linen cupboard at the Station Hotel here plays the role Miss Prism's handbag fulfills in *The Importance of Being Earnest*. Another influence present in the play seems to me to be that of Dürrenmatt's *The Physicists*, similarly set in an asylum and similarly bent on showing that among all the madmen in the play the mad psychiatrist who runs the clinic is the craziest. Here we have *two* psychiatrists mutually accusing each other of being out of their minds. Naked people are seen running in and out of the numerous doors, convincing the onlookers that the reality they see is hallucination.

Orton's baroque imagination knew no bounds. The climax of the play turns on a story, told by Geraldine at the very beginning, that her foster-mother had been killed by the explosion of a gas-main which also destroyed a newly erected statue of Sir Winston Churchill. In fact, the death of the woman was caused—as later becomes clear—by the statue's penis entering her abdomen. The statue has almost been completely reconstructed; only that vital part is still missing. At the end of the play, Sergeant Match discovers that a box Geraldine has been carrying and which she believed to contain some old clothes of her foster-mother, actually harbours the missing part of the statue. (In the 1969 stage performance this was changed to being Churchill's cigar.) The play, therefore, ends with a reconciliation of Dr and Mrs Prentice, the discovery of their children, and the restoration of the nation's fertility symbol to its rightful place. Orton thus saw himself as having written a farce which, at the same time, was heavy with myth, the anthropology of *The Golden Bough* and allusions to classical drama.

It is certainly a dazzling performance. And yet, on reflection, does it amount to more than an impressive piece of juggling, of prestidigitation? Feydeau's characters, however mechanically they are moved about, still embody a satirist's insights into the realities of human nature. But even in this, undoubtedly Orton's most accomplished play, no insights are vouchsafed: the characters are simply not of this world, being pure constructs. That psychiatrists might be crazier than their patients is not an insight, not even an observation; it is simply an old, oft-repeated cliché. But there is not even a hint of a genuine critique of psychiatry or psychoanalysis in the play. This aspect of it is no more than one of those semi-obscene seaside postcards blown up to giant size: the lecherous doctor who orders his patient to undress is a stock character of folk humour. So is the titillation derived from boys dressed up as girls, girls as boys, culminating, as it does here, in the demand 'Take your trousers down, I'll tell you which sex you belong to'. (p. 413)

V

This is not to say that Orton's work does not provide material for a psychoanalyst: his pre-occupation with incest, with sexual ambiguity, equally evident in *Head to Toe* and in the film script *Up Against It*, with homosexuality and murder, might be a fit subject for investigation in greater depth (although at first sight the indications it provides seem fairly obvious) but that does not mean that the *oeuvre* as such provides insights as literature or art.

To all who met him in the period of his ascendancy Orton appeared as a young man of immense charm. The destructiveness of his vision of society showed itself in a certain cockiness, in pleasure at being able to deceive and manipulate the stuffed shirts. He seemed the embodiment of the cheerful practical joker who wrote letters to the newspapers complaining about the obscenity of his own plays in grotesquely exaggerated terms, signing them with names like 'Edna Welthorp (Mrs)', or inserted in his plays passages deploring the decay of decency:

> Society must be made aware of the growing menace of pornography. The whole treacherous avant-garde movement will be exposed for what it is— an instrument for inciting decent citizens to commit bizarre crimes against humanity and the state! (p. 427-8)

Yet there is not the slightest suggestion in all that of any positive reasons *why* the fight against the anti-pornography campaigners is, as it surely is, part of a crusade to humanize and reform society. Behind Orton's attack on the existing state of humanity in the West there stands nothing but the rage of the socially and educationally under-privileged: having risen from the working classes of an ill-educated mass society that has lost all the religious and moral values of earlier centuries and has been debauched by the consumerism of a system manipulated by the mass media, Orton exemplifies the spiritual emptiness and—in spite of his obvious brilliance and intelligence—the thoughtlessness, the inability to reason and to analyse, of these deprived multitudes. This is neither the bitter laugh of which Beckett speaks, the laugh about that which is bad in the world; nor the hollow laugh about what is untrue; nor that mirthless laugh, the *risus purus*, about what is unhappy and tragic; but the mindless laugh which reflects the deprivation of the dispossessed and amounts to no more than an idiot's giggle at his own image in a mirror.

As such Joe Orton's *oeuvre* is both symptomatic and significant.

Note

Life and Writing

Tom Stoppard was born in Zlin, Czechoslovakia in 1937 but was taken to Singapore by his family in the following year. He arrived in England at the end of the war in 1946, where he attended a preparatory school in Nottinghamshire and a boarding grammar school in Yorkshire. In 1954 he began his career as a journalist, working first for the *Western Daily Press* and subsequently for the *Bristol Evening World*. For part of his time he worked as a theatre reviewer and became interested in writing for the stage. In 1960 he resigned his job and wrote *A Walk on the Water*. This was purchased by a commercial television company and transmitted on the day of John Kennedy's assassination. The play eventually reached the stage two years after the success of *Rosencrantz and Guildenstern Are Dead*.

Stoppard's work is published in Britain by Faber and Faber and in the United States by Grove Press. British publication dates of his work are as follows: *Lord Malquist and Mr Moon*, a novel (1966), *Rosencrantz and Guildenstern Are Dead* (1967), *Enter a Free Man* (1968), *The Real Inspector Hound* (1968), *Tango*, by Slawomir Mrożek, adapted by Tom Stoppard from the translation by Nicholas Bethell (1969), *Albert's Bridge* and *If You're Glad I'll be Frank*, a radio play (1969), *A Separate Peace* (1969), *After Magritte* (1971), *Jumpers* (1972) *Artist Descending a Staircase* and *Where Are they Now?*, two plays for radio (1973), *Travesties* (1975), *Dirty Linen* and *New-Found Land* (1976), *Every Good Boy Deserves Favour* and *Professional Foul* (1977), *Night and Day* (1978), *Dogg's Hamlet* and *Cahoot's Macbeth* (1979).

Articles by Tom Stoppard include 'The Writer and the Theatre: The Definite Maybe', *Author*, 78, Spring, 1967, 18-20.; 'Something to Declare', *The Sunday Times*, London, 25 February, 1968; 'Doers and Thinkers: Playwrights and Professors', *Times Literary Supplement*, 13 October, 1972, 1219.

Criticism

Only one book on Stoppard has been published to date, Ronald Hayman, *Tom Stoppard*, (London, 1978 updating an earlier edition). An intelligent essay appears in the British Council series: C.W.E. Bigsby, *Tom Stoppard* (1976). My essay refers in its notes to other essays.

VI

Tom Stoppard: Light Drama and Dirges in Marriage

RUBY COHN

Stoppard: What I try to do, is to end up by contriving the perfect marriage between the play of ideas and farce or perhaps even high comedy.[1]

Beckett: I say farce deliberately . . . . That's what our best authors do, designating with that word their most serious work in case they won't be taken seriously.[2]

Stoppard on Beckett: There's a Beckett joke which is the funniest joke in the world to me. It appears in various forms but it consists of confident statement followed by immediate refutation by the same voice. It's a constant process of elaborate structure and sudden—and total—dismantlement.[3]

I

A Czech-born, India-Englished autodidact, Tom Stoppard left school at the age of seventeen, and yet he is our brightest university wit. His plays sparkle with puns, polysyllables, language games, quid pro quos, distorted quotations. His parodies puncture academic lectures, sports reports, news broadcasts, theatre reviews, detective stories, and especially aesthetic problems. Classics and celebrities are grist to his wit. Thanks to Stoppard, Rosencrantz and Guildenstern aren't dead at all. In *Jumpers* a second Duncan is slain—'Woe, alas! What, in our house?' *Artist Descending a Staircase* closes on Gloucester's celebrated simile: 'As flies to wanton boys . . .,' and *Travesties* snaps up several Shakespeare lines. Sophocles's *Philoctetes* is metamorphosed into Stoppard's spy thriller *Neutral Ground*. Wittgenstein's *Philosophical Investigations* are the building materials of *Dogg's Our Pet*. *After Magritte* greets the Belgian Surrealist painter, and *Artist Descending a Staircase* invites recollection of Marcel Duchamp. Agatha Christie's *Mousetrap* and Anton Chekhov's *Ivanov* hover in the backgrounds of *The Real Inspector Hound* and *Every Good Boy Deserves Favour*. The philosopher George Moore, the explorer Robert Scott, Aesop's hare and Zeno's tortoise haunt the stage of *Jumpers*. Rumanian Tzara, Irish Joyce, and two English consular officials acquiesce in the importance of not being earnest in *Travesties*. Through two decades of playwriting Stoppard teases these figures into light drama, a genre analogous to light verse.

[1] Tom Stoppard, 'Ambushes for the Audience', *Theatre Quarterly* (May-July, 1974) 7
[2] Samuel Beckett, *Eleuthéria* (unpublished), my translation
[3] Ronald Hayman, *Tom Stoppard* (London: Heinemann, 1977) 7

Stoppard's first two stage plays seem seriously intended. In *A Walk on the Water* a Rube-Goldberg inventor derives from Arthur Miller's Willy Loman and Robert Bolt's James Cherry. Stoppard jokingly refers to this early play as 'Flowering Death of a Salesman',[4] but a more accurate title would be Deflowering of the Fantasies of a Would-Be Inventor. Stoppard's unpublished *The Gamblers* tilts toward the absurd, since a prisoner and his jailer exchange roles, leaving us uncertain of who is executed.

Germinating from an extended joke, *Rosencrantz and Guildenstern are Dead* is Stoppard's most popular play, at once for its spirited entertainment and its impression of depth—it debates the relativity of truth, the inscrutability of fate, the problematic nature of identity, the fluidity of art-life boundaries. Another play about a play soon appeared—*The Real Inspector Hound*—which Stoppard has described as an attempt to bring off a 'comic coup in pure mechanistic terms'.[5] As in the Agatha Christie mystery it burlesques, the detective proves to be the murderer, but Stoppard's Hound is also the long-lost husband of the beautiful Lady Muldoon in the play within the play, and, outside that play, he is the third-string drama reviewer Puckeridge, who murders to become the lead reviewer. Adroit rather than mechanical, Stoppard leads us through a rollicking labyrinth of pastiche and cross-conversations. Only the humourless will dig for ideas.

By 1970 Stoppard was producing approximately a play a year—for theatre, radio, or television. On stage his agile dialogue is backed up by sight gags. *After Magritte* is the appropriately titled bravura example. It opens on furniture barricading a door, a basket of fruit counterweighting a lamp, an elderly towel-covered woman lying supine on an ironing-board with a bowler on her stomach, her barechested son standing on a chair with green rubber boots over his dress trousers, his wife in evening-gown crawling on the floor. At the play's end lamp and fruit are still in delicate balance; the elderly woman stands on one foot on a chair on a table while she plays the tuba; her son, also on the table, also on one foot, wears his wife's evening-gown and a cushion-cover on his head; the wife in bra and panties crawls along the floor. By that time, however, we know the reasons for this farcical scene, in which Inspector Foot joins, also on the table, having just rehashed his 'bitch of a day', which reveals the inspector as the play-long figure of contention between husband and wife. Like the real Inspector Hound, Inspector Foot is satisfyingly the culprit, and we have the last laugh at the puzzled policeman Holmes, since we are in rational control of the incongruous scene.

A genial acceptor of invitations, Stoppard composed a short play for the opening of the Almost Free Theater of Ed Berman, nicknamed Professor Dogg. *Dogg's Our Pet*, an anagram of Dogg's Troupe, leans on Wittgenstein's language games to dramatize preparations for an opening ceremony. Characters are generated by code-words for the first four letters of the English alphabet—schoolboys Able and Baker, workman Charlie, and

[4] *Theatre Quarterly*, 4
[5] *Theatre Quarterly*, 8

schoolmaster Dogg. Charlie calls to an offstage aide for objects to build a speaker's platform for an opening ceremony—plank, slab, block, brick, cube. His building rhythm is interrupted when schoolboys Able and Baker or Schoolmaster Dogg violate the linguistic code. Although Charlie's language disintegrates, he manages to complete the platform while mischievous Able and Baker build a wall with lettered slabs and blocks, arranged in Dogg-insulting messages. Under Dogg's ministrations, a Lady delivers a sound-linked series of hostile phrases. After the cast exchange insults, Charlie climbs on the speaker's platform to address the real theatre audience: '. . . if there's one thing I can't stand, it's language.'

These visual highjinks give way to audible puzzles in the radio play *Artist Descending a Staircase*. On this blind medium a dead blind woman Sophie haunts the memories of three visual artists Beauchamp, Martello, and Donner. The last of these descends the titular staircase, falling to his death. Is it murder? Each of the surviving two artists suspects the other. The play moves back through time, then circles to Beauchamp's last tape, which proves to us (but not to the artists) that Donner's death is an accident. Losing his balance after swatting a fly, Donner had a fatal fall, which is lightly mocked by the play's title.

Eight years separate Stoppard's first and second major plays, *Rosencrantz and Guildenstern Are Dead* (1964) and *Jumpers* (1972). Two years later came his third, *Travesties* (1974). In 1976, to celebrate the American Bicentennial and the American-to-British nationalization of director Ed Berman, Stoppard wrote *Dirty Linen* on sexual misadventures of members of Parliament, and, with a soupçon of American flavour, *New-found-land* about a British Parliamentarian's parodic discovery of the United States.

In 1976, too, Stoppard came out of the political closet. Earlier, he had craved 'the courage of [his] lack of convictions',[6] but by that year he shelved his wit for sober lectures and essays on political repression in his native Czechoslovakia and on psychiatric abuse in the Soviet Union. Three plays are freighted with this new commitment. *Every Good Boy Deserves Favour* is a mnemonic for the treble clef. The play is Stoppard's response to a request by André Previn, then conductor of the London Symphony Orchestra, that the dramatist should write a play featuring an orchestra. The result was an orchestra which was presumed to be the fantasy of a mad Russian, Alexander Ivanov. The musician's asylum cell-mate, also named Alexander Ivanov, is a political dissident. A Communist Colonel deliberately confuses their identities, and since the mad musician makes no political statements,and the sane dissident hears no orchestra, both are freed.

The television play *Professional Foul* blends politics with football and philosophy. A Cambridge University professor of ethics, in Prague for a philosophy meeting and a football cup game, is asked by a former student, a Czech liberal in disgrace, to carry his dissertation to the West. Reluctantly, the professor becomes increasingly involved in the former student's fate. A

6 Hayman, 2

colleague from Stoke University later drunkenly insults an English foot-baller who has committed a professional foul in the afternoon game. When the Cambridge professor helps his battered colleague to his room, he slily slips the offending dissertation into his briefcase. Both professors then pass undetained through Czech exit customs. Free speech triumphs through this academic professional foul.

Politically committed though they are, these short plays are anecdotes, but *Night and Day* is more ambitious. A veteran journalist arrives in a fictional African country on the brink of civil war, only to find that he has been scooped by a neophyte who has published an exclusive interview with the rebel leader. The veteran, Dick Wagner, recognizes with distaste that the neophyte, Jake Milne, is notorious for working during a newspaper strike. When Jake leaves for another rebel story, Dick remains behind for a scoop interview with the dictator on a secret visit. In the presence of their hosts—a British businessman and his ubiquitously tempting wife—journalist and dictator differ sharply on the freedom of the press. When news arrives of Jake's death, and the dictator departs, Dick Wagner sends the story to London, but learns that his newspaper is on strike. Jake died for an unprint-able story, but veteran reporter Wagner is thereby converted to the open shop. He will cover the incipient civil war, although he is *persona non grata* to the dictator.

II

In spite of Stoppard's espousal of a press free from any constraints, it is unlikely that *Night and Day* would elicit serious critical attention, were it not for his three preceding full-length plays, the main depositories of his attempt to contrive 'the perfect marriage between the play of ideas and farce or perhaps even high comedy'.[7] Or perhaps even burlesque.

The burlesque origin of *Rosencrantz and Guildenstern* . . . is often noted, and the play's debt to *Waiting for Godot* often traced.[8] Shakespeare burlesque has been popular through the centuries, and no less a playwright than W.S. Gilbert was attracted to Rosencrantz and Guildenstern. It is, however, thanks to Beckett that Stoppard sped to celebrity. From Beckett Stoppard borrows two puzzled friends in an unlocalized time and place. Like Beckett, Stoppard infiltrates their vaudeville-type exchanges with passages of metaphysical yearning. From Beckett Stoppard learned rising interrogative rhythms and swift disjunctive replies. In Stoppard's drama, as in Beckett's, the two friends play while they wait; they probe coins instead of hats and shoes; they meet more people, but the meetings are similarly

[7] See Note 1

[8] C.W.E. Bigsby, *Tom Stoppard* (Harlow: Longman, 1976); Anthony Callen, 'Stoppard's *Godot*', *New Theatre Magazine* (Winter, 1969-70)

Ruby Cohn, *Modern Shakespeare Offshoots* (Princeton: Princeton University Press, 1976)

C.J. Gianakaris, 'Absurdism Altered', *Drama Survey* (1968-9)

Ronal Hayman, *Tom Stoppard* (London: Heinemann, 1977)

Jill.Levenson, 'Views from a Revolving Door', *Queens Quarterly* (1971)

Thomas Whitaker, *Fields of Play* (Princeton: Princeton University Press, 1977)

repetitive; they too ask questions and make a game of asking questions; they too tell jokes and impersonate their betters. Like Beckett's tramps, Stoppard's noblemen try in vain to understand their situation, which is meant to reflect our own.

Like Gogo and Didi, Rosencrantz and Guildenstern rack their brains for things to do or say. At first barely distinguishable from Rosencrantz, Guildenstern is modelled on Didi—'quicker than [his] friend'. Rosencrantz resembles Gogo—more docile and vulnerable. But Beckett's Didi and Gogo never confuse their own identities, as do Guildenstern and Rosencrantz, to our amusement. Many of their trivial phrases are pregnant with extensible significance. Common to the two plays are: 'I forget', 'Even chance', 'What are we doing here?' 'Time has stopped', 'It's the normal thing', 'I'm going', 'Don't leave me', 'Off we go.' Even a scenic direction echoes *Godot*: '. . . *resumes the struggle*'. Both plays are lyrical about leaves, and both plays descend to fallen trousers and other innocent obscenities. Beckett's 'We're waiting for Godot' is transmuted by Stoppard to 'We were sent for.' A light tone governs most of this.

More melancholy are intimations of mortality. Beckett shades his tragicomedy with bone imagery; Pozzo's awareness of human destiny is echoed in key-words of Didi—birth, astride, grave. Stoppard's couple are more loquacious in expounding on death; his tragedians enact death scenes; two letters of *Hamlet* exact death sentences. Although Rosencrantz and Guildenstern 'disappear' from Stoppard's stage, the English Ambassador declares them dead—in Shakespeare's line that gives the play its title.

Both Beckett and Stoppard arouse affection for their twin protagonists, but we feel superior to Rosencrantz and Guildenstern because we know *Hamlet*. Laughing down at them, we tend to forget that they acquiesce in Hamlet's death, however unattractively Stoppard presents him. Moreover, Rosencrantz and Guildenstern accept their disappearance with relief, whereas Didi and Gogo go on interminably.

Through the histrionics of the Player, Stoppard underlines what Beckett hints at—that *homo sapiens* is *homo ludens*. (The first of many puns in *Rosencrantz and Guildenstern* . . . is, fittingly, 'game'.) Also through the Player, Stoppard highlights the old life-role *topos*; all the world's a stage, and all the men merely players in an incomplete drama. The show must go on, without rhyme or reason. *Godot's* pauses, negatives, interrogatives, and circularities convey the very texture of absurdity. Similarly, Guildenstern's questions rise unanswered, courtly characters burst into and out of sight, corpses revive with the alacrity of *commedia dell'arte*. In spite of absurdities in the absurdist landscape of *Rosencrantz and Guildenstern* . . ., the ungiving frame of *Hamlet* imposes the strictures of tragedy.

Deftly dovetailing the *Hamlet* scenes into the *Godot* condition, Stoppard appropriates Beckett's comic devices—puns, poses, jokes, games, aphorisms, direct address to the audience. Although he wisely eschews Beckett's few lyric passages, he also exploits the characters' uncertainties—time, place, logic, memory, language—to suggest ontological and epistemological uncertainty. But Stoppard is much freer with the jargon of philosophy

—syllogism, hypothesis, pragmatism, laws of averages, probability, and diminishing returns. Despite swift exchanges of dialogue, the play lags at such academic moments.

Rosencrantz and Guildenstern Are Dead dramatizes ordinary men in an extraordinary situation—'Well, we're nobody special'—whereas *Waiting for Godot* dramatizes the endless waiting of ordinary men whose situation is our own. With hindsight, we can see that *Godot* was stylistically rather than philosophically seminal for Stoppard—ping-pong dialogue between twinned opposites, rhythmic pauses between beats, lack of answers to many small questions, lack of dénouement to the large plot line, metaphysics partially camouflaged by farce. Neither Beckett nor Stoppard labels his play as farce, but both playwrights exploit devices of farce—pun, joke, sight gag, double take, double talk, cross-conversation. Beckett enfolds philosophy in farce (e.g. Lucky's speech) to build a large agnostic question. Stoppard slows his farce tempo by philosophic jargon in Act I, and by the aesthetics of *Hamlet* criticism in Act III. His play closes on the Shakespearean announcement of his protagonists' deaths—a foregone conclusion within the *Hamlet* frame. Stoppard believes that he learned from Beckett 'elaborate structure and sudden—and total—dismantlement'.[9] The deaths of the courtiers are not, however, dismantlement, and, despite their deaths, they emerge as likeable little men. The chasm is unbridgeable between the deaths of Rosencrantz and Guildenstern and the continued wait of Gogo and Didi.

III

In *Jumpers* Stoppard dispenses with Shakespeare-cum-Beckett non-heroes. From the British philosopher George Moore, Stoppard borrows name and profession for a stellar protagonist of his Moon lineage. Kenneth Tynan distinguishes between Stoppard's Boots and Moons: 'As a double act, they bring to mind Lenin's famous division of the world into "Who" and "Whom"—those who do and those to whom it is done.'[10] Although Lenin's division may not be famous to all of us, Stoppard has played with the idea *passim*. In *Jumpers* Moon and Moore are related phonetically, and Mrs Moore is fixated on the moon. Often ridiculous, usually well-meaning, possibly mismatched, the Moores, like Rosencrantz and Guildenstern, are 'done to' rather than 'doers'. Their ineptitude arouses our sympathy as well as our laughter. In contrast, Vice-Chancellor Archie Jumper is a Boot character, a doer who excels in physical and mental gymnastics.

The plot of *Jumpers* recycles Stoppard's television play *Another Moon Called Earth*, in which an ailing wife (Penelope) of a historian (Bones) is treated by a perhaps adulterous doctor (Pearce). She has pushed her old Nanny (Pinkerton) out of the window to her death on the day of a parade to honor the lunanauts. In *Jumpers* Penelope mellows to Dotty Moore, who may or may not have murdered philosopher-jumper Duncan McFee. At the

[9] See Note 3
[10] Kenneth Tynan, 'Withdrawing with Style from the Chaos', *The New Yorker* (19 December, 1977) 57

play's flamboyant opening Dotty tries to croon while another woman performs a strip-tease on a swing. Yellow-clad acrobats build a human pyramid that collapses when a bottom-row jumper is shot. In George Moore's terse summary: 'McFee jumped and left nothing behind but a vacancy'.

There is no visual vacancy in *Jumpers*, which opens and closes on acrobatic kaleidoscopes. In the body of the play a huge television screen shows a takeoff from the moon. A professor of philosophy utilizes a bow, arrows, target, hare, and tortoise. A corpse is draped on a chair, or swung from a door, and, finally, is stuffed into a bag to the tune of 'Sentimental Journey'. Dotty Moore has a charade compulsion which inspires sight gags. More modestly but consistently, George Moore falls into sight gags; like Inspector Foot, of *After Magritte*, he appears in shaving foam; he composes a lecture from a snowstorm of notes, and he rehearses it facing the audience before an imaginary mirror. Since he keeps his pencils in a glass tumbler, he inadvertently tries to drink them. Only in the coda is he reduced to mere words.

A party of visual surprises, *Jumpers* also pulls verbal rabbits out of hats (literally a dead hare out of a cupboard). Cross-conversations, extended quid pro quos, engage George and Bones, George and Crouch, but mainly George and Dotty. The last is enlivened by film-type crosscuts when Stoppard shifts mid-scene from Dotty's bedroom to George's study.

Honed through earlier Stoppard plays, pun and parody are sharp in *Jumpers*. Mrs Malaprop casts her shadow on both Dotty—panache for panacea, rationalize for nationalize—and Inspector Bones—magician for logician. Archie condenses actual and academic chairs, and in the Coda he puns in a passage of Joycean prolixity but political double-talk. George's puns are singular: his late friend Bertrand Russell was punctual, his wife's hair reminds him of his hare Thumper, consummate artist suggests sexual consummation.

Jumpers leapfrogs around names. Neurotic Mrs Moore is Dotty, and an obsequious porter is Crouch. Sir Archie Jumper, Vice-Chancellor and panjandrum, can be read as both main mental acrobat and chief officer of villainy. Diagnosing Cognomen Syndrome, Archie admits: 'I've got it.' He is also the victim of 'it', since Inspector Bones (whose osteopath brother has married into the Foot family) calls him Sir Jim, Sigmund, and Bouncer. Inspector Bones also reels off names for George—Charlie, Jack, Ferdinand, Sidney, Clarence, Wilfred, mate. The Moores' invisible housekeeper is variously Thing, Doings, Thingummy, Whatsername.

Inspector Bones confesses to George Moore: 'Show business is my main interest, closely followed by crime detection', and Stoppard closely parodies both interests; Dotty and Bones are crooner and fan, suspect and detective. Unlike Stoppard plays in which the detective is the culprit, *Jumpers's* crime goes unsolved. We never learn who killed Duncan McFee, but we do learn that humane philosopher George Moore probably killed his hare, Thumper, and certainly stepped on his tortoise, Pat. In the play's Coda the inference is strong that the new Archbishop of Canterbury, who has replaced McFee in the pyramid, is killed by the Vice-Chancellor's order (in parody lines from *Richard III*).

In parodying mysteries, crooners, and Shakespeare, Stoppard is on sure ground, but his footing slips in his play-long parody of philosophy. Physical gymnastics is a witty metaphor for mental gymnastics in a play that purports to jump to no conclusion, but polysyllables are dull weapons with which to cut at logical positivism. Yet it is with them that George is armed in his lecture on God and ethics. Sight gags and clever similes scarcely leaven his tedious arguments, and the play grinds down at those periods, to the pace of Pat the tortoise.

Beneath Stoppard's visual and verbal agility in *Jumpers* lies the subject of *Rosencrantz and Guildenstern Are Dead:* the cards (or charades, or academic chairs) are stacked against humble, lovable non-heroes. In *Rosencrantz and Guildenstern* the cards are dealt by Claudius, but in *Jumpers* the dealer is Archie Jumper. Perhaps a murderer, perhaps a seducer, he is certainly a chancellor of vice. As the Player of *Rosencrantz and Guildenstern* is on neutral ground, between the sympathtic courtiers and the unsympathetic royal family, so Dotty Moore languishes between her sympathetic husband and unsympathetic doctor-lover. Sometimes a dumb sexy blonde, she is shattered by man's landing on the romantic moon. Since she is stained by suspicion of murder, however, it is finally George Moore who alone bears the standard for unregimented humanity among totalitarian jumpers.

In spite of his often ridiculous appearance, in spite of constant interruptions to his lecture rehearsal, and in spite of an inability to prove his most fundamental contentions—'There is, first, the God of Creation to account for existence, and, second, the God of Goodness to account for moral values' —Stoppard's George Moore sticks to his own hard path. He does not jump. Archie calls him a 'tame believer', and at the play's beginning and end George tamely, unbravely ignores totalitarian murder, retreating to his ivory tower of universals. Nevertheless, he is still our only Moon in a world of wicked jumpers, and he shines more or less brightly.

IV

For all its technological sophistication, *Jumpers* belongs to an old genre— satire—in which, to quote Webster, 'vices, abuses, or follies are held up to scorn, derision, or ridicule.' So, too, more subtly, does *Travesties*, where satire is intertwined with burlesque. From *Midsummer Night's Dream* to *Rosencrantz and Guildenstern* burlesque deflates tragedy, but Stoppard's burlesque of comedy—*The Importance of Being Earnest*—thrives on farce.[11]

A serious substratum of *Travesties* derives from Stoppard's radio play

---

[11] Bigsby distinguishes comedy from farce, 'the one implying a world in which values exist, the other an antinomian world of ethical relativity' (p. 9). It would be digressive to list exceptions to this approximate guideline. Enoch Brater in 'Parody, Travesty, and Politics in the Plays of Tom Stoppard' (in press) distinguishes parody from travesty by the former's 'critical commentary on the original' and the latter's gratuity. The intentional fallacy renders this distinction unserviceable.

Artist Descending a Staircase. To his protagonist Henry Carr Stoppard assigns lines originally spoken by fictional artists of *Staircase*, notably lines that contrast views of art. The descending artist Donner confuses Tzara with Duchamp: 'He used to beat Lenin at chess. I think he had talent under all those jokes. He said to me, "There are two ways of becoming an artist. The first way is to do the things by which is meant art. The second way is to make art mean the things you do." ' In *Travesties,* set in Zurich during World War I, the first way is exemplified by Joyce, and the second by Tzara. Lenin wishes to subjugate art to social utility.

In *Rosencrantz and Guildenstern Are Dead* the protagonists ponder philosophy, and the Player epigrammatizes on art. *Jumpers* continues the philosophic strain, and *Travesties* the artistic. Stoppard himself has outlined the structural similarity between his satires: puzzling prologue, funny long monologue, scenes in which 'people are playing ping-pong with various intellectual arguments', final monologue.[12] Whoever engages in the ping-pong of ideas, the winner/loser continues to be an appealing non-hero. That is to say, although Stoppard's protagonists may lose out to fate, history, or villainy, they compel our sympathy.

Travesties repeats the structure of *Jumpers,* and it refines the comic devices of Stoppard's earlier plays. From the radio plays *Where Are They Now?* and *Artist Descending a Staircase* Stoppard sharpens what Henry Carr calls 'the cheap comedy of senile confusion'. Part of that confusion revolves around playing with another play—Oscar Wilde's *Importance of Being Earnest.* The historical Joyce persuaded the historical Carr to play 'not Ernest—the other one'. In history and Stoppard's travesty the two theatre dilettantes fall out and sue one another, but only in Stoppard's play does Carr career in and out of Wilde's comedy. *The Importance of Being Earnest* belies its title in every line, whereas the travesties of *Travesties* camouflage Stoppard's familiar themes—the unverifiability of truth, the fluidity of art/life, the grace and skill of art, the inscrutability of fate, the treachery of memory, and especially the charm of the vulnerable non-hero.

Through *Earnest* Stoppard moves into his highest comic gear. The bluestocking heroines bear Wilde's names, Cecily and Gwendolyn, but Wilde's Algernon and Ernest become Carr and Tzara. Stoppard expands Wilde's symmetrical couples to symmetrical triangles. Carr is romantically entwined with Cecily who helps Lenin with his book on Imperialism. Tzara is enthralled by Carr's sister Gwendolyn who helps Joyce with his work in progress, *Ulysses.* (The two manuscripts in identical folders are another source of farcical confusion.) Predictably, love wins out over learning.

Before that happens, however, learning peps up the ingenuities contrived by this non-university wit. Parallelling the visual extravaganza that opens *Jumpers* is the verbal extravaganza that opens *Travesties*—without a single sentence of comprehensible English. The fun begins with Tzara's French words in English nonsense garb:[13]

[12] Hayman, 12
[13] I am grateful to co-translator Hersh Zeifman, but we are both stumped by Stoppard's middle lines.

Eel ate enormous appletzara
Key dairy chef's hat he'll learn oomparah!
Ill raced alas whispers later nut east,
noon avuncular ill day Clara!
(Il est un homme s'appelle Tzara
. . .
. . .
Nous n'avons que l'art, il declara.)

This quatrain cedes to Joyce's 'Oxen of the Sun', which yields in turn to Tzara's Dada nonsense, which is supplanted by the Lenins' Russian, which is punctuated by miscellaneous Joyce, which is climaxed by a limerick about Cecily—intelligible English at last. Cecily later puns through a catalogue of polysyllabic 'isms'. Learning marks the frequent puns, mainly Carr's: mucus mutandis, post hock propter hock, face to face in Spiegelgasse, belle-litter, Boche he replied, mystical swissticality, Gomorrhaist, Elasticated Bloomers, eructate a monument. The word Dada inspires no less than five puns: father, hobby-horse, artistic movement, Russian affirmative, stutter of 'dàrling'.

Travesties feeds on literature—Shakespeare, Wordsworth, Tennyson, La Rochefoucauld, Gilbert, a litter of limericks, the question-and-answer mode of the Eumaeus chapter of *Ulysses*. Insults crackle sonically and comically, as in the ancient art of flyting:

Carr about Joyce: 'a liar and a hypocrite, a tight-fisted, sponging, fornicating drunk.'

Carr to Tzara: 'you little Rumanian wog—you bloody dago—you jumped up phrase-making smart-alecky arty-intellectual Balkan turd!'

Tzara to Carr: 'you bloody English philistine—you ignorant smart-arse bogus bourgeois Anglo-Saxon prick!'

Tzara to Joyce: 'you supercilious streak of Irish puke! You four-eyed, bog-ignorant, potato-eating ponce!'

Carr is also afflicted with a virulent case of Cognomen Syndrome, addressing Joyce as Doris, Janice, Phyllis, Deirdre, Bridget.

Although *Travesties* is more subdued visually than *Jumpers,* Joyce is showered with Tzara's snipped sonnet; out of his hat the Irish word-magician pulls a carnation, handkerchiefs, flags, and a rabbit. Carr sneaks around like a spy, and Tzara smashes crockery. We see Carr's garish fantasy of Cecily as a stripper. Gwendolyn and Cecily perform a tea ceremony. Even Lenin appears in a wig, and he delivers a speech in the pose of a familiar photograph.

Obliquely related to sight gags is Carr's obsession with clothes. He orders his manservant Bennett to prepare sumptuous outfits; he is in Savile Row when he hears about the outbreak of war; he recalls that trench warfare ruined his wardrobe; he is invalided to Switzerland by 'a bullet through the calf of an irreplaceable lambswool dyed khaki'. Above all, it is costume that persuades him to play in *Importance*: 'You enter in a bottle-green velvet smoking jacket with black frogging—hose white, cravat perfect, boots elastic-side, trousers of your own choice.'

Versatile in these comic effects, Stoppard directs us by title to the play's spine—parody. Over a dozen quotations from *The Importance of Being Earnest* are skillfully spliced into Stoppard's own dialogue. Graceful epigrams combine with elegant costumes to create an Ivory Tower background for this revolutionary underworld in World War I Zurich. Bennett's war bulletins and Carr's war reminiscences are further parodies in this never-never milieu ostensibly based on fact.

Carr himself is a triumph of English triviality. More or less impressed by his famous coevals, Carr makes several false starts on his memoirs, which parody the rambling reminiscences that are a staple of genteel English literature. Stoppard charges this unlikely character with a defence of art in the play-long pirouette around its definition. Against Tzara in Act I Carr proclaims: 'Wars are fought to make the world safe for artists.' In a complete about-face Carr then attacks art to Tzara, and it is Joyce who finally carries the artist's day. In Act II, however, Carr is back at art's defence against Cecily's socialist onslaught. Soon he is defending democracy against Marx and Lenin.

Like his predecessor George Moore, Henry Carr is well-meaning and ineffectual, well educated and absent-minded, self-centred and wide-ranging. Like Moore, too, he doesn't lift a finger against a totalitarianism he feels is dangerous. He is funnier than Moore because of his clothes-fetish, name-dropping, social snobbery, and incorporation into a classic of comedy. Blending several parodies—memorialist, jingoist, fashion-plate, philistine, defender of the artist though he ignores the arts—Henry Carr may be Stoppard's most endearing character. In contrast, Joyce and Tzara are candid caricatures, both making outrageous claims for their art, neither scratching its surface (in the play).

The play's problem character is Lenin, especially in Act II. The confusion of the play's opening scene might amuse an English-speaking audience with incomprehensible Russian, but Cecily's laborious translations weigh down Act II. Carr early parallels Lenin with Joyce, strawmen in their respective triangles: 'To those of us who knew him, Joyce's genius was never in doubt . . . To those of us who knew him, Lenin's greatness was never in doubt.' Bennett's Act I report of the Russian Revolution blurs into parody, and Lenin can be viewed as a titular travesty. By Act II, however, discordant tones sound loud—not so much serious as dull. Even abridged for performance, Cecily's lecture is pure lead. Lenin on art is self-contradictory, but Stoppard makes no comic point of this, nor of the disproportionately large role he is assigned.

The first act of *Travesties* displays Stoppard at his most scintillating—puns, games, jargon, pastiche, sight gags, limericks, vaudeville, misquotations, cross-conversations, mistaken identity. Act II bogs down undramatically.

Tom Stoppard seems to be as likable as his protagonists. Friends, acquaintances, audiences, reviewers, and serious critics join in a chorus of praise. The philosopher A.J. Ayer and the Joyce scholar Richard Ellmann have lavished encomiums on their relevant plays.[14] A book has been published on Stoppard's work, and dissertations are rolling through typewriters. In the two most searching essays on Stoppard, C.W.E. Bigsby pays tribute to the performance quality of the plays, which he reads as a generalized meta-phoric response 'to the bewildering vagaries of existence'.[15] Hersh Zeifman pays tribute to Stoppard's language ambiguities which he reads as a metaphor for metaphysical ambiguity[16] Metaphor-happy myself, I see this in Stoppard's first play—the fantastic impractical inventions of *Enter a Free Man*. Stoppard's puns, parodies, and performance strategies *are* inventive, but they serve no purpose except entertainment in the light drama that constitutes the bulk of his work. In his three major plays, ideological prose burdens his endearing, indomitable, and doomed protagonists; their ideas seem comically murky, but they prove to be quirkily conventional. Failing to achieve 'a perfect marriage between the play of ideas and farce or perhaps even high comedy', Stoppard belabours ideas—aesthetics, politics, philo-sophy—until they resemble funeral baked meats that coldly furnish forth the marriage tables of farce of perhaps even high comedy.

[14] A.J. Ayer, 'Love among the Logical Positivists', *The Sunday Times* (9 April, 1972) Richard Ellmann, 'The Zealots of Zurich', *Times Literary Supplement* (12 July, 1974)
[15] Bigsby, 28
[16] Hersh Zeifman, 'Tomfoolery: Stoppard's Theatrical Puns', *The Yearbook of English Studies* (1979). I thank Hersh Zerifman for generously sending me Stoppard's unpublished works.

Note

Life and writings

Edward Bond was born to a working-class family in London, 1934. His formal education ended at the age of 15 when he left secondary school, and he wrote his first play at
the age of 32. In 1958, he was invited to join the Writers' Group at the Royal Court
Theatre, then under the direction of William Gaskill. Both *Saved* and *Early Morning*
were censored by the Lord Chamberlain, and when his powers were rescinded in late
1968, Gaskill responded with a 'Bond season' at the Royal Court. While the majority
of his plays have been produced by the Royal Court, *The Woman* enjoys the distinction of being the first contemporary play to be performed on the Olivier stage at the
National Theatre (1978). His most recent play, *The Worlds*, was performed at the
Court's Theatre Upstairs by the Young Activist drama group in December, 1979.

With the exception of *Early Morning*, which is published by Calder and Boyars, the
following are published in England by Eyre Methuen: *The Pope's Wedding* (1971),
Saved (1966), *Early Morning* (1968), *Narrow Road to the Deep North: A Comedy*
(1968), *Lear* (1972), *The Sea: A Comedy* (1973), *Bingo: Scenes of Money and Death*
(1974), *The Fool: Scenes of Bread and Love* (1976), *A-A-America!* (*Grandma Gaust: A
Burlesque and The Swing: A Documentary. Also Stone: A Short Play*) (1976), *The
Bundle: Scenes of Right and Evil or New Narrow Road to the Deep North* (1978), *The
Woman* (1978). His collected works are also available from Eyre Methuen: *Plays: One
(Saved, Early Morning, The Pope's Wedding)* (1977), *Plays: Two (Narrow Road to the
Deep North, Lear, The Sea, Black Mass, Passion)* (1978), *Theatre Poems and Songs*,
selected by Malcolm Hay and Philip Roberts (1978).

Criticism

Among the more valuable secondary material:
Ruby Cohn, *Modern Shakespeare Offshoots*. Princeton, N.J. 1976. Discusses *Lear*
and its relation to Shakespeare's *King Lear*. Tony Coult, *The Plays of Edward Bond*.
1978. Best thematic study of Bond's plays to date. John Elsom, *Post-War British
Theatre*. 1976, p. 188-99. Brief consideration of Bond's technique and general impor-
tance. Malcolm Hay, and Philip Roberts. *Edward Bond: A Companion to the Plays*.
1978. Includes invaluable material from Bond's letters and programme notes and
includes an extensive bibliography of articles and reviews. Richard Scharine, *The
Plays of Edward Bond*. Lewisburg 1976. Provides information on early reactions to
Bond's plays and discusses the plays through *Lear*. John Russell Taylor, *The Second
Wave*. 1971. Devotes a chapter to Bond and considers the plays up to *Passion*. Simon
Trussler, *Edward Bond*. 1976. Brief analysis of plays through *Bingo*. Katherine
Worth, *Revolutions in Modern English Drama*. 1972. Offers an analysis of the plays
through *Lear* with attention to Bond's language.

VII

Edward Bond's Dramatic Strategies

JENNY S. SPENCER

I

Edward Bond is undeniably a part of an active and innovative period in modern British theatre. The issues he is stirred by—the dehumanizing, violent effects of a class-structured, technocratic society; the alienation of the individual under capitalism; the destructive contradictions of our social and political institutions; the seeming impossibility of rational and effective political action; the need for a working-class culture—all appear in various forms in the theatre of his contemporaries. Bond's stylistic diversity testifies to the technical alternatives opened up for British playwrights by the work of Beckett, Artaud and Brecht, much of it within the experimental atmosphere of a proliferating and increasingly popular fringe theatre. The political content and didactic intention of Bond's plays link him to the broader tradition Eric Bentley has labelled 'theatre of ideas'. His controlled and realistic dialogue has been compared to both Chekhov and Pinter, his concrete and often violent imagery has precedents in both Shakespeare and the agit-prop theatre of the 1960s. He writes prefaces like Shaw and theatre-poems like Brecht. Perhaps the most technically ambitious of the contemporary British playwrights, Bond has managed to create a distinctive voice in the theatre, one which resists easy definition in terms of the post-Osborne trends identified by such critics as John Russell Taylor and John Elsom.[1]

Bond calls his theatre a 'rational theatre' primarily in order to distinguish his own literary practice from that of his contemporaries. Firmly committed to humanistic values, he has little use for the avant-garde trends (catalogued by Martin Esslin in *The Theatre of the Absurd*) which assume life is meaningless and human action absurd. His protest, like that of Arden and Wesker, is strictly social and political. For Bond, playwriting is an unquestionably moral activity; his aim, he states simply, is 'to tell the truth'.[2] Few playwrights, however, have elicited responses which vary so widely from outrage to polite dismissal. He is described at times as deliberately confusing, at others as overly simplistic, as both daringly innovative and deeply conventional.[3] Sixteen years after the controversial appearance of *Saved*, Bond now commands more than a grudging respect from the critics, but he remains something of an enigma to even the most enthusiastic students of the

---

[1] See *The Second Wave* (Eyre Methuen, 1971) and *Post-War British Theatre* (1976).

[2] Author's conversation with Bond, 1 December, 1979, Royal Court Theatre.

[3] Practically any sampling of reviews of Bond's plays will substantiate this point. For a complete bibliography, see Malcom Hay and Phillip Roberts, *Edward Bond: A Companion to the Plays* (1978), pp. 79-100.

theatre. Bond himself is quick to note that much of the resistance he encounters lies in deeply rooted cultural biases or class differences. Those who have a stake in the status quo will necessarily be discomfited by the political import of his plays and his tone of moral urgency. But Bond's literary practice presents problems for his left-wing sympathizers as well, problems which are located in how the plays work and how they should be read, rather than in the general and explicit themes with which he deals. Before we can ask whether Bond is a success or failure (or even important), we must first take a closer look at what he has set out to do, and what he has in fact accomplished.

The very breadth and range of Bond's dramatic work makes a traditional overview extremely difficult; and we cannot expect a catalogue of recurring themes, images and motifs to get us very far in the study of his unique contribution to the theatre. The most fruitful approach is one which abandons at the start certain critical assumptions: that the artist's work will retrospectively present a coherent pattern of growth and development; that the work of art must turn on the notion of unity, harmony and organic wholeness; that what can be said of the text is the same as what the text itself is saying; that the work is reducible to the literary message it encodes.[4] Bond himself has articulated some important differences between his early and later plays, and in the course of this chapter we should be able to distinguish certain distinctive techniques and recurring strategies. But while Bond's ultimate purpose remains unchanged (to create a rational society), his style and particular methods will shift in both emphasis and effect, resisting any logic of even artistic development. Also, Bond's political ideas and thematic concerns are for the most part simple and direct. They provide the subject matter for his numerous essays, prefaces and programme-notes, and on them Bond is his own best explicator. His theatrical idiom, however, is often complex, and stands in need of a more thoroughgoing analysis than has been offered to date. This is not to imply that Bond's politics can or should be separated from his aesthetic practice. One measure of his success will depend upon the extent to which these two categories remain interdependent.

II

As the gesture of designating his theatre a rational one suggests, Bond sees himself as a realistic writer. When we think of the various kinds of exaggeration and verbal-visual poetry Bond is noted for (the caricatures of *Early Morning*, Lear's language, Shogo's mutilation in *Narrow Road to the Deep North*, Hatch's madness in *The Sea*, Clare's hallucinations in *The Fool*, Trench's party in *The Worlds*, and so on), or the number of genre types Bond has used (social comedy, Noh-play, parable, epic, history play, tragedy, etc.), such a definition must appear more than mildly inappropriate. The term 'realism' is, of course, as troublesome as the age-old problem of the relationship between art and truth. 'Realism' habitually denotes a reflection

---

[4] This approach is elaborated more fully in Pierre Macheray, *Theory of Literary Production* (1978).

of reality which produces recognition. But just as our immediate perceptions of reality are mediated by ideology, the real in the theatre is mediated
by dramatic convention. The more self-conscious theatre becomes as a self-
reflective, contained, symbolic universe, the more difficult the problem for a
politically conscious playwright who is still interested in 'truthful' representation onstage.

Since Brecht, however, we have at least learned to distinguish between a
bourgeois realism and a critical realism. The former, presenting itself to the
audience as a commodity to be consumed, can be described as integrative
drama. It supports the culture's dominant ideology by posing problems too
limited or easily resolved, and/or presenting reality and human nature as
ahistorical, eternal and unchanging. Naive realism works like ideology to
obscure the kind of dynamic contradictions which could lead to radical
change. By presenting what 'is' as truth (the empirical fallacy), it tends to
naturalize the very conventions on which it depends, to conceal the work's
status as production. To do this, bourgeois realism depends on narrative
continuity and audience identification—a readable discourse with an
entirely appropriable meaning addressed to an audience fixed, unified and
rendered immobile in the act of seeing. Contradictions become conflicts
(static, polar categories) which are displaced to the level of psychology or
resolved through the unfolding structure of the play's plot (usually linear,
teleological, symmetrical).

Like Brecht, however, Bond is concerned with orienting the audience
toward action rather than consumption. As he states in a letter to Tony
Coult, 'Theatre is a way of judging society and helping to change it; art must
interpret the world and not merely mirror it.[5] Bond is less concerned with a
naturalistic surface than with the complex relationship between ideology,
play and audience. His realism is of a Brechtian order: a critical-productive
attitude toward the world which sees reality as historical, contradictory and
subject to human intercession. Thus Bond attempts to present representa-
tions of reality (mediated by theatrical convention in the same way ideology
mediates perception) which are both recognizable as our own world, and yet
untenable (in need of change). Moreover, the audience must become
involved (caught up but not immersed) in the play's narration of events in
such a way that the analysis becomes clear. A successful reading of a Bond
play will rest on the audience's ability to perceive the dynamic which arises
from the dialectical interplay of its elements—between the play's objective
and subjective worlds, between action and language, reason and emotion,
society and individual, the historical process and the experience of the
moment, judgement and description. In other words, we must actively read
how the play produces, rather than simply conveys, its meaning.

Although the particular arrangement and working through of these
dynamics will vary with each play, a number of Bond's strategies can be
elaborated from the general premises outlined above. We might note, first of
all, that the bulk of Bond's plays are historically or geographically distanced

[5] *A Companion to the Plays*, p. 74. See also the Preface to *The Bundle* (1978)

from present-day English life. According to Bond, a dramatist concerned with addressing an audience's immediate situation need not always deal directly with the present. 'The past is also an institution owned by society.'[6] Because our present social problems have a history, the way in which history is taught and understood will either help or circumscribe an individual's ability to recognize and solve those problems. While Bond's first (*The Pope's Wedding* and *Saved*) and most recent play (*The Worlds*) offer a specifically contemporary setting, the rest provide a series of 'history plays' in which Bond re-presents and re-interprets aspects of our historical and cultural heritage in order to create for his audience a more 'usable' past. In fact, Bond sees this activity as one of the artist's primary functions.

Since man not only makes his own history, but is situated within it, the art he creates will always have an historical dimension. Bond states in one essay, 'In literature there are no abstract statements universally true for all time— or if there are, they are trivial until given content and context.'[7] The 'truths' of art will be relativized by such things as the artist's social origins (class position) and his society's state of objective knowledge (e.g., as expressed in science and technology). Bond believes that art which has outlived its historical relevance enters into the domain of myth, and as such becomes both untrue and dangerous. He wants his audience to 'escape from a mythology of the past, which often lives on as the culture of the present'.[8] Thus *Early Morning* is a comic nightmare aimed at disturbing our comfort with Victorian history. The grotesquely caricatured figures of Queen Victoria, Gladstone and Disraeli are attempts to displace the history-book idealizations of such real personages, idealizations which live on to justify our present institutions and obscure the destructive contradictions on which they rest. Likewise, it is against an idealized notion of Shakespeare as a sacrosanct culture hero whose plays are true for all time, that the character of Shakespeare in *Bingo* takes shape. By imaginatively recreating Shakespeare's involvement with the Welcombe enclosures, Bond demystifies the Shakespearean myth, refusing to exempt the bard from personal responsibility for the historical developments of his own time. More importantly, Bond shows how the psychological contradictions which lead Shakespeare to suicide in *Bingo* are the result of the social contradictions of his historical moment. Shakespeare's moral failure is here inextricable from his 'bourgeois consciousness'—the class position won by economic success severely limits both his vision and his ability to act in a politically responsible manner.

Since Bond believes a society that tries to create self-consciousness in its members based on imagery, attitudes and social organizations of the past will only succeed in creating individual emotional crises,[9] he addresses the kind of art which perpetuates that past. In both *Lear* and *The Woman*, for example, we see Bond working within and against older dramatic forms.

[6] Preface to *The Bundle*, p. xiv.
[7] 'The Rational Theatre', *Edward Bond, Plays: Two* (1978), p. xii.
[8] 'Letter to Tony Coult', *A Companion to the Plays*, p. 75.
[9] Preface to *The Bundle*, p. x.

Excursions into 'theatre of quotation',[10] both plays call for the audience's recognition of a counter-text. According to Bond, Greek and Shakespearean tragedy continue to provide cultural and artistic standards for contemporary audiences, long after the plays have outlived their social usefulness. As the backbone of English dramatic tradition, Shakespeare is a figure Bond can neither ignore nor wholeheartedly accept. And, when using him as a source, Bond looks not only to the original texts, but to the modern productions which alternately offer Christian or existential interpretations of Shakespeare's plays.[11] Bond feels that Shakespeare's *King Lear* offers us an anatomy of human values which teach us how to survive in a corrupt world, rather than showing us how to act responsibly in order to change it.[12] The Shakespearean precedents which inform Bond's *Lear* are fairly easy to locate —in Lear's movement to sanity through madness, vision through blindness, and self-knowledge through suffering; in the revitalization of certain patterns of imagery; and in Lear's metaphoric language. But Bond provides wholly new social contexts for Lear's action, replete with the anachronisms which directly relate the narrative to contemporary issues. And audiences can grasp the significance of Lear's actions only by perceiving the way in which Bond reworks the Elizabethan tragic conventions. Likewise, Bond reworks the patterns of classical Greek tragedy when he rewrites the Hecuba story, replacing a psychological study in human suffering with an insight into the historical process. Bond's experiments with older dramatic forms are not limited to tragedy, however. Behind *Narrow Road to the Deep North* stands the tradition of the Noh play, but, through the figure of Basho, Bond criticizes the Noh play's characteristically contemplative stance. While the parable as a literary form seems most appropriate for conveying universal, timeless and unchanging truths, in *The Bundle* Bond uses the parable to examine the historically relative and dialectical nature of morality itself. With Colin's death in *The Sea*, Bond injects a real note of tragedy into what might otherwise pass for a social comedy of manners. And through the figures of Willy and Evens, Bond can present and expose this world from an outsider's point of view. While reminiscent of both the well-made domestic play and Chekhovian naturalism, *The Sea* finally rejects the structure of both forms, and with them, the world-view on which they depend.

Bond claims (and rightly so) that he structures his plays 'with infinite care',[13] and we can recognize Bondian strategies in the way he handles dramatic structure. In order to articulate and represent the contradictions of the real (which are necessarily scattered and diverse), Bond cannot rely on

[10] Shaw, Brecht, Sartre, Giraudoux, Stoppard are among the many modern playwrights who have adapted Greek and Shakespearean 'classics' for their own dramatic purposes. The practice is frequent enough in contemporary theatre to merit a label of its own.

[11] A.C. Bradley has greatly influenced standard Shakespearean criticism with his Christian interpretations of *King Lear* in *Shakespearean Tragedy* (1908) while Jan Kott's existential interpretation of Lear in *Shakespeare Our Contemporary* (1967) has influenced a number of modern productions of the play.

[12] See *A Companion to the Plays*, p. 53.

[13] *Ibid.*, p. 56

the kind of narration which would resolve these contradictions into a specious unity or fix them into permanently irreconcilable categories. To create a literature which is consciously artistic (fictional, structured, and participating in a history of literary forms) without abandoning the project of truthful representation and political effectiveness, Bond must provide within his plays an analysis which breaks up traditional modes of narrative continuity without altogether ignoring narrative conventions. In a discussion of *The Woman*, Bond in fact states, 'We must do that highly subversive thing—tell a story with a beginning, middle and end.'[14] And indeed, Bond not only tells stories, but tells them well, using many of the elements we normally associate with traditional drama: linear chronology, the dramatic reversal, creation of suspense, highly theatrical and emotional scenes, etc. Reacting to what he sees as shortcomings in Brecht's methods, Bond insists that the analysis of an event must never swamp the recording of it. Bond may be an expert at creating discrete scenic units in a Brechtian manner, but he also provides a logical cause-effect structure which links each scene to the next. Because the issues Bond is concerned with can only be resolved in action outside the theatre, we cannot expect to find these issues resolved either within the consciousness of a character or within the structure of the plot. The incidents in Bond's plays are always clarified by other incidents, not by any general or universal principles. Thus we find in the plays a tendency toward uneven development which decentres the central problematic to various levels in order to prevent a wholly satisfactory resolution. This decentred structure affects both character development and plot construction; and with it, Bond succeeds in making his audience actively read, rather than passively receive, the message of his plays.

III

On the level of character, then, Bond will show the kind of understanding and articulation of problems that prevents meaningful action as often as showing what permits it. In the early plays, especially, Bond focuses on the characters' 'pursuit of illusions—of false solutions to personal and political problems'.[15] As a result, more questions are posed than can possibly be answered or resolved within the context set up by the play; the resolutions which are offered in the story's end do not appear as inevitable, but limited and naggingly unsatisfactory. As gestures of hope, Lear's few shovels of dirt to sabotage the wall construction, and Len's action silently mending a chair, seem painfully inadequate under the circumstances. The most obvious example is perhaps to be found in *The Sea*:

> I left the last sentence of the play unfinished because the play can have no satisfactory solution at that stage. Rose and Willy have to go away and help create a sane society—and it is for the audience to go away and complete the sentence in their own lives.[16]

[14] 'Green Room' discussion with Edward Bond, *Plays and Players* (November, 1978),
[15] *A Companion to the Plays*, p. 56.
[16] 'Letter to Tom Wild', *A Companion to the Plays*, p. 57.

The narrative of *Narrow Road* also seems to stop *in medias res*, with a stage picture which vividly juxtaposes several images—Kiro's silent suicide, Shogo's dismembered corpse, a man calling for help and pulling himself out of the river, and Basho's offstage voice making a speech, with distinctly fascist overtones, to the people. None of these characters answer the problem posed by the play—how to act in a morally responsible way. The scene is a key to Bond's use of visual-poetic images in all of his plays, however. Since the poetic image is in itself a synchronic structure, it can perform a potentially mystifying function in the theatre by obscuring specific and analytical relations within a play. Such is Bond's complaint against the 'enigmatic' verbal-visual poetry of absurdist drama. Bond's theatrical images, on the other hand, are concretizations of the very issues he presents in other ways through the characters, structure and narrative movement. In other words, he offers economy of expression which does not abstract/condense/mystify, but represents and clarifies in a concrete and visual way complex dialectical relationships. If we examine carefully the relation of the poetic elements to the historical, time-structured elements of the plays, we find that the former represent without resolving the contradictions of the latter. Though image and event are obviously interdependent, the two aspects do not necessarily contribute to a unifying (tonal, atmospheric) effect, but rather to a kind of dialectical thinking which proceeds by leaps and disjunctions.

Finally, while the early plays present no adequate resolution, most of the later plays rely on a partial resolution accompanied by a scenic 'coda'. These endings are disturbing because they either remind us within the context of one resolution of a problem which the play has not satisfactorily addressed, or they shift the focus of the analysis to an entirely different level. With its story of a successful revolution, *The Bundle* clarifies and optimistically answers many of the questions posed earlier in *Narrow Road*, but ends on a tragic note with the accidental death of a worker. Likewise, in *The Worlds*, Terry diverts the issues of the play to an appropriately unresolved level by refusing to answer Beryl's question (will he condemn terrorist violence?) in the terms offered.

Bond's overall dramatic project is also reflected in his approach to character, and affects the structure of the plays. If the goal of realism is to embody the innate dialectics of social reality, then the truthfulness of the representation will depend, in part, on the broadness of the social picture, and on the kind of contexts offered for the characters' actions. According to Bond, we can't find out about a character's motivation by analysing his soul, and he directs his actors to avoid an understanding of character in terms of psychology. Bond also avoids the tendency of many didactic writers to present characters who are simple functions of the ideas they represent, who are derived from the conceptual in order to illustrate an argument. If art is to provide the audience with knowledge, it cannot be of a scientific nature (theories empirically verifiable), but the kind which arises from history and experience.[17] Marx's description of human consciousness

---

[17] See 'A Rational Theatre', *Plays: Two*, p. xvi.

is directly applicable to Bond's dramatic practice:

> We do not set out from what men say, imagine, conceive nor from men as narrated, thought of, imagined, conceived, in order to arrive at men in the flesh. We set out from real, active men and on the basis of their life-process, we demonstrate the development of the ideological reflexes and echoes of this life process. The phantoms of the human brain are also sublimates of their material life-process, which is empirically verifiable and bound to material premises. . . .[18]

Bond's characters are always determined, in the last instance, by their environment. They are shaped by the social, familial and economic relationships which Bond so carefully articulates onstage. As Bond puts it, 'I show characters in their various social roles and various social relationships (and thus achieving wholeness) rather than developing a character from its *geist*.'[19] In terms of structuring scenes, this often means setting up more than one acting centre on the stage, one situation providing a perspective or frame for another. This multiple focus forces the audience to analyse the relationship between characters and groups of characters, to see the limitations of any one character's perspective, and to avoid the kind of identification that psychological drama encourages. With voices heard from the wings, events undramatized but reacted to, characters absent but determining, Bond often suggests an offstage reality that provides further contexts for the action occurring onstage.

In Bond's plays, an accurate representation must ultimately remain faithful in language and action to the historical situation and class position of his characters. Thus, the conflicts and relationships between characters frequently arise from, and in turn illuminate, the contradictions of a society based on class. Since these relationships are also mediated by a shared ideology (and are therefore complex), the conflicts will rarely appear as head-on, polarized confrontations, but rather as determining factors of behaviour and attitude which define and limit the characters' consciousness. Even in plays where the antagonism between classes is most forcefully presented (*The Fool, Bingo, The Bundle, The Worlds*) Bond is equally interested in exploring the relationships between characters of the same class, in examining the differing ways they react to the same situation, and why. We might note here that the materialist approach outlined above is not only relevant for the more naturalistically presented characters (Len and Pam of *Saved*, Clare and Patty of *The Fool*, etc.), but for the character whose language and actions strain credulity as well. Although he exaggerates or heightens their action for comic or emotional effects, Bond is careful to provide contexts for the violence of Shogo in *Narrow Road*, Bodice and Fontanelle in *Lear*, Fred's gang in *Saved*, and the madness of Georgiana, Hatch, Lear, Trench—contexts which prevent their actions from being read as either arbitrary or tragic (psychologically inevitable).

[18] Karl Marx, *The German Ideology* (1970), p. 47.
[19] *Theatre Quarterly* (Vol. XIII, 1978), p. 34.

Just as the way in which the story is dramatized will affect the audience's ability to interpret it, so the ways in which characters perceive their situation and environment will affect their capacity for changing it. Although not really interested in psychology, Bond *is* interested in subjectivity. While history may determine the individual, and the individual alone can never alter the economic base of the capitalist state, it is individual men, engaged in action, who make history. Since the subject is the location for political practice, Bond must do more than show how subjectivity is created in his characters—he must try to create a radical subjectivity in his audience as well. This intention appears in the shift Bond sees in his own work, from plays which define a problem to plays which try to provide some kind of answer:

> We mustn't write only problem plays, we must write answer plays—or at least plays which make answers clearer and more practical. When I wrote my first plays, I was, naturally, conscious of the weight of the problems. Now I've become more conscious of the strength of human beings to provide answers. The answers aren't always light, easy or even straightforward, but the purpose—a socialist society—is clear.[20]

The change in focus manifests itself in both language and dramatic structure: we see in *The Woman*, *The Worlds* and *The Bundle* a tighter, more symmetrical dramatic structure which closely coheres to the argument being made, and the use (by at least some of the characters) of a more discursive, rational and consciously persuasive language. Moreover, Bond will create characters with whom the audience can more easily identify in terms of offering more plausible models of behaviour.

For Bond, 'human consciousness is class consciousness',[21] and we might distinguish here between characters who belong to a particular class, and those who become class conscious in Bond's sense of the term. It is only the latter (Darkie in *The Fool*, Wang in *The Bundle*, Hecuba in *The Woman*, Terry and the terrorists in *The Worlds*, and to some extent Lear and the Son in *Bingo*) who are able to grasp their situation in a way that allows them to act and to escape (at least temporarily or partially) being the victims of history and circumstance. These characters are not automatically endowed with an enlightened perspective, but come to it through the learning process offered by the concrete experiences and social relationships of the play. It is a practical knowledge, never a purely conceptual one, which issues in and provides a model for action. The kind of knowledge the play offers its audience will be akin to, but not identical with, the knowledge gained by the characters. But in both cases, knowledge is understood as the result of a dialectical process which moves from the realm of immediate sense perception to some kind of conceptual understanding which then issues in action. (That action then provides new sense perceptions which reinitiates the process.)[22] As we shall

[20] 'Letter to Tony Coult', *A Companion to the Plays*, p. 75.

[21] *Ibid.*, p. 74

[22] Mao Tse Tung offers this definition of the learning process in 'On Practice', *Five Essays on Philosophy* (1977), pp. 1-22.

see, this movement is reflected in the time structure of the plays, in Bond's control over the movement and rhythm of narration. It also involves Bond's concern with the individual's relation to history, with the characters' (and our own) ability to grasp an interpretation of events in the process of history in order to understand 'the truth that life need not be an ungraspable flow of experience'.[23]

III

Any playwright interested in change must deal with the problem of time. And the problem of class consciousness for Marx is inseparable from the problem of the subject's capability of perceiving himself as a motive force in history, of obtaining an historical consciousness. In the early plays especially, Bond's characters are limited in their ability to learn from their experience in ways which would allow them to take meaningful (moral, politically conscious) action. This is due in part to Bond's awareness of 'the weight of the problems', one being that objective conditions change faster than subjective consciousness—that there is always a lag between external stimuli and the responses which are dictated by habit and the ideology instilled by family, education, and religious institutions, all of which combine to make one's objective assessment of oppression more difficult. (The problem is registered in these plays in the very language used by the characters to understand and articulate their experience.) But this is also the justification for Bond's sense of urgency, an urgency written into the tempo of the plays. Thus we can identify a characteristic Bondian movement—the calm, analytical pace which builds to isolated moments that are shocking, intensely emotional or naturalistically compelling. (Look, for example, at the baby-stoning sequence in *Saved*, the velvet-cutting scene in *The Sea*, the torture scenes in *Lear*, the parson-stripping scene in *The Fool*, etc.) We are compelled by virtue of the real menace involved in these experiences—when we view a character with whom we at least partially identify, or a situation which we clearly recognize, as 'on the brink' of destruction and increasingly out of control. As opposed to Brecht's alienation-effects, Bond once referred to them as 'aggro-effects'.[24] Hallmarks of his distinctive style, these protracted moments of threatened or disturbingly explicit violence are remembered by the audience long after the performance. Commented upon at length by reviewers (both positively and negatively), they consciously provoke a reaction and play on the audience's fears. These scenes, however, are carefully choreographed by Bond, heightened often to the point of melodrama; and they usually succeed in representing the characters' own subjective experience of history—as an inexplicable concatenation of events which is increasingly overwhelming and out of control. These 'real' and traumatic experiences are determining for the characters involved, and lead to various kinds of reflective assessments (more or less adequate, depending on the

[23] Preface to *The Bundle*, p. xvi.
[24] *Theatre Quarterly* (Vol. XIII, 1978), p. 34.

play), which in turn lead to further action. The audience, of course, is always provided with a social perspective of the whole which permits a clearer understanding of the action than is allowed the characters. But the sense of urgency created by these brutally literal scenes remains—to be channelled into the activity of interpreting the play. The resulting rhythm keeps the plays from being too cerebral, from reflecting the structure of a purely logical argument.

On a more theoretical level, the problem of time and the need for an historical consciousness is registered in many of the plays by Bond's attempts to show a movement away from a symbolic and mythical world to an historical one. The relation between Acts I and II of *The Woman* demonstrates this movement most directly. In Act I, Bond continually invites the recognition of his Greek source as he presents his own version of the last three days of the Trojan War. In Act II, on the other hand, Bond tells a story entirely of his own making which bears little, if any, relation to the acknowledged source with which he began. Here Bond rewrites the consequences of a basically myth-bound action and shows the island village moving from an isolated and ideal community into a Greek-dominated historical world. Thus the annual ritual celebrations on which Act II opens must give way, due to the intrusion of the Greeks, to the future-determining deliberations of the town council on which the play ends. Bond offers a similar description of the three-part structure of *Lear*:

> Act I shows a world dominated by myth. Act II shows the clash between myth and reality, between superstitious men and the autonomous world. Act III shows a resolution of this, in the world we prove real by dying in it.[25]

Both plays begin with an accelerated tempo of events, with actions which appear to have unavoidable and fateful consequences, with a 'tragic' sense of time, only to move into a different kind of tempo—one which allows the characters to reflect on past experience, and to offer alternative models of action.

IV

One aspect of Bond's theatre which distinguishes him most clearly from the plain realism of Wesker and the 'kitchen sink' dramatists is his use of language. The dialogue of Bond's plays ranges from the naturalistic dialect of his working-class characters to the poetic reflections of Shakespeare, Lear and Trench, from the comic exaggerations of Mrs Rafi in *The Sea* and Queen Victoria in *Passion*, to the rational and persuasive discourse of Ismene, Wang and the terrorists. For Bond, language is one register of the characters' social and class position, as well as a tool for measuring their self-consciousness. Moreover, Bond is able to show through his dialogue how ideology intervenes in the consciousness of certain characters and prevents

[25] Preface to *Lear* (1972), p. xiv.

them from understanding the implications of their own actions (e.g., in the case of Mrs Rafi in *The Sea*, the gang in *Saved*, Lord Milton and the Parson in *The Fool*, and the businessmen in *The Worlds*.) In the figures of Lear, Shakespeare, Hecuba and Trench, we find evidence of a consciously imagistic and metaphoric language which does not inevitably lead to moral action (and may in fact prevent it). In the witty and concrete language of Bond's working classes, we find codes of communication which both permit survival and some measure of human group contact, though the kind of joking displacements which also prevent adequate conceptualization of experience. Katherine Worth speaks to Bond's facility with language when she claims he has created a colloquial theatre that is also visionary and poetic'.[26] The equation struck here, however, is not an easy one to maintain. In Shakespeare, for example, the colloquial and energetic language of the clowns and fools, and the visionary, poetic language of kings and heroes, are distinctly separate modes of discourse and reflect similarly distinct (often incompatible) ways of thinking. Bond's problem, and the problem of the modern realist writer, is somehow to combine these discourses without incurring the limitations of either. He would avoid an appeal to a frankly symbolic universe, since it can ultimately have no effect in the 'real' world. And yet brute facts, situations and incidents in themselves cannot offer the kind of knowledge necessary for effective action.

In *The Fool*, Bond addresses this problem in his examination of the ambivalent position of the writer in society. Here, Bond fuses the political and the personal by presenting an analysis which seems to arise from a straightforward dramatization of particular incidents in the life of John Clare. But *The Fool* is perhaps the most carefully structured of all Bond's plays, and, for this reason, belies its own complexity. Unlike *The Bundle* or *The Worlds*, *The Fool* offers no individual or group of individuals who, seeking to understand the socioeconomic laws which govern their lives, clearly articulate the political thought of the play. Despite the historical distancing, its world is closer to that of *Saved* and *The Pope's Wedding*. In all three, the characters respond to situations in a distorted and painfully limited manner because their consciousnesses are so clearly shaped by material and economic forces outside their control. In those earlier plays, however, the meaning of events and their political implications not only remain outside the grasp of the characters, but tend to elude the audience as well—the initial response being that the two plays are exercises in naturalistic theatre, slices-of-life from a fragmented and alienated society. The political message of *The Fool*, on the other hand, appears to the audience by the end of the play as virtually self-evident. This clarity results from the way in which Bond structures scenes and presents relationships so that the actions and the analysis (comment upon the action) occur simultaneously.

The analysis Bond leads his audience to make falls into several distinct, though related, categories. The most obvious, and perhaps most important, is made through the central conflict of the play's plot. Using Clare's life as

[26] *Revolutions in Modern English Drama* (1972), p. 168.

an historically verifiable example, Bond examines the failure of an entire society by showing the contradiction between the positive and necessary activity of writing and the social conditions which make that activity impossible (art as marketable commodity vs. art as productive activity). Secondly, Bond shows how the relation between labour and capital is reproduced in the relation between artist and patron—a relation most vividly illustrated in the boxing match of Scene 5. By making a clear connection between mental and physical labour (and connecting the fate of Darkie to Clare's own), the cause of the artist is understood as the cause of the entire working class. Finally, by showing how Clare's psychology is socially constructed, Bond demonstrates how subjectivity itself is created by social conditions. Without this vital link, the depiction of Clare's madness remains an interesting but socially irrelevant phenomenon. But because the actions of the play so clearly reveal the socioeconomic laws of Clare's world (and our own), we are able to read both the causes of Clare's failure and the political comment of the play through the very images and distortions that will serve to illustrate Clare's insanity.

As the play changes in focus from the perspective of the community (emphasized in Part I) to that of the individual (emphasized in Part II), from objective conditions to subjective consequences, the audience shares Clare's personal experience of increasing enclosure and entrapment in a world over which he has no control. By the end of the play, Clare knows freedom, and with it, health, happiness and mental stability, only through its absence, a perceived lack which he fills with the image of a lost love. Silenced and reduced to the level of a kept animal, his very condition provides the necessary comment on the attitudes expressed by the characters who survive (Patty, Lord Milton, etc.). However, Bond manages to present the 'psychological truth' of Clare's situation in a way which provokes our sympathy without demanding identification. Our learning process is not the same as Clare's own. Unlike Shakespeare in *Bingo*, Clare never gives up hope in the play; but he is, after all, the fool of the play's title. In the eyes of society, his 'madness' grants him that distinction, but he is also a fool by virtue of his limited vision and inability to understand his historical situation. As Bond writes in a theatre-poem: 'Clare, you created illusions/And they destroy poets.'[27]

Given Bond's continued fascination with Shakespeare, however, we may be able to see an even more important function for the play's title. Bond takes up the figure of the Shakespearean fool, not as a romantic myth of the outcast, but as a way of historicizing the problem of the contemporary writer; and he reworks it in order to clarify the very causes of Clare's limitations. As a poet, Clare shares the artistic function of Shakespeare's court-employed fools. We remember these characters for their biting wit, facility with language and worldly wisdom; but their criticism is emasculated by their dependent relation to their patrons. In fact, they are granted immunity from censure by virtue of their role—whatever they say is unthreatening

[27] *The Fool* (New York, 1978), p. 84.

because it is by social definition untrue. What comes from the mouth of a fool must be foolish. So the way society views the function of art invariably determines its effect.

In Clare's society, artistic activity is similarly circumscribed by the tastes and attitudes of the paying public (see Clare's discussion with Lord Radstock in Scene 5), and Clare's very role as a poet becomes a measure of his lack of freedom. Moreover, it is only the poet Lamb who, in Scene 5, is able to see the truth of the situation; but the language he uses prevents him from being understood, and his role as an artist prevents him from being taken seriously. Hence, Mrs Emmerson's response:

> . . . I'm proud to say I didn't understand a single word. Mr Lamb, you're a poet. You have no call to go round putting ideas in people's heads . . .[28]

As the play progresses, Clare (like Lamb) comes to resemble the court-banished fools of Shakespeare's plays. Such a fool (we remember Lear's) invariably speaks the truth, despite the metaphoric and elliptical language he speaks. Patty, however, will accuse Clare of using a language totally inappropriate to their situation, with the implication that if he thought correctly he would speak differently. ('Oon't talk so daft. Talk straight so a body can hev a proper conversation. If you're on fire, you goo up in smoke . . . (etc.)').[29] Patty's reaction suggests that Clare's activity has served to isolate him from his community. But the language he speaks is also a measure of his developing self-consciousness, of a sensitivity that allows him better to understand and articulate the problems he shares with the villagers. Moreover, while the images that make their way into Clare's speech may confuse Patty, those same images, arising as they do from Clare's actual experiences in the play, make brutally literal sense to the audience.

Patty finally reads Clare's actions in terms of an individuality at odds with the general interests of the community (the same reading the upper classes offer). 'Self, allus self', is her complaint against Clare. However, within the society Bond describes in the play, only the characters sufficiently isolated from the community can come to represent the larger individual needs that the community cannot meet. In Scene 7, Mary, Darkie, the beaten boxer, the poet, and the actual experiences of hunger and physical pain become conflated in Clare's mind and lead to a vision which expresses both need and desire, real past and projected future:

> I dreamt I saw bread spat on the ground, and her say: Waste, I risk my life, (shakes his head) No. Birds on't waste. Thass on'y seed so you threw it on the ground. Birds hev it. Or that soak away. Bread goo from mouth t' mouth an' what it taste of: other mouths. Talkin' and laughin'. Thinkin' people. I wandered round an round. Where to? Here. An a blind man git here before me. The blind goo in a straight line. We should hev com t'gither. She git the bread. He crack the heads when they come after us.

[28] *Ibid.*, p. 43
[29] *Ibid.*, p. 56

Then she on't goo in rags. He on't blind. An' I—on't goo mad in a mad-house . . . .[30]

As isolated figures, the three are incapable of effecting the necessary changes in their society, but their very isolation impresses on us the need for change. Thus it is finally through the community's outcasts that the destructiveness of this society's social organization is presented—its inability to provide a fully human existence for any of its members.

With the elliptical, colloquial, non-symbolic poetry of Clare's speech, we return to the problem of the modern artist who, in order to 'tell the truth' and speak for a rational society that does not yet exist, must resist the conventional aesthetic discourse of his own historical moment. The problem, of course, is Bond's own; and perhaps we can see how Bond's dramatic strategies are a response to the postmodernist position of the writer, who, like Clare, would speak on behalf of his society, but finds himself in fundamental opposition to it.

[30] *Ibid.*, p. 73

Note

Little work has been done on the English Stage Company at the Royal Court since 1956, but the best accounts are Irving Wardle, *The Theatres of George Devine* (1978) and Marcus Tschudin, *A Writer's Theatre: George Devine and the English Stage Company at the Royal Court 1956-65 (Frankfurt, 1972)*. Also see John Russell Taylor, *Anger and After* (rev. ed., 1963) and Katherine Worth, *Revolutions in Modern English Drama* (1972).

Christopher Hampton was born in Fayal in the Azores in 1946 and was educated at Lancing College, Sussex, and then at New College, Oxford. His writing career began early, his first play, *When Did You Last See My Mother*, being written before he went up to Oxford. Understanding university authorities then allowed him to intercalate for a year, during which time he wrote his second play.

Hampton's plays are published by Faber and Faber: *When Did You Last See My Mother* (1967), *Total Eclipse* (1969), *The Philanthropist* (1970), *Savages* (1974), *Treats* (1976), *Able's Will* (1979).

There is as yet no full-length study of Hampton's work but a useful analysis is available in *Theatre Quarterly*, III, xii.

David Storey was born in Wakefield in 1933, the son of a miner. He was educated at Queen Elizabeth Grammar School, Wakefield, at the Wakefield Art School and at the Slade School of Fine Art, London, where he received a diploma in fine art. His first novel, *This Sporting Life*, appeared in 1960, a year after he had written his first play, *The Restoration of Arnold Middleton*. The latter was, however, not performed until 1967.

With the exception of *Mother's Day*, which is available in a Penguin collection of three Storey plays published in 1978, all of his work is published by Jonathan Cape: *The Restoration of Arnold Middleton* (1967), *In Celebration* (1969), *The Contractor* (1970), *Home* (1970), *The Changing Room* (1972), *Cromwell* (1973), *The Farm* (1973), *Life Class* (1975).

There is a useful pamphlet, *David Storey* (1974), by John Russell Taylor in the Writers and Their Work series. Both John Russell Taylor and Katherine Worth treat Storey's work in their general surveys quoted above and there is useful interview material in Ronald Hayman's *Playback* (1973)

John Arden was born in Barnsley, Yorkshire in 1930 and was educated at Sedbergh School and King's College, Cambridge. He received a diploma in architecture from the Edinburgh College of Art. He served as a lance-corporal in the Intelligence Corps from 1949-50.

With the exception of a Penguin collection called *Three Plays* (1964), which contains *The Waters of Babylon, Live Like Pigs* and *The Happy Haven*, and *The Non-Stop Connolly Show*, 5 vols (1977), published by Pluto Press, Arden's work is published by Methuen: *Sergeant Musgrave's Dance* (1959), *Armstrong's Last Goodnight* (1965), *Left-Handed Liberty* (1965), *The Workhouse Donkey* (1964), *Two Autobiographical Plays* (1971), containing *The True History of Squire Jonathan and His Unfortunate Treasure* and *The Bagman of Muswell Hill, The Island of the Mighty* (1974). Arden has also published a collection of essays, *To Present the Pretence* (1977).

The best critical study is Glenda Leeming's brief *John Arden* (1974) in the Writers and Their Work series. See also Ronald Hayman, *John Arden* (1968) and Albert Hunt, *John Arden: A Study of His Plays* (1974). Valuable articles are Robert V. Corrigan, 'The Theatre of John Arden', in his *The Theatre in Search of a Fix* (New York, 1973), Susan Shrapnel, 'John Arden and the Public Stage', *Cambridge Quarterly*, 4 (Summer, 1969), and Raymond Williams, in *Drama from Ibsen to Brecht* (1968).

VIII

The Court and its Favours

JULIAN HILTON

I

From the beginning George Devine's policy was to make the Royal Court a writers' theatre: 'Ours is not to be a producer's theatre or an actor's theatre; it is a writer's theatre.' (*New Statesman*, 24 March, 1956) He wanted the Court to achieve two things for the writer: firstly that his play be put on under the best possible conditions, a chance usually denied the new writer at the start of his career, secondly to provide the writer with a workshop where he can test his ideas, even serve an apprenticeship, under skilled supervision. From 1956 to his death in 1966, Devine worked to discover and help new writers and he more than any other single figure in recent British theatre history has been responsible for a growing awareness of the need to repair relations between writers and theatres. But it is arguable just how far in practice such a policy can be realized. How many writers can a single theatre support to the required standard? How do you cope with the highly charged relationships between author, text, director and actors when several productions are in rehearsal simultaneously?

In this chapter I shall be examining some of the work of John Arden, Christopher Hampton and David Storey. They form as diverse a group as one can imagine in modern British theatre yet have two things in common: they all started their careers as playwrights with the English Stage Society at the Court; and they are all concerned with the writer's place in society, a concern that perhaps stems in part from Devine's passionate commitment to the belief that a healthy state needs good theatres as much as good schools and hospitals.

II

Christopher Hampton
Like Devine himself, and indeed like Court directors Tony Richardson, William Gaskill and Lindsay Anderson, Christopher Hampton went to Oxford. After a most successful undergraduate career he began a happy relationship with the Court which culminated in his becoming its first official writer-in-residence. His duties were not new since they involved a large amount of script reading, which other writers like Arden had already done: but what was new was the official status, a measure of how far Devine's ideas had penetrated Arts Council thinking on how subsidized theatre should function. Hampton's work shows many signs of his intellectual origins in its various ways of dealing with the problem of the relationship between artists

and society. *When Did You Last See My Mother* (1966) has two school leavers waiting to go to Oxbridge; *The Philanthropist* (1970) presents the world to which they go; *Savages* (1973) contains a post-graduate student. In *Total Eclipse* (1969) the central figures are the artists Rimbaud and Verlaine; in *The Philanthropist* there is a playwright and a novelist. In *Savages*, West, the diplomat, is a poet and the whole Indian plot is conducted in a poetic mode. There is in both style and content a particular debt to the French dramatic tradition, which is perhaps not surprising in view of Hampton's modern language degree. This is clearest in his use of an epigraph from Molière's *Le Misanthrope* for *The Philanthropist*, whose tone and structure derive much from Molière.[1] But it is equally evident in his sense of drama as a medium of intellectual debate and exploration. Here the debt is both to modern writers like Sartre and the neoclassicism of Racine: Hampton draws from both an interest in purity of form and tightness of construction unusual in British drama. Most obviously this tightness expresses itself in his settings: these are nearly all interiors, some being literally small rooms, others small meta-phorically.[2] Social and intellectual dominance is reflected in the physical domination of that space. Ian drives Jimmy from their shared flat; Philip is left alone in his university rooms; Verlaine lives in his wife's parents' house and is smothered by its middle-class values. The feelings of constriction and claustrophobia reach their most extreme form in the cell in which West is kept by his kidnapper Carlos, in which he is murdered and from which Carlos emerges only to be shot. There are never many people in these cells or boxes, and they seem to be trapped in them, like Philip, the philanthropist, himself. But although the box is constraining, an image perhaps of the cramped state of the Western mind, it also seems to stimulate art in a classic Freudian manner. Energy compressed and suppressed by the West releases itself either in art or violence or, often, both, as key scenes in all the plays show. Escape from the box appears to mean the end of one's career as a writer: Rimbaud 'escapes' to the Middle East and runs guns (vicarious violence perhaps) but stops writing. All the plays show a tight, witty use of language and while there is little physical action there is much in the way of verbal battling to compensate.

When Did You Last See My Mother, staged while Hampton was still an undergraduate, and which, after two Sunday evening showings without decor, rapidly transferred to the West End, is a play founded on such con-finements. In it two adolescents, Ian and Jimmy, share a claustrophobic London flat, having previously shared a study at school. The action never leaves the room, and settles into a triangle of the two friends and Jimmy's mother, who sleeps with Ian as a substitute for her own son, whom she cannot reach. The tension clarifies the despair and contempt all three seem to feel, but the plot is schematic and psychologically unconvincing. But in any case Hampton is, however, not solely concerned with psychological

[1] Molière was in fact Hampton's special subject in his Oxford Finals. *Theatre Quarterly* Vol III no. 12 1973, p. 66

[2] I am indebted to my colleague Tony Frost for this observation, as indeed for many ideas which have emerged in discussion with him of the authors I describe.

naturalism, for the play also displays his preoccupation with theatre and theatricality, with fiction and fictionality. Ian, for example, tells in two forms a story about a lecture he has attended in Paris; the second account at the end of the play challenges the accuracy and truth of the first. The effect is theatrical and intellectual provocation, yet also an awkward but characteristic division in Hampton's attention, between naturalistic and fictionalist concerns. An apparently sincere emotional conflict is subverted by the new idea that one central character may be a pathological liar or an artist in manipulation; but we are then not sure how far to take our new awareness that truth in the play is in question.

The Philanthropist further develops this concern with challenging theatrical forms and conventions. If naturalist plays like Ivanov gradually build up to suicide, Hampton here chooses to begin with one. But not before a remarkable use of anti-climax, another device Hampton had already displayed in his earlier play. The play starts with John, an undergraduate, in Philip's college room with his tutor, aptly named Don. John appears to break down, pulls out a revolver, puts it in his mouth, pulls the trigger, and nothing happens. It is an apparent joke; John is in fact reading the last scene of his play about which Don and Philip are unenthusiastic. However as a result of Philip's well-meant but clumsy and cutting comments, John repeats the scene and this time literally blows his brains out. Since the revolver is the same one it is not clear if the act is intentional or not, but either way the scene is a tour de force generating a whole series of 'play-within-a-play' resonances. Like Ian's art-lecture story, a scene is presented, then represented with a different conclusion and the audience made to consider which of the layers of fiction, if any, is true. The parable is, however, taken a step further for at the very end of the play, when Philip has lost all his friends, he too takes out a revolver and puts it to his temple. As he pulls the trigger the gun becomes a cigarette lighter and the curtain falls (an anti-climax that surely cannot work off the page and must be seen).

Though most effective in performance, the intellectual problems this raises are similar to those in Ian's story. Does Philip lack the courage, or was his whole manner an act, an elaborate lie? Did he wish to 'experience' suicide or was he playing with the audience? Hampton does, in other words, exploit the naturalistic convention of the removed fourth wall for all it is worth, and yet appears at the end to suggest that the whole exercise has been one in which the audience has been consciously manipulated by the actors. We are led by the action and the whole psychological motivation to believe Philip must kill himself, which he does not do. We are not told whether or not his decision to go on living is an acceptance of the constraints working on him and a vision of their necessity. The danger is that the short-term theatrical effectiveness of the anti-climax reduces the whole play in the long run to the one proposition that theatre is a lie.

That Hampton does not believe this is true is surely indicated by his next play, Savages, where the parable or poetic element takes up half the plot. West, a minor diplomat and minor poet, is kidnapped by Brazilian terrorists; this story is then interwoven with legends drawn and adapted from the various rituals of the 'Quarup', an Indian festival of the dead that is linked closely with fertility rituals and seems to be offered as a model of a society where art, violence and sexuality are held in careful balance by ritual in a way now alien to Western man. It becomes evident that the savages are not the Indians but the speculators, the military governments, the well-meaning British and the urban terrorists. Both the kidnappers and the victim are trapped in their box and their only escape is death. Their constriction and oppression contrast strongly with the sunlight and space in which the Indians move, a concept hard to represent on stage, which is perhaps why, as Hampton indicates in his introduction, scenes were heavily cut for performance. The verse of the Indians is set off against the prose of the 'Westerners' but while the idea of some lost capacity to harmonize the forces of life as an answer to European problems is seductive (and given literal representation in West's poems) it does not come across as effectively as it might in view of the very strongly naturalistic presentation of a kidnap. West himself, and the West from which he comes, are in decline, boxed in and constricted. Even the constriction does not produce great art, though West does write in captivity and his death seems cruel if not particularly wasteful.

Once again Hampton cannot resist the ending that exposes all that we have seen as a lie. From the epigraph on, this time from Lévi-Strauss, and from his own passionate introduction about one of the great scandals of our time, we are invited to respond, both intellectually and emotionally, to the plight of the Indians, and quite rightly so. Then we learn at the end that more babies die in the slums of Brazil each year than all the Indians ever killed. Why, then, all the fuss about the Indians if their problems are relatively unimportant? And after all, according to Hampton, the Indians know better than the West how to live and die, and so should be better able to handle suffering than we.

Total Eclipse, Hampton's earlier and perhaps best play, deals with the relationship between two poets, Rimbaud and Verlaine, both of whom stopped writing; and does so in a way both satisfying as a character study and stimulating in the symbolic acts and gestures he uses to structure the work. The central themes are again art, violence and sexuality, and again all three are determined by constricting spaces: the elaborate French drawing room with its smotheringly bourgeois atmosphere, the seedy London lodging room, the Belgian prison; and the sequence is a neat downward progression. Violence is confined to a few moments but is the more powerful for being so: Verlaine punches his pregnant wife, and later shoots Rimbaud. Rimbaud responds in perhaps the most effective of all Hampton's uses of the dramatically repeated gesture. He comes into a cafe where Verlaine is drinking and cuts Verlaine's palms with a knife. At the very end he returns in a dream to Verlaine and, taking his hands, appears to be going to slash them again. Instead he kisses them with a delicacy that is both moving and brilliantly theatrical.

The key intellectual issue is why one writes and why one stops writing. The answer for Verlaine seems relatively simple: he is bought up by the French middle class, made respectable, and given enough money for absinthe, so that he does not need to struggle and hence to write. His resistance to this smothering by comfort takes the form of odd violent outbursts, as we have seen, but it is also expressed in his initial invitation to the young Rimbaud, whom he had never met, to visit Paris. Rimbaud confronts him with the need to choose between sexual and financial ease and struggle, an opposition perhaps a little oversimplified but nevertheless crucial to the artist, perhaps even more so now in the days of pension funds and the welfare state. The more Verlaine drinks, the less he can write, but he needs drink to quiet his conscience about not writing. Rimbaud's case is more complex, in that his art is more an act of exuberance, a channelling of his rich sexuality and violent temper into taut and intense form. He is not seduced by luxury, though he is perhaps unduly impressed for a while by Parisian bohemian life. But most obviously his life is a kind of art, of which writing is no more significant a part than making love or gun running. He stops because he no longer wants to write and it does not cause him the soul searching it causes Verlaine.

Rimbaud's returning to kiss Verlaine's palms is an unusually hopeful and conciliatory gesture for Hampton and is the one instance in his work where expectation is reversed without risking a violation of the coherence of form. It seems a pity there is not more of this hope in his other work—not hope for its own sake, but as a challenge to the mind apparently exhausted by the constrictions of its own limits; a mind so many of his central characters share.

III

David Storey

One of Devine's hopes was that writers whose social and educational background had not given them the entrée to the West End theatre world might be found and promoted by the Court. As it happens, Osborne, the first major Court discovery, was one such man, but there have been very few others. David Storey, whose life on leaving school was split between professional rugby league and the Slade, was perhaps cast in this mould, but he, like many of the very early writers for the Court (e.g. Angus Wilson), came to it as an established novelist. More important, however, was the fact that it was Lindsay Anderson, who had been asked to direct the film of *This Sporting Life*, who brought Storey to the Court and subsequently directed most of his plays there. It is of course hard to assess the exact contribution made by a director in a long and fruitful working partnership like Storey's with Anderson, but the fact of the partnership (like Gaskill's with Bond or Hall's with Pinter) is vital both to an understanding of the workshop process in action at the Court and to an appreciation of Devine's philosophy of production as an ensemble activity, in which the writer was to be both a partner, and to some extent an amanuensis, to what is created in rehearsal.

It is perhaps too neat to see the rugby player and the artist at conflict in Storey, and that conflict expressing itself in writing: but Storey's interest in Nietzsche's early views, as expressed in *The Birth of Tragedy*, on tragic drama as the synthesis of Apollonian and Dionysian forces—forces of lyricism and linguistic creativity on the one hand against those of ecstatic movement on the other—does suggest that one of the keys to understanding his highly distinctive blend of the poetic and the naturalistic, and his concern for communal acts of a physical kind (team games or erecting tents), lies in the Nietzschean model. Nietzsche, unlike Freud, places the study of dreams in the Apollonian, conscious and rational part of the mind. The mind has the job of recovering and contemplating dream images which, if rightly interpreted, explain our actions and desires. Many of Storey's protagonists engage in this contemplative activity, though many do come increasingly to realize that in the process they have become alienated from society and from their families. Arnold Middleton, Steven, Reardon, Jack, Harry, Allott, all contemplate, but some have already gone mad in the process, and others are close to it. Against them are set those whose response is more physical and intuitive, father Shaw and his son Colin, the contractor Ewbank, and many of the team in *The Changing Room*. In all cases a study of behaviour is located within the Nietzschean, and ultimately Feuerbachian, vision of identity as being established through sexual, family and kinship ties, where the individual expresses himself in and through membership of, and loss of self in, a larger 'communitas': indeed, he derives his nature from it.

There are in fact very few individuals in Storey's plays, but rather families or teams. The rooms in which they are shown are family spaces, like drawing-rooms, or shared spaces, like a changing-room, full of a continuous history of that group and its ancestors. Generations are frequently in conflict and the plays deal mostly with liminal moments in family evolution: marriages, anniversaries, home-comings after long absence and the upheavals associated with them. These respond well to simultaneous treatment on a naturalistic and a poetic level, and Storey's use of complex metaphors, like the erection and dismantling of a tent, do invite one to contemplation in the Apollonian manner. But the Dionysian side is equally important and indicates how difficult it is to recover Storey's meanings fully without seeing his plays staged. The contractor's gang, the rugby team, the life class and all the family gatherings bring relatively large numbers of actors onto the stage at once. As the characters they portray know each other well the dialogue between them is by no means confined to the verbal. Groups like rugby teams and working gangs develop, as a matter of course, close physical cooperation and their dialogue, like their threats, is as often physical as verbal. There is no way this sense of the simultaneity of words and actions and the complexity of meaning created in this way can be recovered from the page. This is perfectly consistent with the Nietzschean scheme: societal movement is Dionysian and must be witnessed and ideally participated in to be understood.

With the exception of *Arnold Middleton* (1967), we do not see the celebrations around which the early plays are set. Middleton is waiting for the return of his parents after ten years and throws a party, a 'celebration', the day before their arrival. Their telegram to say they will not after all be coming triggers a breakdown in him. In *In Celebration* (1969) the Shaws are celebrating their fortieth wedding anniversary and their three sons have returned home, curiously without their wives. The celebration is dinner at the top local hotel, but this occurs off stage. In *The Contractor* (1970) Ewbank's daughter is getting married, but we do not actually see the wedding or the reception that is held in the tent. In *The Changing Room* (197 –) the main action of the play, the rugby game, goes on throughout, but is of course never seen. The result is that one is forced by Storey into considering why he so deliberately and often presents, as it were, the two outside panels of a triptych, but consciously removes the middle. The answer in part lies in the fact that he is shifting our attention from the 'rites' and 'celebrations' to the preparation for and the reactions to them, which in fact reveal more of the truth than the events themselves. But in part the structure derives from the logic of the Nietzschean model: the actual celebrations are Dionysian and therefore 'abstract', like music, or beyond memory, like acts committed in drunken ecstasy. The artist knows these forces and is inspired by them, but does not, indeed cannot, describe them as they are an intrinsic part of life. His job is rather to recover images for contemplation from those areas of experience that operate on the conscious rather than unconscious mind; that is, the 'before' and 'after' of familiar and societal ecstasies.

In this context the settings all have emblematic significance; the family sitting room becomes a sort of museum of family history, the store place of family wisdom. Articles in it, the typical knick-knacks, are all rich in association. A tent becomes, in its newness and size, both a huge extension of the white bridal gown and an image of 'communitas', a womb, even, that bears a newly formed family. The intense scrutiny of family objects and the endless retelling of family history that always characterizes such events is also not that far removed from the process of investigation of the model in *Life Class*—and, as its title suggests, in that play Storey makes explicit the implication in his other works that everyone is an artist to the extent that he creates his own identity through contemplation of his past, at vital moments reassessing and even reshaping it. It is, however, a frequently violent process. Middleton breaks down, as do, however briefly, most of the Shaw family, Violence is never far from the surface in *The Contractor*, though it is always controlled, for Storey makes it clear from his comments on *In Celebration* that he does not see any particular need to show violence as it is always present:

> In a way the explosion has already taken place, off or outside or away, and this is really the aftermath of battle. If you compare it with Ibsen in terms of approaching emotional realities, Ibsen is writing about what happened before the explosion: the bomb is festering away inside, and it does go off. *In Celebration* is after the bomb has shown what it can do. (*Drama*, Spring 1971)

Storey's own choice of violent images suggests a turbulent mind, as does his use of the rather strange character Reardon in *In Celebration*, whose apocalyptic visions of a whole world burning seem oddly incompatible with the tense but far from cataclysmic Shaw family row. Despite the upheavals

and visions there are no deaths, few serious fights and the plays end tran-
quilly if somewhat depressed or dazed in mood. In other words, the Nietzschean logic, and indeed Storey's own description of the violence of the
human condition, is not carried through to its necessarily destructive conclusion. For Storey, compromise and resignation are always possible, and
when Allott, the artist of *Life Class*, is confronted with the notion that art
may be destructive he appears with his ironizing 'they tell me', to retreat
from the consequences: 'Violation, they tell me, is a prerequisite of art . . .
disruption of prevailing values . . . reintegration in another form entirely.'
(p. 89) The 'other form' is perhaps here the novel, Storey's other strength;
but in none of his plays does he go through with the complete restructuring
of experience and personality that his Nietzschean view of art suggests.
Instead he closes the play with a question about the role of the artist not
through Allott's mouth but through that of his pupil Saunders: 'Perhaps
there isn't a role left for the artist . . . perhaps in an egalitarian society—
so-called—an artist is a liability . . . after all he's an individual: he tells you
by his gifts alone that all people can't be equal . . .'. (pp. 48-9) The artist
emerges then from this 'life-class' as an Übermensch, a superior being by
virtue of his art—a view that clearly conflicts with Storey's concern for social
class, which is for him one of the chief causes of alienation in society. In *In
Celebration*, for example, one of the chief tensions between the parents is
that the mother is from the middle class and the father is a working-class
miner. The family, therefore, is divided and uncertain about which class it
belongs to. Ewbank, the contractor, is rich and an employer, but still working class; while his daughter, who is marrying a doctor, and his university
educated son are clearly middle class in their attitudes. In *The Changing
Room*, there is a less obvious class pattern, but a very clear metaphor of the
alienation between labour and capital: the owner of the team has never
watched a game in his life, yet exercises close control over his men. In its
most extreme form the alienation of labour is expressed in the character
Harry, whose whole life is the changing room but who has never in his life
seen a game, the fruits of his labour. But in *Life Class* Storey himself is
brought up against the central dilemma of the egalitarian socialist artist. The
artist's talents are not ones in which all can share; they are not widely accessible even with the best educational opportunities.

In *Home* the Storey-Anderson partnership perhaps reached its peak, for
with Ralph Richardson and John Gielgud taking the lead roles the work had
the optimum performance conditions Devine would have wished for it. Set
in a mental hospital, where problems of class and of socialist realism are less
obviously important than in studies of coal miners, it achieves, especially in
the superb first act, a remarkable blend of wit, Beckett-like lapidary dialogue
and pathos:

Jack: Nice to see the sun again.
Harry: Very.
Jack: Been laid up for a few days.
Harry: Oh dear.

Jack: Chill. In bed.
Harry: Oh dear. Still . . . appreciate the comforts.
Jack: What? . . . You're right. Still . . . Nice to be out.
Harry: 'Tis. (p. 10)

For a long time it is not clear that the play is set in an asylum, and it perhaps loses when the setting is made explicit. But here, as indeed everywhere in Storey's plays, the central problem is one of communication, parents with children, bosses with men, teachers with pupils and, as here, people with themselves. Crises are provoked by broken communications consequent on the lack of a common language through which to talk and release aggression. This is why each man must in some degree be an artist, and above all one in language, for it is through language we define ourselves and what we see and experience about us. Nowhere is the failure of communication put more clearly than in an exchange from *Home,* structured like a typical two-man comic routine joke and yet as sharply ironic as anything in Storey's dialogue:

Kathleen: I don't know what you're saying half the time. You realize that.
Harry: Communication is a difficult factor.
Kathleen: Say that again. (p. 56)

Kathleen's reply is beautifully poised between her own inability to listen ('Say that again') and what could be an abbreviated form of affirmation ('You can say that again'). In its ambiguity and its sharpness the exchange reflects a delicacy in much of Storey's work that his comments about bombs and violence would seem to belie.

IV

John Arden

The range of John Arden's writing over twenty-five years is remarkable. He has written for major professional companies and the most inexperienced of amateurs, for the stage, television and radio; his style can be fiercely polemical and politically engaged, but also quiet and reflective, charged with metaphysical conceits; and he has explored a wide spectrum of staging techniques. His achievement is not, however, simply one of range, for in all his work there is that essential quality of critical self-appraisal that has kept his writing consistently fertile and challenging. In concluding his 1968 description of Arden's plays, Ronald Hayman lamented the fact that Arden had not by then found a company with which to work regularly, something he felt would not only have greatly enriched our national theatre but also been of benefit to Arden himself. Certainly when one considers the development of playwrights like Shakespeare, Molière and Brecht, this regular association with a single company seems of great benefit. Yet at the same time it may be that one source of Arden's inventiveness lies in the fact that, through his long-standing conflict with the theatre establishment, he has had to improvise and has never been able to rely on efficient professional staging to cover any deficiencies in his conceptions.

Strictly speaking, perhaps only three plays properly belong to a study of

Court writing: *The Waters of Babylon*, (1957) *Live Like Pigs* (1958) and *Sergeant Musgrave's Dance* (1959): A fourth, *The Happy Haven*, (1960) first produced at Bristol University during a writing fellowship there, came to the Court; and *The Workhouse Donkey*, (1963), which started off as a Court commission but was actually first seen at Chichester, may be counted a possible fifth. But while Arden's physical association with the Court ended in 1960, he—perhaps more than any other of Devine's initial circle of writers —has remained true to Devine's idea of the theatre as a workshop. In the Court plays one can see how Arden lays out the ground for his subsequent work, for certain early preoccupations have remained at the forefront of his mind. Yet then, as since, the main purpose of his plays has been to ask questions, not to answer them, and where answers have been offered for the most part they are tentative and formulated as yet further questions. This does not mean, however, that Arden is stuck in an intellectual treadmill, for one of the most exciting aspects of his *Non-Stop Connolly Show* (1975)—a cycle of six plays about the Irish labour leader Jim Connolly—is the way Arden's conviction that one of the fundamental 'answers' lies in the dialectical nature of history, moving towards the inevitable triumph of the oppressed over the oppressor, informs the whole cycle with immense energy:

> We were the first to feel their loaded gun
> That would prevent us doing it any more—
> Or so they hope. We were the first. We shall not be the last
> This was not history. It has not passed. (No. 6, p. 106)

These words, which close the work, indicate the most important single theme in Arden's writing—the pursuit of what Ernst Bloch characterizes as *das Prinzip Hoffnung*, the principle of hope and optimism. This is not the glib socialist realist aesthetic that demands bright enthusiastic heroes of the revolution, free from doubts and thoughts of material prosperity, but a hard-won formulation of a moral, political and intellectual strategy of hope. Where Arden differs from the logic of Bloch's thought is that while Bloch's utopias must be presented in 'concrete' and naturalistic shape, Arden's are accessible more through metaphor and implication.

Arden's background and education are in many respects a mixture of Hampton's and Storey's: born in Barnsley in 1930, he has in several of his plays drawn on his knowledge of life in the northeast. The sorts of community and politics he encountered there form the core of his long internal debate on the function of such closed societies and the role of artist and thinker within them. Equally important, however, was his university experience as a student of architecture, an art form which one might characterize as the art of applied ideas. Arden also sees applied ideas as the chief purpose of theatre, an aim he shares with Brecht: 'We would emphasize finally that the play will work only if the actors are more concerned with undertaking the political arguments and implications of the story than with "creating character" in the normal theatrical sense.' This sort of statement, in fact part of the introduction to the *Non-Stop Connolly Show*, might well be taken as a general comment on how to approach Arden's work. Equally important, however, is his commitment to the business of writing itself, and this he owes to some extent to Devine. It was Devine who 'rescued' him from a career as an architect and had faith enough in his work to allow it to lose large sums of money. It was his 'writer's pass', Devine's system of allowing his writers access to the theatre at all times, that Arden counted his first great present in life:

> The other was a job reading manuscripts at a flat rate of a bob a script. I was accordingly able to leave the architect's office I was working in and spend all my time in or around a theatre. The point is that the theatre had come out and asked me in. I don't suppose I would have ever really got going as a proper playwright if this had not happened. [3]

Not only therefore was the invitation to the Court of great significance to him, but the close and regular contact with it developed him as a writer. Arden is often concerned with reflective men, whose thoughts, however inarticulate, lead them to some sort of action. Arden's suspicion of intellectuals persists to this day, so it is important to see that thought is not necessarily for him the clear and logical activity required of the trained mind. Rather, men like Musgrave work, sometimes grope, through a mixture of images and intuitions towards some truth which, when they face it, they may baulk or not even recognize. The intellectuals, like Blomax in *The Workhouse Donkey*, David Lindsay in *Armstrong's Last Goodnight* (1964), and the poet himself in *The Bagman* (1971), all in some way discover the inadequacies of thought as compared with action, and the men of action like Musgrave, Butterfield, and King John, are portrayed as much more likeable and sincere if misguided or deluded men. The common pursuit of all these character studies is, however, towards a man who is both intellectually committed and capable of translating thought into action, and these virtues are united in Jim Connolly, who, like Lenin, could not only write a socialist paper but also fight for the cause. Connolly in fact loses his life for it, but in a way that gives Arden grounds for optimism.

Just how hard-won the optimism was is shown by the prevailing sense of disappointment in opportunities lost that all four Court plays have in common. Each one contains a number of figures who seem at first to be successful or wise or who have a message that is irresistible, but each one ends with the social, psychological or intellectual failure of their hopes and the sense that a vision of a better world embedded in the plays, is for the time being lost. Even in *Connolly* in fact the vision is apparently lost, but what is gained is the hope that the struggle is worthwhile. In *The Waters of Babylon*, the central figure, Krank, is a rapacious landlord, exploiter of his friends and veteran of a concentration camp extermination squad. As his German name suggests, his devious mind is sick, but not in a way that enables one to dismiss him as mad: rather his cynicism confronts us with a question. Throughout the play he has promised to reveal who he is, like the villain of some melodrama; but in the end he does not:

So many thousands of people

In so large a cold field.
How did they get into it?
And what did they expect to find? (pp. 96-7)

The cold field, with its suggestions of concentration camps, its echoes of the storm scenes in *Lear* and feeling that it represents the total world, is a typically complex image: and the closing question, echoing Christ talking to the disciples of John the Baptist, then turns attention from the 'many thousands' back to the individual, who must, like John the Baptist, ultimately make up his own mind as to what he believes. The agony and loneliness of having to make a decision can only be borne if balanced by the overriding principle that allows one to hope one is acting for the best.

Live Like Pigs is similarly rich in complex images, the most important of which are generated by the setting, the rooms of a council house, and not the spoken text. The Sawneys are a problem family, moved into a well cared-for council estate in an attempt, through improving their living conditions, to make them conform socially. The experiment is a disaster, and they finally flee the house before the enraged neighbours set fire to it, hoping to burn them all. (The play has assumed an oddly prophetic note as three children were recently burned to death on a council estate for similar reasons.) But while it has a naturalistic aspect, dealing with the difficulties of such social engineering, its metaphors yield other kinds of meaning, ones located in particular rooms of the house, which, rather like Storey's rooms, assume emblematic force. The living room is the social space, the place of meeting and conflict; the bedroom represents sexuality, feverishness and death. The stairs are not only the link between these experiences but also a place where the Sawneys drink. The bathroom, with its image of flowing water, represents both plenty and a profusion which becomes so rich as to overwhelm and drown this menace. The Sailor feels and articulates this menace as the neighbours close in at the end:

> You don't know this bastardy-like folk like I do. I've lived longer girl so listen. Aye, Aye, they live inside their hutches their houses and all. And they don't fight strong. But when they're out and calling you out, they don't run home soon, neither. They're in their crowd and they'll swarm you and drown. (p. 175)

Here again the meanings are complex and even contradictory. The British middle classes, or the respectable working class, will, if provoked long enough, rouse themselves to fight and engulf their enemies. But in the tone there is both admiration for the spirit that defeated Hitler as well as dismay at the rejection of the Sawneys.

By far the best known play of this group is *Sergeant Musgrave's Dance*, produced in 1959. Like much of Adren's work, however, it appears to contain within it two contradictory styles and points of view. On the one hand, there is the real possibility that Musgrave's plan to hold a town to ransom with a new and dangerous weapon will work, will in fact spark off some sort of revolution among the disaffected colliers of the town. After all, it is no more absurd a prospect than a group of Bolsheviks declaring themselves to be the new rulers of Russia in October 1917 with little more support than Musgrave had to muster. On the other hand, Musgrave's failure to capitalize on the situation he creates seems both to confirm the elderly Marx's pessimism about the time-scale for the coming revolution, and also to demonstrate how thought—in this case Musgrave's sudden awareness of the ambiguity of violence—prevents action. In one sense this is a reflection of Arden's desire to be intellectually fair, to show both sides of the case: in another, it is simply being honest to history. Here he is most obviously at odds with socialist realist aesthetics, which would demand some sort of triumphant vision of success from Musgrave rather than the bewildered steps towards the gallows which close the play. But he also refuses to simplify issues in a way demanded by socialist realism: when at the end of the play Musgrave is hesitating it is not because his anger evaporates or his vision of the evils of imperialist capitalism in any way diminishes but because he cannot be sure that those people he has lined up in front of his gun are guilty of creating such a system. Are they not also innocents, like Billy Hicks whose skeleton he has displayed above the market place? This is just the difficulty Marx had to face, for it is the fact that in a revolution it is invariably the oppressed who suffer most, which places severè moral constraints on any would-be revolutionary. The resolution of the play's opposed views lies in a strong implicit demand for pacific protest. Musgrave's gun, pointed, as it is, not just at the on-stage audience but at the auditorium, must suggest immense destructive potential, even nuclear threat. What holds Musgrave's hand at the end is a vision that, once started, violence would destroy the whole race, a perception that the glorious societal recruiting dance of the middle of the play is only the first movement in a dance that ends in death. This is, then, a weakness in Nietzsche's idealized vision of the Dionysian ecstasy-destroying self, that it has, built within it, loss of control, surrender of moral values, of the sort that overtook fascist Europe in the 1930s and led to the Second World War.

Early critical incomprehension of *Musgrave* stemmed largely, however, from its mixture of styles—seen as a fault in the first two plays as well. What appears to be a naturalistic work about soldiers and colliers is also a poetic dance of death, and a series of political statements about imperialism. All these themes have their commensurate linguistic registers—plain north-country dialect for the colliers contemplating strike action, Musgrave's rich imagery and Sparky's haunting songs—but none of these on its own seems to offer a complete picture. Arden's answer, of course, was that he was not attempting any unity, that the whole point of his experiment lay in the diversity of theme and language and the tensions that engendered and for this very reason he achieves the Brechtian ideal of getting his audiences to think about his ideas rather than about his characters.

Though *Musgrave* was actually the last wholly Court piece, his next major work, *The Workhouse Donkey*, started off as a Court commission. The idea was

for the audience to come and go throughout the performance, assisted perhaps by a printed synopsis of the play from which they could deduce those scenes or episodes which would interest them particularly, and those they could afford to miss. A theatre presenting such an entertainment would, of course, need to offer rival attractions as well and would in fact take on some of the characteristics of a fairground or park. (p. 8)

The constraints of the Chichester festival stage and resources, the demands of the Lord Chamberlain and Arden's own problems made the final version, both as performed and published, remote from the original drafts but it does point to the essential difficulty about Arden's work as published, that so much of its effect depends on the staging, the use of scenery, costume, props, of music and dance that the printed text can at best be only an indication of what the theatrical experience is like. In this he shows himself closest to one of the major influences on him, Ben Jonson, and in particular Jonson's *Bartholomew Fair*. One of the decisive experiences for Arden was, by his own account in *To Present the Pretence*, the 1950 Edinburgh festival production by George Devine of *Bartholomew Fair*: 'the main impression I retain is of having actually *been at a fair* (rather than having seen a play about some fictional people at a fair) . . .'[4] The writer himself is a craftsman come to sell his wares like any other skilled artisan. The importance of this for an understanding of Arden's political attitude is that writing for the stage is seen as a pre-capitalist form of labour: the worker is not alienated from the product of his labour but remains in contact with it from conception to execution.

Set, like *Musgrave*, in the north, in a tight, 'closed', community, *The Workhouse Donkey* describes the fall of ex-mayor Charlie Butterthwaite from 'Napoleon' of the town to an outcast. The agent of the fall is the 'intellectual' Colonel Feng, the new head of police whose uncompromisingly strict sense of public morality leads to his own fall as well, leaving the field clear for the capitalists to regain control of the town they had lost. In a sense, Butterthwaite is like Musgrave, and his grip on the local community an indication of where Musgrave might have reached had he been more decisive.

The scene which focuses the play's problems comes when Butterthwaite, deeply in debt to his machiavellian adviser, Dr Blomax, decides to steal the outstanding money from the council safe. In naturalistic terms this is not that plausible a move for an astute politician, though it does reveal Butterthwaite's arrogance reaching maniacal proportions; much more important is the information it offers about Arden's nature as a writer, one which is both Jonsonian and Swiftian. The artist's role is to be the conscience of society, a thorn in the flesh: he is both caustic and scurrilous; he may opt for simultaneous use of naturalistic and imagistic modes, a technique one finds in *Gulliver's Travels*. Indeed the image of the donkey itself has both these levels, as Butterthwaite's song makes clear:

Oh what a shock, I nearly died,
I saw my ears as small as these,
Two feet, two hands, a pair of knees,

[4] *To Present the Pretence* p. 32

My eyeballs jumped from side to side,
I jumped right round. I bawled out loud,
You lousy liars, I've found you out!
I know now why you're fleeing . . .
I am no donkey never was,
I'm a naked human being. (p. 99)

Like Krank's closing questions, Butterthwaite's song is rich and resonant. The sudden shock of recognition is structurally presented like a conceit, whose force, as Donne said, was left to the 'shutting up'. It is also a similar shock to the one Gulliver tries to ward off when he begins to sense that he too is a Yahoo, though Arden's optimism makes him see the recognition as a positive acceptance of being human in a way Gulliver always resists. But the resonances are also tragic, in the fulfilling sense of tragedy that Nietzsche identifies in Oedipus's question 'who am I?' The point of the tragic experience is to make everyone ask who he is: but where Nietzsche's answer is aesthetic, 'I am my art', Arden's is more political, 'I'm a naked human being'. All privilege and class advantage is, in other words, a fiction of the rich.

Arden's concern with the writer's role in society comes to a head in two works stemming from the late 1960s, *The Bagman*, his short and intensely personal radio play, and the huge cycle of three plays grouped under the heading, *The Island of the Mighty* (1974). The total failure of relations between Arden and the Royal Shakespeare Company over the latter led to Arden and Margaretta D'Arcy picketing the production as a result of what they saw as a recreation of the idea, by the director, in a spirit totally alien to their conception. The Ardens give their side of the story at some length in *To Present the Pretence* (1977) which, apart from anything else, shows just how important to Arden's sense of his work the precise details of staging are. But the whole episode marks what was perhaps the lowest point in his dealings with the 'Establishment'. The plays themselves explore, through the Arthurian legends in their early Celtic form, the relations between the artist and poet (like Merlin) and the state. Merlin is brilliant but dishonest, and his dishonesty leads him to disaster and madness. While one cannot read a precise psychogram from this, there is no doubt that Arden puts much of himself into Merlin, arguing with himself over whether the poet should have a place in society or be locked in a cave like Merlin; and, if he should have a place, whether it is right that he play conscience to the state. Much tauter, and more incisive, is his analogous analysis of the same issues in *The Bagman*, a first-person narrative poem where Arden has a brief experience of the sort of encounters Swift created for Gulliver.

Once again the mood is one of Oedipal questioning: who am I? If I am my art, what will people make of it?

If on this soggy Thursday, I should fall down dead,
What of my life and death would then be said?
'He covered sheets of paper with his babble,
He covered yards of stage-cloth with invented people,

He worked alone for years yet was not able
To chase a little rat from underneath the table.' (pp. 37-8)

Arden falls asleep and in a dream buys a mysterious bag from an old crone.
In the bag are figures who perform, without prompting, exactly what their
audiences wish to see. The people want hints of revolution, but only hints:
the nobility want sex-shows, and new ones every night. This is of course a
well deserved attack on the staple diet of West End audiences, but it also
raises questions directed at himself. These come to a head when he is kidnapped in the dream by terrorists. When he opens the bag for the figures to
perform they refuse, knowing that:

Men of war do not require
To see themselves in a truthful mirror
All that they need to spur them to action
Is their own most bloody reflection
In the white eyeballs of their fire. (p. 86)

The moral, therefore, for the writer is to *do* more, and yet also to realize that
writing is, if rightly approached, an act as well. The writer is as able to fight
for the cause as the man of action because writing is action. Out of this realization grew the Connolly cycle.

The première of the *Non-Stop Connolly Show* took place in Dublin over
Easter 1975, in celebration of the anniversary of the 1916 rising. A further
measure of the extent of the breach between Arden and the 'Establishment'
was the fact that the event passed almost unnoticed and the plays—despite
being perhaps the single most impressive achievement of the British theatre
in the 70s—are still unknown. There are six in all, based around the life of
Jim Connolly, his talents as thinker and organizer of labour, his trip to
America, his contacts with international socialism and his martyr's death at
the hands of the British government. The style is a remarkable blend of
melodrama, living newspaper, political propaganda and music hall, all
bound up in an historical sweep of world-historical proportions. Connolly
himself may not be the Hegelian figure who moves history, but the issues
which he symbolizes are. His adversary, the all-purpose pantomime villain,
is the capitalist Grabitall, but the melodramatic shape he is given intensifies
rather than diminishes his menace. The show is avowedly emblematic,
requiring: 'stylized, easily changed, strongly-defined costumes and possibly
stock masks for recurrent social types'.

The success of the work depends substantially on two factors, Connolly
himself, and the staging. In Connolly, Arden for the first time chose a
protagonist who was writer and thinker and a man of action, and also one
whose conduct he could endorse: as such, he grew directly out of the conclusions Arden had drawn from *The Bagman*, a writer whose words were also
deeds. Connolly also has the Bagman's power to look at himself with witty
detachment; he returns home one day after selling newspapers in the cold
and explains that to be an activist 'you must wear woollen gloves upon each
fist.' (n. 2 p. 49) This double aspect to the joke reflects Arden's confidence

in his hero: even the most fiery activist needs woollen gloves to keep warm, but also to soften the blow to their adversary. It is as if the violent solution that Musgrave contempleted is here finally rejected.

The staging has much in common with rapid cross-cutting techniques of film. Characters come and go quickly and are usually only figuratively represented. This places great demands on the actors, of course, not least on their stamina: but more importantly it captures the feeling of history being made. It suggests an uncanny feeling that fragmentation and myriad-mindedness offer a truer reflection of how the individual experiences history than any great holistic theory: and yet, through the vision of men like Connolly, the organizing principle can be glimpsed. Here perhaps is the role of the artist, and one that seems almost Aristotelian in concept: the artist can organize, recreate and represent history in a way that makes us realize that history is not safely located in the past. Because what Connolly was trying to do still has to be done, he is not past. The artist sees this truth and finds a way to present it. The key difference between Aristotle's and Arden's view of the artist lies, however, in their understanding of what type of experience he examines. Oedipus is a man on his own, and the questions he asks emphasize his individuality and particularity. True, he stands metaphorically for us all, but he is still an individual. Connolly, by contrast, is a product of a particular society, and what is shown is not his individual efforts but the society he is trying to reform. Where Aristotle sees poetry as embracing and containing history, Arden sees only the immediacy of history and its specificity. This is why it is 'non-stop', a structural rejection of the Aristotelian principles of 'beginning, middle and end' in favour of the continuing movement of history.

V

Even though early critics were puzzled by Arden, they recognized that whatever he did he took them along with him. This is still true, for Arden has the great writer's ability to demand of his reader or audience that he listen, even when his tale appears as erratic and bewildering as the Ancient Mariner's. Arden has not created a character more striking than Musgrave, but that is largely because Musgrave was the last *character* in a naturalistic sense that he tried to create—and even then character was only part of the purpose. But that is perhaps one major reason why Arden is still known essentially for one play. British audiences, with the same suspicion of 'ideas' in art that enraged Mathew Arnold, resist what they feel may be the preacher in Arden. Storey and Hampton, by contrast, who do appear to create characters, have as a result fared rather better than Arden in terms of popular esteem, because for all their interest in stylistic experiments and in breaking naturalistic modes of writing still they use naturalism enough for audiences not to feel bewildered or insulted. Arden is not the first writer this century to write in exile, and exile does contribute some of the passion with which he writes. Yet it would be a great day for British theatre in the 1980s if another George Devine could be found to go out and ask Arden back into his theatre.

Note

Though political theatre covers a large part of contemporary British drama, many of the standard works—John Elsom's *Post-War British Theatre* (1976) or Kenneth Hurren's *Theatre Inside and Out* (1977)—hardly refer to it. Peter Ansorge's *Disrupting the Spectacle* (1975) is a notable exception; and the topic is dealt with extensively in my own book—however in German—*Das englische Theater der Gegenwart* (Düsseldorf, 1980). Catherine Itzin's book *Political Theatre* (1980) fills a gap; also see *Theatre Quarterly* and *Gambit*.

John McGrath was born in Birkenhead, Cheshire in 1935. He was educated at St John's College, Oxford and was conscripted into the army in 1953. His first play, *A Man Has Two Fathers*, was produced at Oxford in 1958. He subsequently worked for the BBC where he created *Z-Cars*, an attempt to create a realistic series based on the police force in a northwestern town. He has directed films and television programmes and was the founder of the 7:84 theatre company.

His plays have been published by a number of different companies: *Events While Guarding the Bofors Gun*, Methuen (1966); *Bakke's Night of Fame*, Davis Poynter (1968); *Random Happenings in the Hebrides, or, The Social Democrat and the Stormy Sea*, Davis Poyntery (1972); *The Fish in the Sea*, Pluto Press (1977); *The Cheviot, The Stag and the Black, Black Oil*, West Highland Publishing Company (1974); *The Game's a Bogey*, EUSPB (1975); *Little Red Hen*, Pluto Press (1977); *Yobbo Nowt*, Pluto Press (1978).

Caryl Churchill read English at Oxford University. Her first one-act play went to the National Union of Students festival in 1959. She has written several radio plays but her breakthrough in the theatre came in 1972 when *Owners* was produced by the Royal Court's Theatre Upstairs.

Owners was published by Methuen (1973); *Light Shining in Buckinghamshire*, Pluto Press (1978); *Traps*, Pluto Press (1978); *Vinegar Tom*, Theatre Quarterly Publications 1978; *Cloud Nine*, Pluto Press (1979).

Trevor Griffiths was born in Manchester in 1935 and graduated in English from Manchester University in 1955. He served in the army for two years and then worked as a teacher and lecturer for eight years. He was an education officer for the BBC from 1965 to 1972.

Occupations was published by Calder and Boyars (1972); *The Party*, Faber and Faber (1974); *Comedians*, Faber and Faber (1974); *Apricots and Thermidor*, Pluto Press (1978).

IX

Three Socialist Playwrights: John McGrath, Caryl Churchill, Trevor Griffiths

CHRISTIAN W. THOMSEN

So why why why—
WHAT MADE YOU THINK YOU
COULD FLY?
Adrian Mitchell,[1]

I

It has already been argued in this book that the English theatre in recent years has seen a remarkable rise in political theatre, starting in the 1950s, but accelerating during the 1960s and 1970s. It is a theatre that has generated great interest in international terms, has invigorated both mainstream and fringe theatre, film and television. But to whom or what has this rise of political theatre given wings? To the theatre in general? To particular play-wrights? To new or old audiences? To the political issues discussed? To the development of a more mature political consciousness? The present essay attempts, in the light of these questions, to consider the work of three of the leading socialist playwrights—John McGrath, Caryl Churchill, Trevor Griffiths: an outspoken Marxist, a socialist-feminist, and a socialist play-wright of disillusionment—all of whose work is indicative of a clear ideo-logical perspective, yet which indicates too a wide variety of possible approaches to the artistic issues their interests and commitments raise.

II

John McGrath
Now an outspoken representative of Marxist group theatre, John McGrath, coming from a Birkenhead working-class background, enjoyed the benefits of an officer's training in the army and an education at St John's College, Oxford—a training that gave him a literary education but also some sharp awarenesses of the workings of British society and its class structure. He began to write plays in 1958, and can now look back on a remarkable record of activity in stage plays, in television production, and in film. When he produced his play *A Man Has Two Fathers* at Oxford in 1958, Kenneth Tynan wrote on the performance in a friendly review in *The Observer*, and directed the attention of George Devine at the Royal Court to this promising

---

[1] Mitchell, Adrian: 'Icarus Shmicarus' in *The Annotated OUT LOUD, London, 1976. No pagination.*

student of English. It was a typical start at this time, and one that was to link him with the new developments in British theatre in a vigorous season. The result of his connections with the Royal Court, with John Arden, and the intellectual and theatrical scenes of Oxford and London, was a number of plays, never published, produced in a variety of places—plays like *The Tent* (London, 1958), *Tell Me* (London, 1958), *Why the Chicken* (Edinburgh, 1959) and *Basement in Bangkok* (Bristol, 1963). But there were frustrating experiences with the Court and with prospective West End productions. McGrath now joined the BBC, directing features and documentaries, and then went on to concentrate on single plays. He also established himself, together with Troy Kennedy Martin, as the father of the now ledgendary *Z-Cars* series. However, *Z-Cars* wore out; its innovations became formulaic and, as McGrath himself felt, as a consequence of BBC bureaucracy it became more and more alienated from the original idea, which was 'to use the cops as a way of getting into a whole society'.[2] So McGrath now turned to directing plays and films, becoming heavily involved with the American film industry between 1967 and 1972, when he directed *Billion Dollar Brain, Virgin Soldiers, Bofors Gun*, and *The Reckoning*. He earned enough money from this to found the 7:84 Company in 1971, and finance a tour through Scotland and Northern England with his new play *Trees in the Wind*.

This development marked the end of the first part of his career as a play-wright—a period characterized by plays which concentrate on individual characters and their relations to, and conflicts with, society: *Events While Guarding the Bofors Gun* (London, 1966), *Bakke's Night of Fame* (London, 1968), which is an adaptation of William Butler's novel *A Danish Gambit*, and *Random Happenings in the Hebrides* (Edinburgh, 1970).

In the early 1970s, during a time of close cooperation with the Everyman Theatre, Liverpool, there followed a kind of transition period during which McGrath wrote *Soft or a Girl* (1971), *Underneath* (1972), and *Fish in the Sea* (1973)—plays which combine a close-knit plot and individual characters with topical political questions. Working with 7:84, he then began to experiment with popular forms, resulting in a revue-like style—a mixture of Highland ceilidh, pop and pub culture, music-hall and Brechtian techniques. Character is deliberately flattened, plot dissolved into a series of performances, events, facts. Politics was central; it is the dialectic of the historical process rather than the individual which counts in *The Cheviot, the Stag, and the Black, Black Oil* (1973-74), *Boom* (1974), or *The Game's a Bogey* (1974). In *Little Red Hen* (1975) and *Yobbo Nowt* (1975-76), the fighting working-class individual is taken as an example and model of an alternative working-class culture, arising out of the collective consciousness and the individual strengths of men and women who, autodidactically, have become aware of ways and means of attacking the ruling-class ideology which permeates the mass media and almost every aspect of daily life. Thus, on another, more

[2] McGrath, John: 'Better a Bad Night in Bootle . . .' in interviews with *Theatre Quarterly*, 19, p. 43. 1975.

articulate and specific, level, McGrath finds his way back in the latest of his published plays to a form of drama that combines his starting points with the experiences derived from five years of touring with 7:84.

Among his early plays, *Events While Guarding the Bofors Gun* achieved particular popularity, not so much through Ronald Eyre's 1966-67 Hampstead Theatre Club production as through McGrath's film version (1968). *Events* reflects the frustrations of McGrath's army experiences in northern Germany, the foreign environment amplifying the feeling of futility that pervades an army life which in itself represents ruling-class structures and interests more clearly than any other institution. The play shows certain parallels with Wesker's *Chips with Everything*. It is not as powerful and well-constructed as Wesker's best work, but does derive considerable impact from the polarization of the two protagonists, Lance-Bombadier Evans, 'who is climbing out of a working-class mentality into a middle-class one, with everything that entails',[3] and Gunner O'Rourke, whose maniacal vitality and positive aggression turns into a fanatic death wish. O'Rourke runs amok against himself, thus symbolizing both frustration and suppression, but also the inability of a working-class individual to cope with his situation through any other means than adjustment or self-destruction.

McGrath stresses the importance of ambition, contrasted with homesickness, 'an emotion, an overwhelming, overpowering emotion—something you find in Anglo-saxon poems, *The Wanderer* or *The Seafarer*, the whole atmosphere of longing for home.'[4] *Events* is a modern tragedy of passions, of perverted, suppressed, neurotic passions breaking loose in borderline situations. The influence of French existentialism is clear: crisis is the source of revelation; man is thrown into a world of absurdity where everyone fails. Like the social playwrights of the late 1950s, a generation to which McGrath was a latecomer, he portrays his characters in a realistic way. In the end everything is a fraud, a cheat, a bogey: the Bofors Gun, the situation in British society, the individual mastery of life. In this respect Griffiths anticipates the analysis of a later play, *Bakke's Night of Fame*.

This is another exercise in mental and 'metaphysical gymnastics'[5] (as McGrath called the novel, by William Butler, from which it was adapted) which demonstrates his skill in constructing plot, creating character, and building a dramatic tension based on an ambiguity concerning the protagonist and his fate. Whereas Behan's *Quare Fellow* derived its tension and specific atmosphere from the 'hero's' absence, Bakke is a loquacious delinquent. The theme is a macabre one. The night before his execution, Bakke develops his talents as an actor to the limit. He plays with his own life in a kind of Russian roulette in which neither the player nor the audience knows how many bullets are in the revolver. The play revolves around the theme of fatherhood, father-son relationships, guilt, revenge, and sacrifice. The audience are never really in possession of the full facts, only facets, allusions, from which everyone can draw his own conclusions, only to have them

[3] Ibid., p. 44.
[4] Ibid., p. 44.
[5] Ibid., p. 44.

undermined by Bakke's next turn of the screw. Just as in James's famous story, the intellectual thrill lies in the audience's uncertainty as to the nature of reality. Is Bakke simply a criminal who has committed rape and murder? Are we being offered a perverted version of Hamlet? Is he able to differentiate between fact and fiction, reality and imagination; or is he a metaphysical sufferer offering a Christ-like sacrifice, taking the sin of mankind upon himself, obsessed by desperation and death wishes, in all his blasphemies calling on God for a revelatory sign?

The most political play of McGrath's early period is *Random Happenings in the Hebrides*, dedicated to his wife Elizabeth MacLennan, who comes from the Highlands and for whom the part of Catriona was written. *Random Happenings* shows McGrath's characteristic strengths and weaknesses in a traditionally constructed stage piece. His attitude towards politics and society is more definite than before. Much to the discontent of East German critics,[6] the play offers sober analysis of rather than revolutionary perspectives on the chances of a left-wing Labour politician bringing about any decisive change in British society. Later on, under the influence of Marxist studies, of sociological research, of 7:84 and the many discussions with friends and audiences, his fighting working-class heroes offer more of a socialist outlook—an awareness of the need to fight in the name of an irreversible historical process, despite the difficulties which must be overcome in prevalently capitalistic surroundings. Labour is no longer seen as a force one can seriously count on. Self-assured and immune to doubts, McGrath's recent protagonists do not reflect on the potential fragility of their convictions. In *Random Happenings*, however, there are still fragments of Jimmy Porter in the person of Jimmy Litherland, and echoes of resigned Weskerian analysis. The play is strongly rooted in the local situation, and in the first part individual conflicts and sociopolitical problems are interwoven in a tragic constellation which combines individual psychology, modern politics and the traditional forces of a closed island society:

> The play is about the whole complex issue—which I feel in myself—of organized political activity, which is in conflict with the richness of experience.[7]

Jimmy Litherland, political Casanova of the Outer Isles, is attracted alike by politics, by his desire to unionize the fishermen, and by women. Jimmy's political rise means an almost simultaneous degeneration of his ideals; he realizes that organized politics are synonymous with compromise. McGrath objectively scourges Labour politics during the 1960s. Pragmatism and social democratism are contrasted with the real interests of Socialism, through the positive description of Jimmy, thus mirroring the disappointment of those who had set such hopes on the 1964 Labour victory. But the complexity becomes almost impenetrable not only for Jimmy, but for McGrath, too, and the result of this is something of a collapse of style and

[6] cf. Günter Klotz: 'Alternatives in Recent British Drama' in *Zf. AA*, vol. 25, Heft 2, pp. 152-61, 1977.
[7] McGrath, John: 'Better a Bad Night in Bootle . . .', p. 48.

form in the second act. It gets more and more difficult to pull the different threads of the subplots together: the outburst of primitive sexuality in old McPhee degrades him too suddenly from his former position as a noble, integral socialist to a human animal with purely bodily needs. Jimmy's political career at Westminster remains colourless until Rachel turns up, and the conflicts between Jimmy's women—Mary, Pauleen, Rachel, Catriona—parallel the political layers of the play. All the women are powerful characters in their own right, McGrath being one of the few contemporary playwrights with the ability to create powerful and original women's parts, but they also mirror different aspects of Jimmy and his oscillating sympathies towards the female sex as well as towards politics. Jimmy tries to evade clear decisions and a straight course in both fields. His sexual and his political energy is unfocused. Once in Westminster, he becomes uprooted and his dilettante handling of the last conflict is deeply suspect. His final decision to resign from his parliamentary career and try a new start as an independent local politician supported by Catriona looks very much like wishful thinking. At all events it is unsatisfactory from any artistic point of view.

Even if there are clearly marked stages in McGrath's development, his work is organic; seminal motifs and themes of later plays appear in all the earlier ones. In this sense the colourful McPhee family is a prelude to the much more colourful Maconochie family, from *Fish in the Sea*. The latter play and *The Cheviot, the Stag and the Black, Black Oil*, show McGrath reaching the peak of his skill as a writer.

A product of his cooperation with Alan Dossor and the Liverpool Everyman Theatre, *Fish in the Sea* is a play (with international appeal) about Merseyside working-class people. As McGrath explains in his foreword, the title is taken from Mao's well known analogy of the Party as the head and body of a fish, and the population as the water through which it moves. More decidedly than before, this play aims at changing political attitudes and maturing political thought:

> The main elements I wanted to set in some form of dialectical motion were—the need for militant organization by the working class; the anarchistic, anti-organizational violence of the frustrated working-class individual in search of self-fulfillment here and now, the backwardness of some elements of working-class living: attitudes to women, to socialist theory, to sexual oppression, poetry, myth, etc.; the connections between this backwardness and Christianity; the shallow optimism of the demagogic left, self-appointed leaders of the working-class; and the intimate realities of growing up and living in a working-class home on Merseyside.[8]

McGrath is successful in creating a modern-day working-class saga; he is less successful in his depiction of a factory occupation. Its political implications suffer by oversimplified anti-American clichés; the psychological strain such an occupation imposes on the characters' private behaviour and

[8] Foreword to *Fish in the Sea*, Pluto Press Edition, London, 1977.

on their actual quality of life is less convincingly worked out. The more abstract character of such an occupation fails to work on a large stage, while aspects of the second half of the play, where MeGrath intentionally uses Brechtian techniques, relate uneasily to the realism of the rest. The three Labour MPs, for instance, are obviously modelled on the three Gods in *The Good Woman of Setzuan*, but the humour poked at them undercuts the potential political complexity of this scene. Apart from the occupation subplot, *Fish in the Sea* gains its impact from the fact that McGrath here finds a dramatic form of his own, drawn from various sources like the documentary, music hall, pop and pub tradition, and realistic comedy. He blends and fuses these influences into something powerfully original, a form of semi-epic, semi-realistic tragi-comedy with a positive socialist perspective. The characters suffer, and can be defeated, but not broken. His epic realism therefore is entirely different from Mike Leigh's photographic naturalism, in *Ecstasies*, for example, which offers a merciless vivisection of working-class characters for the ambiguous delight of a sophisticated Hampstead audience.

In *Soft or a Girl* (1971), McGrath uses rock-based music extensively for the first time, along with broad Liverpool comedy. In *Fish in the Sea* comedy and music are integrated in a more subtle way in a serious sociopolitical context. Some of the songs have a strong poetical and Brechtian flavour, e.g. the title song 'Fish in the Sea' or 'Sandra's song', where models from Brecht's earlier poetry, from *Threepenny Opera* and *Mahagonni*, have successfully been transposed into a Liverpool context; others, like 'Lonely as the Dark Side of the Moon', show more contemporary influences from Liverpool rock and beat to Donovan, Bob Dylan and Jimi Hendrix. And then there are music hall numbers like 'Enter the Maconochies', 'Totties, judies, Jumbo-jumpered beauties etc.', which, taken together with the various other forms of songs and music, provide the play with its distinctive vitality, mixing entertainment and political analysis.

The Maconochie family is entirely believable, both individually and collectively. McGrath carefully contrasts the male and female reactions, attitudes and points of view in situations of political and family crisis: mother Maconochie, stout and down-to-earth, but not without tenderness and understanding for the problems of the younger ones; Mary, who takes everything deeply and is hauntingly serious, who has sensitive antennae for the dark-poetic sides of life; Fiona, the family genius with ambitions to be a student and climb the social ladder; Sandra, the prototype of a sensuous, working-class girl with a *carpe diem*-attitude who is aware that happiness is relative and may be short-lived.

The male characters are equally convincingly portrayed. Old Maconochie, Willie, Yorrick and Andy are representatives of different socialist standpoints, ranging from the pathos of father Maconochie's straightforward socialist convictions, to Willie's awakening socialist consciousness, from Yorry's intellectual communist enthusiasm to Andy's anarchism. Andy is the individual with the death-wish who has appeared in all of McGrath's other plays, but here he displays not merely articulateness but a wild poetic vision. Yet there is no sentimentality in the presentation of Andy's desperate and futile rebellion.

Since his involvement with the Liverpool Everyman, McGrath writes with particular audiences in mind, with the intention of achieving a lively interaction between stage and audience. *The Cheviot, the Stag and the Black, Black Oil* (1973-74) is, up to now, the best example of the kind of theatre developed by 7:84 and which later on, with characteristic variations, was imitated by other socialist groups like Belt and Braces, Red Ladder or North West Spanner. The play describes British exploitation of Scotland since Culloden: the expulsion of the Highlanders by British and Scottish land-owners, first to gain pastures for the Cheviot cattle, later on to offer the aris-tocracy unspoilt hunting pleasures, and nowadays, through an unholy alliance between British and American big business, to rob the country of its oil resources and to leave it, after a couple of years, sucked out, without improvement of its infrastructure, poorer than ever. The play not only describes, it calls for political action. In unfolding an historical panorama it does without individually shaped characters.

McGrath's principal model is the Highland ceilidh, a kind of on-going scene with quick changes, alienation effects, varying styles of acting, didac-tic comments, documentary material, direct addresses to the audience, often interrupted by songs which explain, entertain and warm the audience up. Among the forerunners, besides local traditions, are Brecht's epic theatre and Piscator's political revues. Leo Lania wrote, in the programme for Piscator's revue adaptation of Alexei Tolstoy's *Rasputin,* that it was the intention to describe the most exact and most comprehensive epic course of the story from its roots to the last consequences and results.[9] The description could apply with equal force to *The Cheviot, the Stag and the Black, Black Oil.* It is first-class agit-prop theatre, which avoids that monotonous dullness which often characterizes didactic socialist plays. But it is non-Brechtian in its reliance on an emotional identification which excludes any considera-tions other than those of actionist partisanship. McGrath is indeed consider-ably closer to Piscator than to Brecht. If one looks at Brecht's famous remarks on *Mahagonni,* where he contrasts epic and dramatic theatre, it becomes obvious that McGrath creates a mixture of those theatrical forms identified by Brecht in an antithetical manner. Yet in the end it is epic theatre which predominates. McGrath's characters change and are change-able. He creates dramatic tension, but each scene is closed in itself. The world is not taken as something given; instead motivations, causal connec-tions, perspectives are laid open. Though perhaps intellectually less eman-cipating than a strictly Brechtian form this theatrical mode is particularly effective.

The shows following *The Cheviot, the Stag and the Black, Black Oil* are less convincing and less carefully constructed. To an extent this may be partly a matter of his practical working conditions. In his introduction to *Boom* (1974) he tell us:

[9] cf. Heinrich Goertz: *Piscator,* rowohlts monographien, No. 221, p. 63. Reinbek, 1974.

> When we began to work with four weeks to go, nothing was written. I had
> a framework and the line of the play in my mind.[10]

He explicitly uncovers 7:84's production methods:

> Firstly we do not 'improvise'. Virtually every thing, down to the smallest
> throwaway, is written or discussed before the performance.
> Secondly, the actors do not write their own material. The shows are
> conceived and controlled down to the smallest detail by the writer/
> director with the fullest consultation, discussion and contribution from
> the collective company.[11]

Boom, The Game's a Bogey, Little Red Hen move along lines similar to those
developed in *The Cheviot*. Fiercely satirical, they are even more obviously
agit-prop.

With *Yobbo Nowt* (1975-76, published 1978) McGrath's style underwent
a further development. Setting his play in the England of the 1970s he
sought to tell a story similar to that contained in Gorky's *The Mother*, and
Brecht's adaptation of that novel.

> In form it is not exactly a musical comedy—though it is definitely musical
> and a comedy. With Mark Brown, who composed the music, I set out to
> explore several ways of relating music to speech and story-telling: the
> sung-narrative, straightforward character- and situation-songs, plus
> scenes in which the characters cut from speech to song, and scenes com-
> pletely set to music.[12]

Again Brecht comes to mind, and in particular his cooperation with Kurt
Weill in the *Threepenny Opera* and *Lukullus*. The plot is relatively independent of the Gorky/Brecht model. McGrath returns to the individual
character who undergoes an emancipating process. Mary, a working-class
nobody, discovers her individuality and political consciousness, gains
independence from her husband and learns to fight sexual, social, and economic suppression. It is this emancipation which is the purpose and subject
of McGrath's work. Asked in 1975 whether he would see himself as a developing writer, John McGrath answered:

> I don't think I've begun to write properly yet—I'm all the time searching
> for meaning through various forms, exploring music and comedy . . . But
> I don't think that I've developed the form or the chain of thought that will
> work in a big way and be right and fulfill and capture all the levels of
> experience that I'd like to capture in a play.[13]

---

[10] *Boom*, 'An introduction by John McGrath' in *New Edinburgh Review*, No. 30, August,
1975, p. 10.

[11] Ibid., p. 9.

[12] Foreword to *Yobbo Nowt*, Pluto Press Edition, London, 1978. No pagination.

[13] McGrath, John in 'Better a Bad Night in Bootle . . .', op. cit.

III

Caryl Churchill
Yobbo Nowt offers a convenient transition to our second playwright, Caryl ‸
Churchill, who regards herself as both a socialist and a feminist, increasingly
so in the last few years.[14] As such she represents a decisive change in
European drama. Though there is an outstanding tradition of women novel-
ists in a number of countries, most notably in England, Germany and
France, there have been few major women dramatists. With Ed Berman's
pioneering *Women's Theatre Season* (1974) at the Almost Free Theatre, it
became apparent that there are in fact a number of noteworthy women playwrights able to continue what Shelagh Delaney and Ann Jellicoe started in
the late 1950s. Caryl Churchill, Pam Gems, Mary O'Malley and Michlene
Wandor have established reputations as writers of some stature, while
Margaretta D'Arcy, with male chauvinism, continues to be regarded as her
husband's annex (she is married to John Arden) rather than an author in
her own right. At the same time female groups like Women's Company,
Monstrous Regiment and Mrs Worthington's Daughters have developed
their own style and professional skill, producing women's plays dealing with
women's topics.

Caryl Churchill started writing plays when reading English at Oxford
around the same time as John McGrath. Her first one-act play, *Downstairs*,
went to the NUS festival in 1959. In the following years she wrote a number
of radio-plays, broadcast on Radio 3: *The Ants* (1962), *Lovesick* (1966), *Identical Twins* (1968), *Abortive* (1974), *Not . . . not . . . not . . . not enough oxygen*
(1971), *Schreber's Nervous Illness* (1972), *Henry's Past* (1972). Her breakthrough came in 1972, when *Owners* was produced at the Royal Court
Theatre Upstairs. With the exception of *Perfect Happiness* (written in 1973,
and performed at the Soho Poly, Lunchtime, 1975), all her subsequent plays
have been performed at the Royal Court with her growing reputation being
mirrored in the fact that, since *Objective to Sex and Violence* (1975), her plays
have moved from the Upstairs theatre to the main auditorium.

Caryl Churchill plays are usually centred on a single image or metaphor
which provides the key theme. A number of other themes are clustered
around this core. This is true, for example, of her early radio play *Ants*,
where the insects offer a powerful image for human relations, human insig-
nificance, cold-blooded cruelty and mass society. *Ants* also sets the tone for
the predominance of the conflicts between individual and society in her
plays.

Ownership, on many levels, is the central theme of *Owners*, which, as
tragic farce, attacks capitalist society and the means by which capitalist
materialism perverts human relations. There is a grim linguistic ambiguity
about the story of Clegg (the family butcher, who is a family butcher in every
sense of the word) and his wife Marion, property agent and developer, who,
having consented to her lover's murder, offers the concluding observation
that:

---

[14] Churchill, Caryl in an interview with the author of this article, 6 November, 1979.

> *Marion:* I'm not sorry at all, Alec. Or about that other baby. Not at all. I
> never knew I could do a thing like that. I might be capable of
> anything. I'm just beginning to find out what's possible. (p. 73)

Owners shows decidedly Ortonesque qualities. In *What the Butler Saw*
Orton depicted England as a brothel and the English as sexually obsessed; in
Caryl Churchill's play, ownership, treated in Ortonesque manner, is the
central obsession of her characters. They own, or want to own, property,
human relations, human bodies, with a fierce, petrified heartlessness that
points out the psychological defects and reified humanity which are the product of a society which regards ownership with a quasi-religious awe. In
such a context human relations are degraded, as is apparent in Clegg's blunt
petty-Shylockian butcher's language:

> She is mine. I have invested heavily in Marion and don't intend to lose
> any part of my profit.
> She is my flesh. And touching her you touch me.
> And I will not myself be touched. (p. 62)

And then there is Worseley, Marion's marionette. He is the Vice figure from
medieval drama, who in the farce directs part of his evil intentions on himself. He limps through the play as a symbol of crippled humanity; all his
efforts to destroy himself only result in self-mutilation. *Owners* is not yet a
feminist play, even though Marion destroys her butcher-husband's peace of
mind by violating the rules by which a woman is not allowed to be commercially more successful than her husband. In *Vinegar Tom* and *Light Shining
in Buckinghamshire*, however, where Caryl Churchill worked together with
Monstrous Regiment and Joint Stock, one finds in her a mature socialist
writer with a personal style and strong interests in history and feminine
questions. David Zaine Mairowitz writes in his review of *Light. . .*:

> She gets her sharpened hook into God . . . and does not relent until she
> has pulled Him (decidedly Him in this case) down to face the social out-
> casts of the misfired English Revolution. . . .[15]

In *Vinegar Tom*, by contrast, she gets her hook into the male devil thereby
utterly denouncing a male-oriented religious and secular system which
treats women as inferior beings, as scapegoats for social shortcomings and
defects caused by men.

Light . . . tells the story of the revolution in 1647 which was extinguished
before it really began. It is the story of the Levellers, the Ranters, the Putney
debates, which led common people to outbursts of quasi-democratic belief
in religious, economic and sexual freedom, outbursts withstood and finally
crushed by Cromwell and Ireton. From a socialist perspective it marks the
collapse of fixed hierarchy, the recognition of betrayal by king and Church,
the beginnings of social doubt, which is the prerequisite for fundamental
change. In David Mairowitz's words:

[15] Mairowitz, David: 'God and the Devil: David Zaine Mairowitz assesses the latest work of
Caryl Churchill' in *Plays and Players*, February 1977, p. 24.

One of the dramatic virtues of this magnificent play is that it can assume a certain given historical foundation and proceed to de-emphasize specific characters and events.[16]

Caryl Churchill's power often lies in scenes where a lurid light is cast on the seventeenth century but where the audience is forced to draw analogies to the contemporary situation. She is concerned with the suppression of women, of the poor and the powerless, with the displacement of social and political evil onto sexual morality.

The seventeenth century is painted as an age of horror, of cruel punishment, hypocrisy, exploitation and feudalism; the puritans, as Christ's soldiers, preach revolution in the interest of the new rulers. Churchill dissects the perverse logic of Cromwell's sermons, where the self-appointed chosen are justified in persecuting those who are not. The puritans, from the beginning, deploy the usual tools of revolutionary regimes: brain-washing, prohibitions and suppressions.

In a very Brechtian sense women relativize official statements, expose inconsistencies and reveal the similarity of old and new structures of government. The scene *Hoskin interrupts the Preacher* is typical of this method:

> *Preacher:* For St Paul says, 'I suffer not a woman to teach nor to usurp authority over the man, but to be in silence.' . . .
>
> *Hoskins:* How can God choose us from all eternity to be saved or damned when there's nothing we've done? . . .
>
> *Hoskins:* God's pleasure? that we burn? what sort of god takes pleasure in pain? . . .
>
> *Preacher:* Woman, you are certainly damned. (pp. 9-10)

Compared with McGrath, Churchill's historical analysis proceeds without comic relief. Her commitment is clear, as is her assault on what she clearly sees as a pernicious christianity.

With great seriousness she unfolds the background of documentary material, reconstructing the Putney debates which suggest advanced attitudes in questions of electoral law and property. She deliberately takes sides with the poor and suppressed, as in the scene *A Butcher Talks to his Customers* which betrays an echo of Swiftean toughness and severity. Some characters, like Cobbe, the historical Ranter whose writings have survived, find release in revolts of blasphemy, pulling the Son of God, who has been politically misused in the interests of the ruling class, down to the level of the common people where he belongs:

> Stick your fingers in Christ's arsehole. He had an arsehole. Christ shits on you rich. Christ shits. Shitting pissing spewing puking fucking Jesus Christ. Jesus fucking—(p. 30)

In the end the real revolution consists in religious emancipation. The poorest of the poor recognize God in themselves, thereby cutting a mendacious metaphysical sphere down to the physical needs of men:

[16] Ibid.

Cobbe: You are God, I am God, and I love you, God loves God. (p. 38)

In *Light Shining in Buckinghamshire* Caryl Churchill uses an historical situation to exemplify on-going issues about human rights and democracy. In this play she avoids alienation effects, such as the songs of *Vinegar Tom* which stress parallels with the present. The latter play only gradually unveils itself as the description of a typical example of British witchhunting in the seventeenth century. It is another play that has much to do with the development of a collective subconscious, the witches being those women of all classes who dared to act rebelliously or lustily according to their own physical and psychological needs, and thereby provoked the wrath, intensified by feelings of guilt, of the emotionally suppressed community. *Vinegar Tom* is steeped in a mood of resignation and failure, and deals more with specific female problems than any other of Caryl Churchill's plays. The dominant tone is that of sinister hopelessness about a sex-ordained fate. It expresses a sense of aggressive, superstitious helplessness, a furious but powerless assault against the injustice of a world whose history has been, and is still, directed by men. Caryl Churchill and Monstrous Regiment retaliate for centuries of female humiliation. In *Vinegar Tom* the devil does not only act as a convenient tool in the historical suppression of women, in the opening line the generalized figure of *Man* already asks the crucial question:

Man: Am I the devil?
Alice: What, sweet?
Man: I'm the devil . . .

One can understand the fiercely feminist politics of a group like Monstrous Regiment, but on occasion their work becomes somewhat shrill, as perhaps it is here.

Compared with these two plays *Traps* is neither particularly socialist nor of great literary or dramaturgical interest. It is a play very much dependent on Joint Stock's excellent acting; otherwise, the audience is kept in the dark as to whether it is meant as a serious alternative to bourgeois forms of living or as a parody on alternative forms of living, the ceremonial bath in the end providing the most cogent image in a dramatically not very significant play. Its strengths lie more in an experimental use of language, in subtle ambiguities where plays on words set traps for the audience and actors alike.

With *Cloud Nine* (1979) Caryl Churchill returns to Joe Orton and polished, exuberant farce, using techniques which may seem experimental, but are in fact firmly rooted in the tradition of farce—British theatre anyway being disinclined to formal experiments.

Hugh Rorrison headlined his review, '*What the Boy Saw*, a Victorian colonial farce', an allusion to Orton. The implicit question is whether there is a serious concern under the motley of farce. The central metaphor of *Cloud Nine* is sex-obsession. As Rorrison observed:

It starts in Africa where the local commissioner's family, complete with resident mother-in-law, is visited by Harry Bagley, explorer and bounder, and Mrs Saunders, a widow of amazing spirit. This cast of

Boy's Own Paper caricatures is then permutated in pairs to show what a variety of passions throbbed behind the Imperial façade. Clive's wife Betty melts into the arms of Harry, who has already bestowed his favours on her adolescent son, Edward, and on Clive's African boy, Joshua, though he ends up, for decency's sake, marrying the governess Ellen, who for her part loves Betty. Cross-casting of Jim Hooper as Betty and Julie Covington as Edward underlines the artificiality of the characters who are crisply sent up by their own clichés.[17]

In the second half we meet more or less the same characters, now played by different members of the cast. The play is set in contemporary England, where imperialistic bourgeois behaviour has apparently deferred to modern petty-bourgeois pseudo-enlightenment. Sexual taboos have been dissipated and the characters are confronted with the problem of finding suitable sexual levels of their own, no fixed standards being available.

The middle of the road turns out to be bisexuality, though homosexuality and masturbation are equally proposed as routes to identity. But to reduce Victorianism and Imperialism to sexual totalitarianism seems no more valid than Osborne's reducing the reformation to Luther's indigestion. The difference between the two plays lies in Osborne's serious form and intent contrasted with Caryl Churchill's farce. But nevertheless she presses her conviction that remnants of Victorianism persist while the permissiveness of the so-called permissive society is more verbal than actual, more an expression of insecurity than cheerful composure. Under the veil of caricature on the Victorians she attacks the self-ordained godlike superiority of the British male:

> *Clive:* You are thoughtless, Betty, that's all. Women can be treacherous and evil. They are darker and more dangerous than men. The family protects us from that, you protect me from that. You are not that sort of woman. You are not unfaithful to me, Betty. I can't believe you are. It would hurt me so much to cast you off. That would be my duty. (p. 22)

Every statement is an insult; humiliations are mixed with threats. The hidden fear is that women might free themselves from male tutelage. Caryl Churchill unmasks the still norm-setting attitudes of the upper-middle-class husband who cloaks his sexual instincts with myths and language.

Caryl Churchill is an intellectual farceur as well as a committed cultural critic, but by no means a mouthpiece of any party line. In its contrapuntal structure *Cloud Nine* shows a consciousness of dramatic form which might lead to more experimental, perhaps more musically structured, work in the future.

IV

Trevor Griffiths
Like John McGrath, Trevor Griffiths was born in 1935, but, unlike the

---

[17] Rorrison, Hugh: 'Cloud Nine' in *Plays and Players*, May 1979, p. 23.

other two playwrights, he did not find his way to the theatre via reading English at Oxford. The son of a poor Manchester working-class family, he stayed there most of his life and still feels rooted in northern traditions. He graduated in English at Manchester in 1952; after that it took him fifteen years to write his first play for television—*Love Maniac* (not produced)—and seventeen years until he saw the first production of his play *The Wages of Thin* and secured a radio production for *The Big House*. As a teacher and BBC Further Education Officer, Griffiths spent many years studying sociology, anthropology and political history until he emerged as the critical Marxist and articulate political and cultural critic that he is today.[18] The major part of Trevor Griffiths's work was written or adapted for television, and in plays like *All Good Men, Absolute Beginners, Through the Night*, or the eleven-part *Bill Brand* series, Griffiths proved that it is possible to write plays which are complex and demanding in a language and a manner acceptable to millions of viewers.

Before concentrating on his full-length plays *Occupations* (written and performed 1970), *The Party* (1972, first performed 1973) and *Comedians* (1974, first performed 1975), it is worth considering *Apricots* and *Thermidor*, two one-act plays written and performed in 1971 by 7:84 at the Edinburgh Festival. These two plays are in many ways seminal for Griffiths's work, dealing in a basic manner with two of his main themes: sexuality and love on the one hand and a critique of Stalinism on the other. *Apricots* is a play about sexual relationships in a loveless, failing marriage, 'perverted', thwarted sexuality being offered by Griffiths as a metaphor for an entire socially conditioned situation. In the three short scenes between Anna and Sam, they talk, copulate, masturbate and in the end fail to communicate at all. There is a Beckett-like loneliness and barrenness in the middle scene when Sam switches on a cassette recorder with attached microphone during love-making and later on uses the re-play as stimulus for his masturbation. *Krapp's Last Tape* brought up to date. The play is nevertheless distinguished by a certain poetry of frustration, masturbation serving as a metaphor for an isolating society. Behind the sterile action is a longing for a complex personality which can integrate sexual, emotional and rational instincts. Sex is here the symptom of alienation. There is no escape and no perspective. Griffiths thus uses the play as a perverse image of bourgeois society.

Thermidor, named after that month in the French revolutionary calendar beginning on 19 July (from the overthrow of Robespierre which took place in that month in 1794), is a unique metaphor for Stalinism, not only in so far as Russia in the 1930s is concerned, but for Stalinist attitudes everywhere where, in Yukov's key sentence, 'Enemies . . . are no longer people'. Predictably it is not a play which has endeared him to East European critics but it is not an anti-socialist play. Its target is the ossifying power of bureaucracy,

---

[18] cf. the long interview Trevor Griffiths gave to Catherine Itzin and Simon Trussler: 'Trevor Griffiths, Transforming the Husk of Capitalism' in *Theatre Quarterly*, vol. 6, No. 22. pp. 25-46, summer 1976; also *Theatre Facts*, vol. 3, No. 179, 1976, with a theatre checklist on Trevor Griffiths.

the anti-human power of an idea allowed to dominate the human personality. Anya is interrogated by Yukov. They have known each other as party members for many years but instead of friendship and solidarity the encounter is dominated by that terrorism of the word, that absolute inversion of rationality which characterizes the inquisition. Perverse charges, neither rooted in reality nor justifying investigation, pervert human relations until the whole system is inverted. *Apricots* and *Thermidor* are thus complementary pieces, which by implication define the kind of socialism for which Griffiths fights. And that socialism includes freedom of opinion, freedom to develop one's own creativity and personality, the rights of error, discussion and opposition.

Occupations, Griffiths' first full-length play, is another proof of the importance Griffiths attaches to historical analysis of socialism and the workers' movement. Set in Turin during the Italian workers' occupation of factories in 1920 under the leadership of Gramsci, the founder of the Italian Communist Party, it is also a play about two men and their attitudes towards politics, the working-class and revolution. Gramsci, the tough, dwarfish Italian, fervently dedicated to the revolution and his Turinese workers, is challenged by Kabak, the Bulgarian representative from the Communist International in Moscow, tougher still, revolutionary by profession, a matter-of-fact politician without visible emotions and sentimentality, a pragmatic tactician who never gives battle unless he is sure of success. The revolution of heart and idealist imagination is contrasted with that of power politics; revolutionary identity rooted in regionalism is contrasted with chess-like manoeuvres on an international plane. As Trevor Griffiths explained in his interview with Catherine Itzin and Simon Trussler:

I've always thought in terms of dialogue, or dialectically if you want to enhance that a bit. I've always thought about opposites, about the possibility of opposites for ideas.[19]

Emotionally audiences are likely to be drawn to Gramsci. But has his revolution any chance of succeeding? Kabak, on the other hand, who puts on a masterful demonstration of Machiavellianism for the Italians, may be right from any logical point of view, but behind him opens the gulf of Stalinism, indicated by Griffiths in the photographs projected after Angelica's closing speech: the Fascist takeover in Italy, Stalin, and the signing of the non-aggression pact between Germany and Russia. Kabak stands for the dangers of a suffocatingly bureaucratic communism which may represent the interests of a clique of functionaries but hardly those of the people.

The occupations having failed, Kabak reveals to Valetta, the Fiat representative, the alternative purpose of his mission: to negotiate a loan from the Fiat bosses in return for trading concessions in Russia. Valetta's toast after having signed the agreement, 'Business as usual', suggests an understanding among the ruling few over the heads of their subjects; it also may suggest an

[19] Ibid., p. 32.

East-West detente based on mutual profit, as Peter Ansorge suggests.[20]

John McGrath attacks capitalism and the ruling class, satirizing them and exposing their deeds through carefully researched facts. Caryl Churchill proceeds with irony and sarcasm, aiming at a double target—the ideology of male supremacy and of the ruling classes. Trevor Griffiths is more complex; his plays are multi-layered, his technique relies on multiple perspectives. *Occupations*, therefore, is not only a play about different forms of Marxism or different attitudes towards revolution, it is also very much a play about the adaptability of capitalism. Unlike the other two playwrights, Griffiths never underestimates his enemies and shows the historical, collective and individual obstacles on which socialism may founder. This makes any clear-cut judgements about Kabak difficult.

Moreover, *Occupations* is also a play about love. Gramsci and Angelica are the representatives of different forms of love.

> *Gramsci:* But then I thought, how can a man bind himself to the masses, if he has never loved anyone himself, not even his mother or his father. I thought, how can a man love collectively, when he has not profoundly loved single human creatures. And it was then I began to see masses as people and it was only then that I began to love them, in their particular, detailed, local, individual character. (p.50)

Both their loves are connected with a sensibility heightened by physical defects: Gramsci, the dwarfish hunchback with a heavy head, and Angelica, the countess hooked on cocaine, dying of cancer, who frenetically loves the gravediggers of her class. The critics did not like her and perhaps there is too much of a Chekhovian flavour in this dying representative of a dying class. But, beyond a question of mere dramaturgical convenience she also constitutes another emotional counterweight to Kabak's brutal matter-of-factness. There is an inherent feeling of sadness, even tragedy, about Anglica and Gramsci which challenges the audience to consider the forms of political change Griffiths wishes to initiate, forms which should lie somewhere between Gramsci and Kabak.

Occupations marked the beginning of a critical alliance between a Marxist playwright and the established theatre. His next play, *The Party*, was produced by the National Theatre, with Laurence Olivier playing the lead.

> It started with a number of images, really. It started with 1968, and what happened to me in 1968, in France. . . . It started with the experience of the Friday night meetings at Tony Garnett's where sixty or seventy people would cram into a room. . . .[21]

Griffiths's predilection for ambiguous titles again appears in this play and the double meaning of *The Party* throws an ironic light on a play which alternates between seriousness, comedy, frustration and impotence. Since

[20] Ansorge, Peter: *Disrupting the Spectacle: Five years of experimental and fringe theatre in Britain*, London, 1975, p. 64.

[21] Griffiths, Trevor in 'Transforming the Husk', op. cit., p. 40

Shaw, nobody in the British theatre has demonstrated such a fondness for theoretical discussions and brilliant intellectual analysis. Griffiths's method of dialectical thinking reaches its climax in this play which is full of clever puns, beautifully coined phrases, convincing aphorisms of a kind which show him to be a master of language. Because of the pervading irony there is no *ultima ratio* in any of the speeches and statements, yet there is a more comprehensive analysis of the situation of the Left, imbedded in the complex structures of present-day society, than in any other post-war play. Against the TV-background of French students marching through Paris and mounting the barricades on the night of the 10-11 May 1968, the British left-wingers discuss the situation on their island and possible joint revolutionary ventures. Since, with the exception of Tagg, they are all intellectuals, this consists of nothing other than the parading of rhetorical attitudes. They are theorists, nothing more. In the mouth of sociology lecturer Andrew Ford, Marx's words achieve an irridescent ambivalence, suggesting that the Western industrial proletariat has lost its revolutionary potential.

He is countered by Joe Tagg, a veteran Glaswegian Trotskyist, who has dedicated his life to building up the Revolutionary Socialist Party. The part is dramaturgically very skillfully constructed on a crest of rising expectation, during which he sits modestly and says little, before launching into a twenty-minute speech illustrating the Trotskyite position as the way to 'put the proletarian revolution back on the agenda of European history'. (p. 52) He fires broadsides of disdain at the intellectuals:

> You're intellectuals. You're frustrated by the ineffectual character of your opposition to the things you loathe. Your main weapon is the word. Your protest is verbal—it has to be: it wears out by repetition and leads you nowhere . . . (p. 48)
>
> In an objective sense, you actually stop believing in a revolutionary perspective, in the possibility of a socialist society and the creation of socialist man. . . . Finally you learn to enjoy your pain: to need it, so that you have nothing to offer your bourgeois peers but a sort of moral exhaustion. (p. 49)

But Tagg's position is undermined by Kara and others before he even starts to deliver his speech, and, convincing as it sounds as long as he talks, the limitations soon become obvious: the worn-out slogans, the obsession with the past, the fruitlessness, unnecessarily emphasized by the cancer which consumes him.

In the end Malcolm Sloman, the drunken writer in the role of devil's advocate, emerges from his stupor and, suddenly sober, delivers the only realistic perspective on revolution presented in the play:

> There'll be a revolution, and another, and another, because the capacity for 'adjustment' and 'adaptation' within capitalism is not, contrary to popular belief, infinite. And when *masses* of people, masses mind, decide to take on the state and the ruling class, they won't wait for the word from the 'authentic voice of Trotsky' or anyone else. They'll be too busy 'practicing the revolution'. (p. 71)

There is no change at the end of the play; Joe and Angie are still impotent; frustration and blind aggression continue to reign. There is no suggestion that the play's leftists would be able to build a society more humane than that of capitalism. The melancholy clown's attitude from the prologue prevails: 'Je suis Marxiste, Tendance Groucho.' (p. 12)

Less lachrymose, Griffiths's analysis resembles that of Wesker in the early 1960s, and it is because of this realism that he is attacked by a Left which refuses to accept that disillusioned analysis as a necessary first step.

Comedians pursues this line in even more subtle ways. To a large extent it is a play about comedy and comedians. Griffiths has been fond of stand-up comedy since his early youth. Part of the play, indeed, is his tribute to forms of entertainment, based mainly on working-class culture, now endangered by bingo and TV. He has talked at length about his personal commitment to the play[22] which is developed around a class in comic methods in which six adults are taught by a veteran comedian Waters, who has turned teacher because, as he explains, he was afraid of success. Waters's theoretical basis consists of regarding comedy as a cathartic means of liberating the audience's fears and anxieties without supporting prejudice, clichés, hardened patterns of thinking. The apprentice comedians embody different approaches to comedy which are, at the same time, fundamentally different approaches to life: racial stereotypes, sophisticated humour and, finally, Gethin Price's tragi-comic mime, in the style of Grock, which abruptly collapses into violence as he enacts the role of a football hooligan who attacks two dummies dressed as members of the bourgeoisie:

> Price: ... For the lady. Here's a pin. (Pause). I'll do it, Shall I? (He pins the flower—a marigold—with the greatest delicacy between the girl's breasts. He steps back to look at his work). No need for thanks. My pleasure entirely. Believe me. (Silence. Nothing. Then a dark red stain, rapidly widening, begins to form behind the flower). Aagh, aagh, aagh, aagh ... (p. 52)

Price represents a dimension of anarchy in the well ordered realm of comedy, a neurotic frenzy born out of despair, and designed to shock.

Waters's epigrammatic phrase, 'A real comedian—that's a daring man' (p. 20) contains a crucial truth applicable to all his characters but one especially applicable to Price, who not only tries to contrast a liberal attitude towards comedy with a revolutionary one, but, more significantly, tries to tread the borderline between comedy, black humour and anarchic madness.

There is, indeed, a political dimension to *Comedians*. Though integral to the first two acts its didactic aspects emerge most directly in the Waters-Price discussion of the third act. But the power struggle between Waters and Challenor, a cynical ex-comic sent to adjudicate, is also clearly political as are the performances of the would-be comedians. On the whole they see comedy either as mere entertainment or as social anodyne or oblique social comment. Price's daring performance is not accepted by the system because he is interested in truth and the role of comedy in expressing that truth. As such, of course, it is an oblique comment on Griffiths's sense of the role of his own work, as he tries to mediate between the competing demands of his social and artistic conscience, as he endeavours to find a form appropriate to his convictions.

The Left has tended to regard Griffiths as a political opportunist. But in doing so they have disregarded his sincerity, his search for truth, for an understanding and interpretation of the sociological and philosophical questions raised in his plays. They have ignored the honesty with which he has tried to reach that audience towards which he acknowledges a primary responsibility. As he said of *Comedians*, indeed:

> I wanted to write a play that wasn't overtly scratch and scarring the revolutionary theory. I wanted a play removed from that, and therefore, I wanted it to be like some of my television plays, more immediately accessible to people who haven't had a background in revolutionary theory or revolutionary history or whatever.[23]

V

To return to Adrian Mitchell's question; it was doubtless the sociopolitical climate of the late 1960s and early 1970s that made them—playwrights, political theatre and its audience—think they could fly. In their very individual styles, which mirror the colourful variety of socialist drama in Britain, John McGrath, Trevor Griffiths, and Caryl Churchill (Howard Brenton, Steve Gooch, Snoo Wilson, and the collective plays of CAST and the Red Ladder are further examples) had every intention of giving their audiences support in the difficult art of flying. But the political scenery has changed dramatically, not only in Britain but all over Western Europe and beyond; and now it is doubtful whether Mr Maconochie's answer to his wife's final question, in McGrath's *Fish in the Sea*, can be anything but ironic for the British Left:

> *Mrs Maconochie:* Then it's time you started winning, isn't it?
> *Mr Maconochie:* Yes.

---

[23] Ibid., p. 42.

Note

In the nature of things, the more commercial side of the New Drama in Britain has not come in for much sustained critical consideration. *Anger and After: A Guide to the New British Drama* (revised edition 1969) and its sequel *The Second Wave: British Drama of the Sixties* (revised edition 1978) by John Russell Taylor, contain bibliographies of the published play-scripts. General background information may also be found in Arnold Hinchliffe's *British Theatre, 1950-1970* (1974), John Elsom's *Post-War British Theatre* (1976), Oleg Kerensky's *The New British Drama: Fourteen Playwrights since Osborne and Pinter* (1977) and Ronald Hayman's *The British Theatre since 1955: A Reassessment* (1979). From another point of view, *Celebration: 25 Years of British Theatre* (1980), a history of the *Evening Standard* Drama Award, is oddly illuminating.

Robert Bolt (b. 1924) has been the subject of a monograph by Ronald Hayman. His plays *Flowering Cherry* (1957), *A Man for All Seasons* (1960), *The Tiger and the Horse* (1960), *Gentle Jack* (1963), *The Thwarting of Baron Bolligrew* (for children, 1965) and *Vivat! Vivat Regina!* (1970) are all published by Heinemann.

Peter Shaffer (b. 1926) is the subject of a monograph by John Russell Taylor in the British Council 'Writers and their Work' series. His principal plays are *Five Finger Exercise* (1958), *The Private Ear and The Public Eye* (1962), *The Royal Hunt of the Sun* (1964), *Black Comedy and The White Liars* (1965, 1967), *The Battle of Shrivings* (1970, later revised and retitled *Shrivings*), *Equus* (1973) and *Amadeus* (1979). Those up to *Black Comedy* are published by Hamish Hamilton; later plays are published by André Deutsch.

Alan Ayckbourn (b. 1939) has brought most of his innumerable plays to London. Of these, the principal are *Relatively Speaking* (1967), *How the Other Half Loves* (1970), *Time and Again* (1972), *Absurd Person Singular* (1973), *The Norman Conquests* (1974), *Absent Friends* (1975), *Bedroom Farce* (1977), *Just Between Ourselves* (1977), *Ten Times Table* (1978), *Joking Apart* (1979), *Sisterly Feelings* (1980) and *Taking Steps* (1980). All are published in Samuel French acting editions; the first two are also published by Evans; *The Norman Conquests* is published by Chatto and Windus, who also publish *Three Plays* (*Absurd Person Singular, Absent Friends, Bedroom Farce*).

Simon Gray (b. 1936) has often done better in book form than on the stage. All his stage plays have been published: *Wise Child* (1967) and *Dutch Uncle* (1969) by Faber, *The Idiot* (adapted from Dostoevsky, 1970), *Spoiled* (1971) and *Butley* (1971) by Methuen, *Otherwise Engaged* (1975), *Dog Days* (1976), *The Rear Column* and *Molly* (1978), *Close of Play* (1979) and *Stage Struck* (1979) by Eyre-Methuen.

X

Art and Commerce: The New Drama in the West End Marketplace

JOHN RUSSELL TAYLOR

I

Shortly after the opening of *Look Back in Anger*, John Osborne called it in an interview 'a formal, rather old-fashioned play'. He was, of course, affecting to wonder what all the fuss had been about, which was perfectly understandable in a dramatist who, having just become big business, did not wish to be tagged for ever as a wild young experimental tearaway, and who also felt that he was making technical advances in his later plays that the rather sensational nature of his debut prevented anyone from noticing. But at the same time, the observation, though provocatively put, had its measure of truth. The New Drama had begun with a bang with *Look Back in Anger*, but the play's novelty was much more of tone and content than of technique. This meant that it was a lot easier for conventionally trained theatregoers to take: the wine might be new, but it was disguised in a comfortingly familiar bottle.

This should have helped to establish from the outset that 'New Drama' did not have by definition to be cast in some kind of experimental form: the mere fact of being under thirty when one's first play was staged in London did not by any means guarantee that one's dramatic sympathies were nearer Beckett than Rattigan. And though the New Drama in its early years had its quota of experimentalists—Pinter, Arden, Jellicoe, Simpson—the very variety of their approaches to dramatic form forbade—or should have forbidden—critics and commentators to assume any uniformity in the group, or indeed any community of aims and achievements which would justify regarding it as a group at all. Nonetheless, there were spirited debates in the early 1960s as to whether writers like Robert Bolt or Peter Shaffer could properly be regarded as members of the New Drama, even though their first London plays had appeared in, respectively, 1957 and 1958, and they were at the time respectively 33 and 32.

Such a discussion also tended to take in the whole question of whether New Drama ought to be commercially successful. Was it not somehow failing its true purpose and basic ideals if it was in any way comprehensible and enjoyable to more than a tiny minority audience? Naturally, this was overlooking what history tells us about the inevitable course of any revolution: that those who have overthrown the existing Establishment eventually (and sometimes immediately) become the new Establishment. It can indeed sometimes still, all these years afterwards, come as a bit of a shock: I doubt whether I can be the only one who was brought up short for a moment by seeing the drama critic of *The Times*, in his end-of-the-Seventies roundup, refer to Harold Pinter as one of 'our senior playwrights'. Undeniably he is just that, but the image of him as young and wild and incomprehensible, out there on the theatrical fringe somewhere, dies hard.

So, the significant number of straight commercial hits scored by these new dramatists from 1956 on created problems. If it showed they had won their battle, did it also suggest that they were fighting for the wrong things? Must they of necessity have sold out? If they had never shown much interest in whether or not new dramatic modes could be made acceptable to the public at large, did this show they were traitors to the cause? And anyway, what was the cause, if such a thing existed? Fortunately, perhaps, the passage of time has rendered such questions irrelevant. We can see, for instance, that Pinter has been ruthlessly consistent to himself and the internal necessities of his development from one play to another. There was no question that his transition from being regarded as the *ne plus ultra* in obscurity, on the strength of *The Birthday Party* in 1958, to being one of the most commercially successful West End dramatists in 1960, as *The Caretaker* brought in coach parties from Macclesfield to the Duchess for some eighteen months, came about because of some shift in public taste, not from his having shamelessly set out to write a commercial play the second time round.

So, clearly, what would have been rightly regarded as a very advanced and daring play in the early 1960s may well now have become, retrospectively, very easy to take and quite unexceptional to even the most conservative audiences. And yet in some ways a distinction does still exist between plays that have in some vital way benefited from the British theatrical revolution of the later 1950s and plays which, whatever the age of their writers, would surely have come out much the same even if Christopher Fry and Terence Rattigan had continued unchallenged to rule the theatrical roost. It is these latter—those which emphasize the lines of continuity with the past rather than hiding or denying them—that form the subject of this essay. The traditionalists do not form a school of their own, or even a coherent group, and naturally what is felt to be traditional in 1958 is bound to differ somewhat from what is felt to be traditional in 1968 or 1978. There are borderline cases, such as Tom Stoppard, an apparently 'modern' dramatist who has yet managed throughout his career to function in a very Establishment sort of way. But in general the distinction, even if it defies precise definition, seems clear enough.

II

Let us look first at the two dramatists in relation to whom these arguments first came up, Bolt and Shaffer. In 1957 *Flowering Cherry* was a hit, and so was *The Entertainer*. Both featured a theatrical knight, Ralph Richardson in the first, Laurence Olivier in the second. Yet no one was in much doubt which represented the safe and traditional, and which the dangerous and new. In 1958 we have the same sort of situation with *Five Finger Exercise* and

A Taste of Honey. The lines are unmistakably drawn. And the first thing you would have to say about both Bolt and Shaffer is that they are very literary sorts of dramatist. They believed from the outset in the advantages of the well-made play: a plot carefully laid out, with its exposition, its intricate pattern of information given to and withheld from the audience, its satisfactory denouement. They also believed that all this should be put into words. They were not the only ones of their generation who saw drama as primarily a verbal medium, but the ways that Osborne or Pinter or Arden use words in drama are significantly different. Their words do not bear the whole weight of a play's significance, but form only part of a complex whole which comes completely alive only in performance. Bolt's and Shaffer's plays, on the other hand, though they are certainly viable theatrically, work almost equally well in the study, as literary artifacts.

One might guess as much from the parallels cited at the time. *Flowering Cherry* was generally called Chekhovian; *Five Finger Exercise* was like Rattigan with a saving dash of Strindberg. Neither of these judgments is unfair, though they should not be taken to imply similar quality. *Flowering Cherry* is Bolt's *Death of a Salesman,* picturing a smalltime insurance salesman who lives in a world of illusion and his shaky relations with his wife, his two children, and the outside world at large. The story was handled in a fashion which Bolt later characterized as 'uneasily straddled between naturalism and non-naturalism', but certainly leaning much more to the side of naturalism, despite the occasional poetic flight of a big speech and the final vision of orchards as the unfortunate Jim Cherry dies, as he has lived, by a radical misunderstanding of the life around him. If the play seemed experimental at all when first produced, or even a little odd, it was largely the result of a dislocation between the small character of Cherry and the very big, idiosyncratic performance Ralph Richardson gave in the role, but the dislocation was clearly not intended: without it *Flowering Cherry* would have been a much more coherent but also a much more boring play.

Five Finger Exercise, on the other hand, was plotted with good old-fashioned virtuosity. An overheated drama about a semi-incestuous family group—mother, father, son, daughter—and the misfortunes of a German tutor who somehow stumbles into their midst and, guilelessly, comes to believe their protestations that he is just like one of the family, it falls neatly into the same category of 'strong' middle-class theatre as *The Vortex* or *The Deep Blue Sea.* There is no straddling here, not even a hint of it: the play is fairly and squarely in the naturalist tradition, and though each member of the cast is sooner or later handed a big scene in which he or she is allowed to be unexpectedly eloquent, that is, finally, all part of the convention and does not indicate adherence to a brave new theatre just liberated by John Osborne from the strangulation of the old school tie.

This traditionalism on the part of both dramatists may well have something to do with their primarily non-theatrical formation. Whereas many of the new generation of dramatists had come from working-class backgrounds, had never been to university, and had worked in the theatre (several as actors) before they began to write for it, Bolt had come of a solid middle-class background, read history at Manchester and been a school-master until his success as a playwright enabled him to give it up in 1958; Shaffer had been to public school and Cambridge, worked for libraries and music publishers, and been a professional music critic before his first success. Their training being primarily literary, it was natural they should think in literary terms of the drama, and be intensely aware of dramatic tradition. (John Arden, of similar background but very different tempera-ment, shared the intense awareness of tradition, but looked from the outset at different traditions—ballad opera, folk play, Jacobean tragedy, for example.)

If the beginnings of Bolt and Shaffer in the theatre are closely comparable, so, up to a point, are their subsequent careers. In both cases we can see a gradual move away from the simple naturalism of their first efforts. But the accent is on the 'gradual': it is as though they were affected by the changing climate of English theatre at almost exactly the same speed as the average, intelligent member of the ordinary theatregoing public. And so, if they moved to take a chance outside the confines of conventional stage natural-ism, it was a very little chance, very carefully prepared for so that their audi-ences were not in for any nasty shocks. Bolt's third play to be produced in London, and his biggest stage success ever, was *A Man for All Seasons*. This enclosed easy naturalistic scenes telling the history of Sir Thomas More and his problems of conscience with Henry VIII in a non-naturalistic framework involving a Common Man who acts as a narrator and moves in and out of the action, sometimes totally involved in the historical context, sometimes stepping right out of it to provide a twentieth-century gloss on the proceed-ings. This was all put down at the time to the influence of Brecht, his ideas of *endistancement* and the Epic Theatre. No doubt some influence of the sort was present, cunningly and painlessly acclimatized. But the play had in fact started life as a radio script back in 1954, and there the device of the narrator who steps in and out of the play is as old as radio drama itself, and as readily, unquestioningly accepted. If it was still in 1960 slightly out of the ordinary to put such a character on stage, at the same time Bolt obviously knew exactly what he was doing, how far audiences would accept the device with-out question and how far, indeed, it might serve as a talk-provoking gimmick, making people feel that they were boldly accepting a piece of modern theatre when it was in fact not necessarily anything of the sort.

Shaffer's move away from naturalism came later, with *The Royal Hunt of the Sun* in 1964. Again, the subject was historical, which somehow helps (it is much easier to accept some departure from naturalism in a play which deals with a remote time or place than it is in one which concerns the close, familiar and everyday). And the script, after going through many transfor-mations, ended up as the book for a stage spectacle more than a thoroughly worked-out play in its own right. (Interestingly enough, when *The Royal Hunt of the Sun* and *A Man for All Seasons* were filmed, the non-naturalistic elements were in both cases eliminated: *A Man for All Seasons* survived with its fundamental brainwork intact; *The Royal Hunt of the Sun* seemed by comparison paper-thin.) Shaffer's most satisfactory subsequent plays, *Black*

Comedy (1965) and *Equus* (1973), both move away in some vital respect from naturalism. *Black Comedy* does it very simply, by following the inspiration of oriental theatre, where darkness is acted rather than physically created, and reversing the light values, so that when the characters are in the light we, the audience, can see nothing, and when they are plunged into darkness we, on the contrary, see them in a blaze of light. *Equus*, more adventurously, is staged in an indeterminate acting area that may be anywhere or nowhere, and, by a bold stroke of director and designer as much as of writer, presents the dream world of the horse-obsessed boy in strongly conventionalized form, with actors in black leotards with elaborate open-work masks representing the horses of his private ritual.

And yet, for all this demonstration of awareness that the theatre of the 1960s and later (not to mention its audiences) is no longer the same as it was in the 1950s, a sense still remains with both Bolt and Shaffer that they are decidedly old-fashioned dramatists. The words still count above all—much too much so in the case of Shaffer, who does not have a very good ear for dialogue and tends to over-verbalize everything—and there seems sometimes to be a conflict between their traditionalist inclination and their desire to belong, after all, to the present. Perhaps this conflict has something to do with Bolt's virtual abandonment of the theatre in favour of the cinema after the failure of his attempt at a Shaffer-like ritual drama in *Gentle Jack*, and in fact the most notable of his later work in the theatre, *Vivat! Vivat Regina!*, is constructed in a quasi-cinematic form, in a series of short scenes moving betwen its two queens, Mary Queen of Scots and Elizabeth I, so that one wonders if he did not have at least half an eye on an eventual film adaptation.

III

Not that old-fashioned need be in any way a derogatory term. It is amazing how rapidly distinctions are effaced which once seemed all-important: if a play has any lasting value it soon becomes immaterial whether it was originally rather old-fashioned for 1960 or quite advanced for 1950. In any case, there are obvious cycles in fashion: regular exhibitors in the Royal Academy's Summer Show may well have kept right on painting in the same detailed representational way for forty years, only to find themselves suddenly in the forefront of fashion again, as things come round full circle. Dramatists like Coward and Rattigan, whose reputations were supposed to have been exploded for ever in the first gleefully iconoclastic phase of the theatrical revolution, very soon found themselves reinstated as modern classics and great precursors. And audiences' need for a balanced dramatic diet brings about constant slight shifts of taste, so that, for instance, in the mid-1960s audiences starved of sheer plot in the theatre (unless, horror of horrors, they were to stoop to *The Mousetrap*) began to turn towards revivals of recently despised playwrights like Maugham, Pinero and even Rattigan, in search of just that. If audiences felt it, dramatists felt it too, and so the later 1960s show a gradual re-establishment of story-telling in the theatre— often by dramatists of a generation even younger than that of the first young revolutionaries who brushed plot aside.

Some of the plays which came up this way were deliberately commercial, with no claim to deeper motivation or significance. The two most famous were Barry England's *Conduct Unbecoming* (1969) and Anthony Shaffer's *Sleuth* (1970). *Conduct Unbecoming* seems very like some kind of sport, a deliberate throwback to *The Winslow Boy* or something of the sort (*The Winslow Boy* itself being a sort of deliberate throwback to the well-made-play of the 1890s). Set in Imperial India shortly after the Mutiny, it concerns a spruce young officer who is charged by the regimental widow with indecent assault (for reasons of his own and her own which only slowly become apparent) and is defended by a self-made man among his fellow officers, who reveres regimental honour as only a recent convert can. It resolves itself into a neatly plotted courtroom drama with all its surprises and reverses in the right place, and seemed to have nothing whatever to do with the way drama was supposed to be developing at the time, but a lot to do with what real audiences were beginning vocally to want.

Sleuth, the first successful play by Peter Shaffer's twin brother Anthony, refers us to a different kind of theatrical nostalgia, and ingeniously contrives to have its cake and eat it by parodying the Agatha Christie kind of detective fiction and at the same time proving itself to be a most proficient example of it. It can claim to be more in touch with the theatre of its time than *Conduct Unbecoming* in that it involves an elaborate play with illusion and reality, but if it is compared with Tom Stoppard's *The Real Inspector Hound* (1968) the difference can at once be seen: while Stoppard leaves his illusion/reality interplay unresolved, so that we get no more 'explanation' than in any ripe example of the Theatre of the Absurd, Shaffer does eventually explain everything in basic rational terms: he is depicting strategems of characters behaving according to the conventions of naturalistc theatre (whether they are believable is another matter), whereas Stoppard is questioning his audience's whole body of assumptions about what is real and what is not. *The Real Inspector Hound* ends by challenging an audience, *Sleuth* by reassuring it.

IV

This is the cue which two of the most commercially (and, it must be said, critically) successful dramatists of the 1970s happily take up. The main distinguishing feature of the New Drama was that in various ways its writers challenged our view of reality, or even denied that it existed at all ('What have I seen', inquired one of Pinter's characters, 'the scum or the essence?'). Traditional dramatists, on the other hand, however much they might challenge our received ideas about intellectual, social, political or moral issues, usually left reality as such alone: maybe they recognized that it was 'a joint pretence' on which we all depended to continue (Pinter again), but if so they were certainly not going to hint as much to their audiences. In the 1970s two important dramatists at least diverged from the New Drama norm by seeming to assume, and allowing us comfortably to assume, that while the whole truth might not be known, it was not of its nature unknowable.

They were, of course, Alan Ayckbourn and Simon Gray. Apart from their success with a vast, non-specialized public they have virtually nothing else in common. It is altogether possible that Simon Gray nurtures fantasies of deeper significance for his works: his play for the National Theatre, *Close of Play* (1979), certainly roused a lot of discussion of what was real and what was imaginary (were this benighted family on an awful weekend get-together all imagined by the mute father who remains centre-stage throughout, or was he imagined by them, or were they maybe all dead?). But unfortunately the piece gave much too much the impression of having been deliberately devised as a tribute to Experiment to impress the critics (which on the whole it didn't) and dutifully bore National Theatre audiences (which on the whole it did). One could hardly take it seriously as a statement about the identity-crisis of our own times or something of the sort. And at least, once he had got that out of his system, Gray returned cheerfully to his natural stamping-ground in *Stage Struck*, Agatha Christie with intellect.

Ayckbourn, happily, has never been troubled with delusions of deeper significance. Of his whole very theatrically orientated generation (he was born in 1939) he has probably been the most complete, all-round man of the theatre. He began at the age of seventeen as an actor in provincial rep, ending up with Stephen Joseph's Studio Theatre company in Scarborough and Stoke on Trent. Here he did just about everything, as actor, director, ASM, general odd-job man and also, eventually, writer under the name of Roland Allen. His first play to reach London (briefly) was *Mr Whatnot* in 1964; his first resounding success was *Relatively Speaking*, produced in Scarborough in 1965 as *Meet My Father* and in London in 1967. Since then he has established himself as far and away our most prolific dramatist as well as our most staggering commercial success, with, at one point, no fewer than five plays running simultaneously in London. (It might be added, parenthetically, that he seems to be very specifically a British taste; his plays have never done so well elsewhere, and certainly not in New York.) In recent years he has also been in general control of his own theatre at Scarborough, where he tries out many more plays than London theatregoers could ever suspect, more even than see the light of day in the South, difficult though that is to imagine.

At least Ayckbourn's plays are all of a piece, middle-class plays for middle-class audiences, set wherever in the scampi-belt the garden gnomes grow thickest. Certainly he began with out-and-out farce, and has moved little by little into character comedy, but not, apparently, with any of the comedian's traditional desire to play Hamlet. Rather, he has created his own comic world, and if from time to time he feels inclined to probe it a little deeper, he never shows any signs of ceasing to see it as comic at all. One or two of his plays manage a hint or two of melancholy just beneath the surface: *Time and Time Again* (1971-72), perhaps, and *Joking Apart* (1979) begin, particularly the latter, to mirror a certain menopausal dissatisfaction with life on the part of Ayckbourn's characters if not, we may presume, of Ayckbourn himself. But in general he is content to recolonize for the English theatre those territories of society which have been lying fallow since *French Without Tears* began to seem intolerably elitist and out of touch with life (which is to say, some time before it came to look like a charming period piece and long before it began to seem again to be a play which had something of lasting validity to say about youth and growing up and life).

Ayckbourn is in fact an interesting and exceptional dramatist because what turns him on in his plays is so evenly divided between the creation of character and milieu, and the element of purely technical challenge. In *Relatively Speaking* the technical challenge seems to be uppermost: one would guess that Ayckbourn has set out quite deliberately to make the most out of the least, to see just how far one farcical joke (a misunderstanding involving a girl's fiancé in the belief that her older lover is actually her father) can be taken without cracking under the strain. Admittedly this is your basic stuff of farce, and that is the way it is developed. But to make so much capital out of the one simple situation—especially for an author who, as we have subsequently had ample evidence, is hardly short of ideas—does appear to invite comment on the prestidigitatory side of the proceedings: we must, surely, be meant to be aware of (to vary the metaphor) just how dangerous a tightrope our dramatist is treading. Hope/fear that he will fall is all part of the fun.

But since *Relatively Speaking* Ayckbourn has managed to keep his elements in better balance. If the human element is more prominent and important in *How the Other Half Loves* (1970), so is the purely technical. The trick of the play, in fact, resides, as with *Black Comedy*, in one technical device which, once the audience grasps it, becomes an enjoyable talking-point in itself, being not only used, but displayed for all it is worth. In this case it is the notion of combining two households in one set, super-imposed and intertwined. The set is half pseudo-grand, with damask wallpaper and Harrods' traditional furniture, half struggling *Guardian*-reader, with distemper and nappies drying; the two households are equally contrasted, linked only by the fact that the two husbands work in the same firm and that, secretly, Mrs Foster (grand) is having an affair with Mr Phillips (ambitious). The actions that go on in the two rooms alternate and often get inextricably involved with each other as a character in one will narrowly miss collision with a character in the other or apparently (from the audience's point of view) deliver a resounding insult fairly and squarely in the face of his victim, without either party on stage being aware of it. The climax of farcical ingenuity comes with the dinner scene, when an innocent third family, which has been used as an alibi by both philanderers, finds itself embarrassingly involved in two simultaneous dinner parties, full of ambiguity and devastating cross-reference, at a table which is half linen and crystal, half paper napkins and tumblers from the local supermarket.

It is possible to suspect that without the mechanical complication Ayckbourn's plays might turn out to be pretty thin. But one might as well wonder what Feydeau would be like without his clockwork precision of intrigue: that, after all, is the prime source of his creativity. Ayckbourn is a little bit more interested in his people as people than Feydeau, but finally he is interested in them only within the context of the complex structures he devises to set them in motion, and it would be unrealistic to complain that these structures are only an elaborate cover he adopts to disguise from us the limitations of his human vision. Certainly when he does not have the structural complexity, as in, say, *Ten Times Table* (1978), his plays can seem pretty frail and long drawn out. Also one can well see in that play how heavily he may depend on having the right actor to bulk out the role with his or her own personality: a Tom Courtenay or Penelope Keith role may well thin to vanishing point when played by anyone else.

But on the other hand, in one of his really complicated works, like *The Norman Conquests* (1974), the characters do take on intricacy too. The three plays which make up *The Norman Conquests*, played in repertory on consecutive nights, are in some ways an extension of the idea of *How the Other Half Loves*, turning it, in a sense, inside out. This time all the romantic and other intrigues are going on in the same house at the same time, during another ghastly weekend. So while we are watching people popping in and out of the garden at just the right wrong moments, we are probably wondering what on earth can be going on in the dining room or the drawing room. The classical answer is that nothing is: the characters are existent only when and where we see them, and there is no point asking how many children Lady Macbeth had or other such questions which presuppose that there is a larger reality of which what we see in the theatre is but a small segment. But, says Ayckbourn, what if I, the dramatist, know perfectly well what is going on elsewhere, and choose to tell you? Hence, we have these three plays, the action of which is for the most part simultaneous: put them together in your mind, and you know exactly where everyone is and what he or she is doing for just about every moment of the time covered.

Moreover, just in terms of time spent you have that much more acquaintance with the characters than any one play would give you. You come to know them in much the same way that you know your neighbours, and however improbable your neighbours may seem, it would never occur to you to doubt their existence: extent of acquaintance can conveniently stand in for depth and intensity. And thirdly, it is necessary for the complete working of the scheme that each one of the plays shall be self-sufficient and make perfect dramatic sense if seen without the other two. Of course, it may be hoped also that the first one you see (it could be any of the three) will be sufficiently entertaining and intriguing to send you back for more. And if this succeeds, it is a triumph of sheer theatrical expertise: one cannot imagine the effect being equal in any other medium, simply because here the stage's natural limitations are being turned into a decided advantage, whereas in a film, for instance, nothing could be simpler than to shift the locale from one room to another at will, and therefore nothing less interesting.

By the time of Ayckbourn's real emergence as a dramatist the New Drama itself was already old and settled enough to make questions of whether he really belonged to it, or was, rather, an entrenched conservative dressed up in a certain amount of technical gimmickry but none the less catering essentially for the complacencies of Aunt Edna, seem completely beside the point. New drama, old drama, what's the difference? The world is divided into plays that work and plays that don't. Most of Ayckbourn's do, and if he is finally Ben Travers for the 1970s, at least it is for the 1970s, not the 1930s. The New Drama has changed the expectations even of audiences who would never dream of enjoying one of those modern plays—very much as Shaw remarked in the 1890s 'A modern manager need not produce *The Wild Duck*, but he must be very careful not to produce a play which will seem insipid and old-fashioned to playgoers who have seen *The Wild Duck*, even though they may have hissed it.' Even a conservative audience is quite a bit different in its expectations today from how it was ten years ago, and it is ridiculous to berate a commercially successful dramatist for taking advantage of this difference without, as it were, having put in his stint of experimental unpopularity in order to deserve it.

Simon Gray has found himself in rather a similar position with regard to the critics. If Joe Orton did the spadework with *Entertaining Mr Sloane* and *Loot*, winning the vocal support of Terence Rattigan himself and convincing timid theatregoers that the New Drama could be fun, Gray seemed to start as a lightweight exploiter of the Orton vein. *Wise Child* (1967), about a criminal in hiding disguised as a blowsy middle-aged woman, made saucy play with homosexuality and sexual ambiguity; *Dutch Uncle* (1969), selected by the Royal Shakespeare Company for one of its then infrequent brushes with new drama, was a dutifully black comedy about a would-be wife-murderer who wants to make his mark on criminal history and attract the personal attentions of his idol, Inspector Hawkins. *Spoiled* was a bit different: a naturalistic piece leading slowly and carefully to its climactic revelation that the schoolmaster hero is a suppressed (and finally not-so-suppressed) homosexual, it had clearly been bypassed some time before by the average audience, which, far from being shocked and amazed by the turn of events, was in general way ahead of the dramatist.

Then came *Butley* (1971). This, directed by Harold Pinter with Alan Bates in the lead, hit a very happy medium. It was, indeed, a formal, rather old-fashioned play in just the same sense as *Look Back in Anger*, with which it had quite a few things in common, particularly the creation of a central character who is unmistakably a blazing star role, holding the centre of the stage with his rhetoric and reducing all the rest of the characters round him to tatters. Except that, unlike Jimmy Porter, he does get his come-uppance: finally wife, colleague, friend and pupil all turn on him or, what is probably even worse, just turn away. The structure of the play is simple: a series of encounters in which Butley's fund of malicious talk seems to win the day, and then a denouement in which we discover that he is not after all quite so unassailable as we have all (him included) assumed. What distinguished it from the run of traditional commercial plays was the force and intensity of its central monologues (much the same as *Look Back in Anger* or *Five Finger Exercise*). What distinguished it from most plays of the newer kinds was its extreme literateness, or literariness: here was a university lecturer—not exactly a favoured class of character lately—who talked like a university lecturer, or at least as a lecturer of his particular character might. In a theatre newly accustomed to four-letter words, nudity and such, a knowing mention of T.S. Eliot could be far more surprising and explosive.

So, *Butley* was a solidly popular, commercial play for the new conservative generation, those who read *The Guardian* and *The Observer* and *Time Out* and were just as entrenched in their own orthodoxy as the *Telegraph* readers of time past. It seemed to challenge, but ultimately did not, sending out its audiences with the flattering feeling of having been provoked and the comforting feeling of having then been pacified. Not surprisingly, the play (with its star) went on to be a big hit in New York and on tour throughout America. Gray followed it with two more plays featuring the same winning actor-director combination. *Otherwise Engaged* (1975) was rather like a sequel to *Butley*, with a rather similar character beset by the demands of others when all he wants—or all he claims to want—is isolation. *Stage Struck* (1979) chooses an obviously lighter mode: it is a sort of thriller with various showy *coups de théâtre* and quite a bit of intelligent talk as we gradually unravel what the central character, a failed actor who is just going to be chucked out by his tremendously successful actress wife, is really up to. It could make about the same claims to superior intellect applied to Agatha Christie material as could *Sleuth*; as in *Sleuth*, there is a lot of play-acting within the drama (well, two of the principals are actors, after all) and we may, for a moment or two, be left at sea about what is real and what is not. But it is all finally sorted out for us, in true detective-story fashion: nothing is unknowable, nothing even ambiguous. Whether we believe it is up to us, but at least we clearly know what we are being asked to believe.

Simon Gray might well complain that he suffers from his own success: audiences and critics have been too quick to feel they have him taped, and react with quite unreasonable hostility if he tries anything different, as he has most spectacularly with *Close of Play*. But the fact is that he is best at what he is best known for, and applauding his enterprise in trying to do something different is not the same as admitting its success. It would seem that he is self-conscious about being, with Alan Ayckbourn, our most solidly popular, commercially bankable playwright during the 1970s. Like Robert Bolt before him, he would like to be taken differently, more seriously, and from time to time makes deliberate attempts in that direction. It is true that comedians seldom feel they are getting their just desserts: another successful commercial dramatist with higher aspirations, Alan Bennett, remarked when receiving his *Evening Standard* award for *Getting On* as the Best Comedy of 1971, that 'To be given the award for Best Comedy is rather like taking great care and love nurturing your finest marrow but when you take it to the show you find you have won the prize for best cucumber.'

Fortunately no such qualms seem to afflict Alan Ayckbourn. Or if they do, he wisely keeps them to himself. In his work the old and the new, art and commerce, are immaculately fused, so that it does not really matter in what light you choose to see his plays, they are just unarguably there. He offers a model for what the unpretentious but not contemptible commercial theatre of the 1970s (and after) should or may be like. Significantly, it seems that commercial and comic have to be synonymous: we are still waiting to see whether such a thing as a tragedy or even a strong drama can belong just as unmistakably to our own time and still achieve just as indisputable a broad-based popular success. Maybe *Equus* has done it: at any rate, it stands out as the only play of the 1970s which can put in a serious claim. But otherwise, funny can find the middle-brow public, while serious has to be either safely classic or dangerously contemporary. Perhaps the 1980s, and the changes they will inevitably bring in theatregoing tastes and habits, will also produce a playwright who can comfortably bridge the gap and produce that popular, modern, British tragedy that the world has supposedly been waiting for ever since *The Deep Blue Sea*.

Index